THE TEMPLAR MERIDIANS

Richard

Another book on the
St. Clairs,
If you already have a
copy, pass it on to
my cousin, Hal

Best Wishes

THE TEMPLAR MERIDIANS

The Secret Mapping of the New World

WILLIAM F. MANN

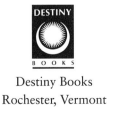

Destiny Books
Rochester, Vermont

Destiny Books
One Park Street
Rochester, Vermont 05767
www.InnerTraditions.com

Destiny Books is a division of Inner Traditions International

Library of Congress Cataloging-in-Publication Data

Mann, William F., 1954–
  The Templar meridians : the secret mapping of the New World / William F. Mann.
    p. cm.
  Includes bibliographical references and index.
  ISBN 1-59477-076-X (pbk.)
  1. America—Discovery and exploration—Pre-Columbian. 2. Acadia—Discovery
and exploration. 3. Sinclair, Henry, Sir, 1345–ca. 1400. 4. Grail. 5. Templars.
6. Freemasons—America. 7. Meridians (Geodesy)—America. 8. Leys—America.
9. Historic sites—America. 10. America—Antiquities. I. Title.
  E103.M355 2005
  970.01—dc22

                                                              2005030727

Printed and bound in the United States by Lake Book Manufacturing, Inc.

10 9 8 7 6 5 4 3 2 1

Text design and layout by Jonathan Desautels
This book was typeset in Sabon with Mason as a display typeface

To send correspondence to the author of this book, mail a first-class letter to the
author c/o Inner Traditions • Bear & Company, One Park Street, Rochester, VT
05767, and we will forward the communication.

Contents

In the plain of Tormore, in the isle of Arran, are the remains of four circles, and by their sequestered situation, this seems to have been sacred ground. These circles were formed for religious purposes: Boetius relates, that Mainus, son of Fergus I, a restorer and cultivator of religion, after the Egyptian manner, (as he calls it) instituted several new and solemn ceremonies; and caused great stones to be placed in a circle: the largest was situated to the south, and served as an altar for the sacrifices to the immortal gods. Boetius is right in part of his account: the object of worship was the sun; and what confirms this, is the situation of the altar, pointed towards that luminary in his meridian glory.

THOMAS PENNANT, *VOYAGE TO THE HEBRIDES*

Where were you made a Mason?

In the body of a Lodge, just, perfect and regular.

And when?

When the Sun was at its Meridian.

As lodges in this country are usually held in the evening,
how do you account for this, which at the first view
appears to be a paradox?

The Sun being the Centre of our system, and the Earth
constantly revolving on its axis, and Masonry being
spread across the whole of its habitable surface, it neces-
sarily follows that the Sun must always be at its Meridian
with respect to Masonry.

EXCHANGE BETWEEN THE WORSHIPFUL MASTER AND
A NEWLY INITIATED MASON, FROM THE YORK RITE
MASONRY 1ST-DEGREE EXEMPLIFICATION

ACKNOWLEDGMENTS

Let me humbly begin by acknowledging the contributions of those authors, from ancient times forward, who have challenged me throughout a lifetime of reading. From Plato to Bacon, Shakespeare to Tolkien, C. S. Lewis to Joseph Campbell, some of my fondest memories relate to the wonderful times I spent dreaming about everything from ancient mariners, the seven seas, dragons, and knights, to castles and mysterious islands. From the voyages of Jason and the Argonauts, the deeds of King Arthur, the mysteries of Middle Earth, and the quest for the Holy Grail, I developed an ability to explore the full extent of my mind and creativity and learned to intertwine and connect what might at first appear to be unrelated facts and events. This has opened up to me a world of amazement and adventure. For this I am truly grateful, and I hope that this love of books and reading has been passed on to my two sons, for I cannot think of any greater gift.

I would be remiss if I did not acknowledge the work of those more contemporary authors who have provided me with their own exhaustive research and conclusions as they relate to *The Templar Meridians*. It is only through their hard work and independent research that I have been able to arrive at my conclusions. In writing about such diverse topics as mythology, geometry, religion, and history, I have been grateful for the influence of such diverse authors as Margaret Starbird, Geoffrey Ashe, Henry Lincoln, Michael Bradley, and Dan Brown, to name but a few. The personal revelations in *The Templar Meridians* may be more the product of the collective conclusions drawn by others than of some miraculous bolt of lightning striking me.

I thank my two great-uncles, Frederic George Mann and Frank Ederic Mann, two of the kindest and gentlest men whom anyone could ever ask for as mentors and guides, for the sense of wonder and curiosity they instilled in me at an early age. These two men, veterans of the trenches of World War I, saw despair and evil at its worse, yet through it all maintained an amazing sense of forgiveness and spirituality. I dedicate this book to their memory.

I acknowledge the overwhelming support and unwavering encouragement and understanding of my wife, Marie. She provided a great deal of objective criticism in her many reviews of early drafts of *The Templar Meridians*. Thanks, too, to William and Thomas, my two sons, for allowing their dad at times to remove himself from his and their surroundings. Merlin, our golden retriever, also deserves a fair amount of credit, as those walks in the woods, which he so eagerly demanded, provided me with the time and excuse to collect and sort my thoughts.

Many friends have also continued to be a never-ending source of knowledge and inspiration, specifically Niven Sinclair, Elizabeth Lane, John Ross Matheson, Bill Beuhler, George Karski, John Coleman, and Aleta and Hamilton Boudreaux. Without good friends, life and this book would not be complete. I also thank E. David Warren, George Fairburn, and Gary Humes of Oakville Lodge No. 400 and White Oak Chapter No. 104 and Godfrey de Bouillon, Preceptory No. 3, for their brotherhood and sincerity. Special thanks go to F. Douglas Draker, Supreme Grand Master of the Knights Templar of Canada, 2005–2006, for his kind encouragement and direction.

Thanks to the Champlain Society, the Louvre Museum in Paris, the Trustees of the Chatsworth Settlement, the Trustees of the Dulwich Picture Gallery, the National Museum of Scotland, the Ashmolean Museum at Oxford University, the Cluny Museum, the Metropolitan Museum of Art, the Cloisters Museum, the University of Toronto Press, the Staatliche Museum in Berlin, the U.S. Library of Congress, and Conservation Halton for their kind and generous use of copyrighted materials.

I also acknowledge those many people who took the time to review my first book, *The Knights Templar in the New World*. I have been truly amazed at the diverging comments made with respect to the information and conclusions presented there. While some people appear to have viewed it as a personal attack on their religious beliefs and educational teachings and, therefore, have felt compelled to attack my personal integrity, many others found it extremely thought-provoking and highly entertaining. To those who have been somehow offended by the extent of connection presented, I must say that my true intent was to challenge the reader to open his or her mind to new ideas and to think about some of the accepted tenets that exist today as well as their true origin. It is my hope that *The Templar Meridians* will continue the debate and extend the challenge into new areas of history.

Finally, thanks go to the team at Inner Traditions • Bear and Company, who constantly exceed my expectations in every manner: publisher Ehud Sperling, acquisitions editor Jon Graham, marketing director Rob Meadows, managing editor Jeanie Levitan, editor Elaine Cissi, art director Peri Champine, and author liaison Patricia Rydle, as well as the many other staff members who have been involved in making this book a reality.

Note: All latitudinal and longitudinal positions stated in this book have been verified through either Natural Resources Canada, Earth Sciences Sector, or through Microsoft's TerraServer USA, which is sponsored by the U.S. Geological Survey.

Introduction
THE GUARDIANS
⊙F THE GRAIL

In *The Knights Templar in the New World** we learned the story of the Scottish prince Henry Sinclair, who, in 1398, almost one hundred years before Columbus arrived in the New World, sailed to what is today Nova Scotia. It was also revealed that, along with approximately five hundred of his trusted knights, he established at Green Oaks, Nova Scotia, a secret "Grail" settlement for the Templars fleeing persecution by the Roman Catholic Church and the French monarchy.

In part, *The Knights Templar in the New World* is a personal story: My late great-uncle was supreme grand master of the Knights Templar of Canada in the 1950s, and it was from him, when I was still a young boy, that I received the "secret" key that would eventually allow me to rediscover the site of the Templar settlement established by Sinclair and his followers in what they considered at the time to be the new Arcadia.

It was in Arcadia (later known as Acadia) that Prince Henry Sinclair and his Knights Templar sought to find a refuge for the descendants of Jesus and Mary Magdalene (otherwise known as the Holy Bloodline), who, through arranged marriage, provided a direct connection between the House of David and the early French Merovingian dynasty. Sinclair's charge was achieved with remarkable simplicity and secrecy until the British exiled the Acadians in 1755. Support for this story of Henry Sinclair is

---

*William F. Mann, *The Knights Templar in the New World* (Rochester, Vt.: Destiny Books, 2004).

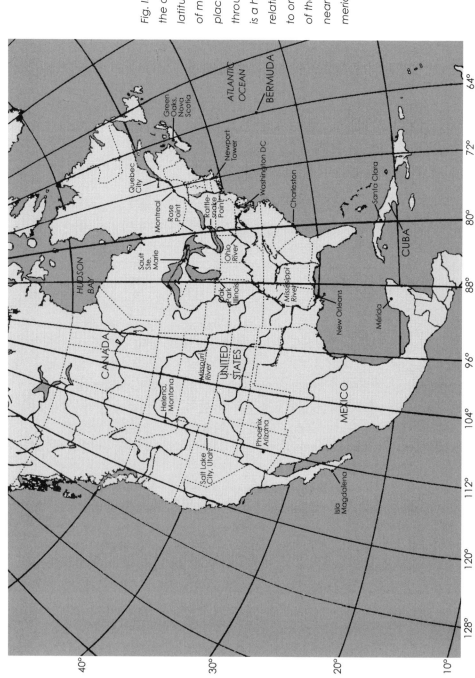

Fig. I.1. This map shows the approximate latitude and longitude of many of the key places mentioned throughout this book. It is a helpful tool in relating these places to one another in terms of their locations on or near important meridians.

found in a historical document called the *Zeno Narrative,* written in 1555 by Antonio Zeno, the great-nephew of the Venetian admirals Nicolo and Antonio, who accompanied Sinclair on his journey to the New World.

Intriguingly, Henry Sinclair was hereditary grand master of the Scottish Knights Templar at the time of his voyage. He was also a direct descendant of the Grail Bloodline through strategic marriages between prominent French and Scottish families, making him the ultimate guardian of the Templar treasure.

But what exactly is the true nature of this Grail treasure so protected by the Poor Knights of the Temple of Solomon, as the Templars were formally called? On one level, it will always be considered to be the descendants of the Holy Bloodline themselves, but on another it may be something as all-encompassing as the knowledge of the ancients, an aspect of which was the knowledge of longitudinal meridians that allowed Sinclair and those who sailed before him to navigate the treacherous North Atlantic and locate "Grail" settlements in the New World. There is a simpler possibility, however, that holds considerable ramifications for the interpretation of the history of the New World and the birth and growth of the United States and Canada. This involves an ancient knowledge of how and where the underground practice of smelting and steelmaking could be conducted in secret.

Many researchers and authors believing in a more "concrete" Templar treasure have speculated that it is either a genealogical record of the Grail family, a firsthand account written by either Jesus or the Magdalene herself, or associated relics—perhaps, even, the bones of Jesus—that ultimately can be tested against the DNA of known Holy Bloodline members. Many of these same people still believe that the Templar treasure lies below enigmatic Oak Island, located on the south shore of Nova Scotia (see chapter 4, page 180). But the deciphering of the ancient Templar code of sacred geometry has determined that Oak Island is not the final resting place of this treasure. Indeed, a whole series of physical treasures may still remain buried along ancient meridians that stretch across all of the Americas, starting beneath the settlement ruins recently uncovered at Green Oaks, the geographic mirror image of Oak Island.

The compelling story and ongoing mystery of the Templar treasure, coupled with the world's current events, which reflect or harken to the historical background of the First Crusades, continue to capture the public's imagination and, in part, have ignited in people an insatiable desire for anything related to the Grail or the Holy Bloodline. With the recent release of Dan Brown's novel *The Da Vinci Code,* this desire has hit an all-time high. Added to this is the ever-more-mainstream understanding of the notion that the founding of the United States was based on Masonic/Templar principles, which include a Grail and goddess veneration.

It is essential to remember, however, that the basic theory on which Brown's book is centered, that Jesus and Mary Magdalene were married, is not new. In fact, through their book *Holy Blood, Holy Grail,* Henry Lincoln, Michael Baigent, and Richard Leigh were probably the first to raise in a modern context the old Cathar belief that Mary Magdalene and Jesus were married and produced offspring. With the advent of the Internet and the arrival of the second millennium, however, it appears that the time is now ripe for general acceptance of this alternative history.

Holy Blood, Holy Grail hypothesizes that after Jesus' crucifixion, the Magdalene, Jesus' wife, either pregnant or with at least one child, was smuggled to an overseas refuge by her uncle, Joseph of Arimathea. Continuing the theory, this means that there existed a hereditary bloodline descended directly from Jesus through the Merovingians, and that this "holy blood" may actually be in existence this very day.

Of course, not everyone is ready for such a dramatic shift in religious direction. The Vatican still clings to the basic history in the gospels as interpreted by the early Church Fathers, while the religious right in the United States is strengthening its "traditional" beliefs through an ever-increasing influence on mainstream politics. In Europe, within the context of a European Union, the remaining royal houses appear to be vying for the ultimate "divine" position. Interestingly, Princess Diana, one of the most beloved royals connected to the House of Windsor, has also been directly connected to the Merovingian bloodline, which has only increased the admiration and even veneration she has been accorded after her death.

Since the publication of *The Knights Templar in the New World,* I've received hundreds of e-mails, letters, and large parcels of information from people all around the world who offer that they too possess a little piece of the vast puzzle that is the Templar treasure. Inevitably, I find that all of these pieces have led to the one question that I am constantly challenged to answer: What was it that the Poor Knights of the Temple of Solomon actually discovered? What could have caused the Church to seek to pursue and eradicate a group and its beliefs two centuries after it had sanctioned all that this group represented? Was it a treasure in the traditional sense or something much more profound and lasting?

Through the encouragement of Bernard of Clairvaux, the twelfth- and thirteenth-century Church initially conferred great favor on the Templars, allowing them to enjoy unprecedented growth and prosperity. But it reversed this position in the beginning of the fourteenth century to the point of sanctioning the arrest, torture, and murder of hundreds of men in the Order. Does the Knights' treasure have anything to do with this change of status? Perhaps the answer to the mystery of the Templars' discovery lies beyond the Holy Bloodline and its descendants. In the course of this book, we will learn more about the possibility that the Knights discovered evidence of an ancient knowledge developed before the Great Flood—knowledge that is still preserved in present-day Masonic/Templar ritual. Among these many pieces of information, the knowledge they may have gained concerning the establishing of accurate latitudinal and longitudinal positions before it became standard practice in the eighteenth century would have had the greatest impact on the Templar refugees' life in the New World, just as similar mapping knowledge would have aided the earlier Vikings, Celts, Phoenicians, Egyptians, and other ancient mariners who—perhaps through secret societies in other ages—were able to navigate the world through continuous observation of the sun, moon, and stars and their relative positions as recorded by stone circles and the like.

Through prehistory and recorded history, this knowledge provided those who were "in on the secret" the ability to enjoy the New World's limitless supply of precious metals, including the much-sought-after copper and gold, and its seemingly unlimited amounts of rare earth minerals such as titanium. It is quite possible, in fact, that access to such materials helps to explain how the Templars were able to develop superior weaponry and thus overwhelming military strength during the First and Second Crusades. It is likely, then, that it was the power and advantage acquired by the Templars as a result of this access to the New World riches—not their supposed position as guardians of the Holy Bloodline—that led to their ultimate downfall within the Church, for access to the New World represented not only unlimited material wealth, but also an opportunity to play a significant role in the establishment of a new world order that could exist free from the oppressive control of both church and state.

Ultimately, what we may infer is that this rediscovered mapping knowledge allowed Prince Henry Sinclair and his Knights Templar to relocate the ancient meridians, or *roselines,* and thereby both establish secret Grail settlements in the New World and safely deposit more concrete "treasure"—artifacts, manuscripts, and relics—that could easily be retrieved centuries later by future initiates of their sacred knowledge, including such men as Verrazano, Jacques Cartier, Samuel de Champlain, and Lewis and Clark.

This knowledge, an awareness of pre-Christian exploration, the journey to the New World of many Europeans after the thirteenth century, the establishment of settlements and a New Jerusalem or Arcadia here, and the subsequent colorful history of the colonization and growth of this part of North America that was to become the United States and Canada, is the context of *The Templar Meridians.* As we become aware of this meridian knowledge and how it has been used in our history, we will see that visionaries such as Pierre Charles l'Enfant and Thomas Jefferson may well have tapped into this grid of concealed energy through their respective designs of Washington, D.C. and Monticello. Such knowledge may also provide a hidden reason for Jefferson's sponsorship of the Lewis and Clark expedition: Perhaps one of its hidden purposes was to search out the final resting place of the grand initiate who "reactivated" these meridians across North America—Prince Henry Sinclair.

As we become more aware of this Templar roseline knowledge, we may see how aspects of secret societies such as the Freemasons in both Europe and the New World, works such as those of the artists Nicolas Poussin and David Tenier the Younger, and stories such as that of the Church of Rennes-le-Château in France and its famous priest, Berenger Saunière, figure in to the puzzle by revealing clues to this ancient information.

As we will see in the pages that follow, it is this meridian knowledge that may well tie together the New World's historical events and provide the thread that leads us to the greatest Templar treasure: the profound and complete knowledge of the ancients and the establishment of an Arcadia, a New Jerusalem, on this side of the Atlantic Ocean.

1

TREASURED SECRETS

From the ninth grade on, former U.S. president Bill Clinton was a member of the Order of DeMolay, a boys organization sponsored by the Masons.[1] The stated purpose of DeMolay was to foster personal and civic virtues and friendship among its members. Only recently has it become widely known that the Order was named after the last grand master of the medieval Knights Templar, Jacques de Molay, who supposedly took to his grave the secret of the Templar treasure after he was burned at the stake in March 1314.[2] (See fig 1.1.)

For close to two centuries in the Middle Ages, the Templars had enjoyed a unique position between the established Church and the French state. According to most books on the subject, the Order of the Poor Knights of Christ and the Temple of Solomon was founded in 1118, nineteen years after the capture of Jerusalem during the First Crusade. The declared objective of the original nine knights of the Order was to keep the roads and highways safe for pilgrims. There is very little evidence of their accomplishing this goal, however, and the true objective of the first Knights Templar may never be known. Many historians do suggest, though, that these first Templars discovered something hidden beneath the Temple of Solomon confirming, among other things, the very existence of Jesus Christ.

According to the established traditions of a number of secret societies, in all likelihood some of the "booty" uncovered by the original nine knights was in the form of the maps known as portolans, which exhibited a mathematical basis then unknown to the medieval world.

Fig. 1.1. This engraving, The Burning of Jacques de Molay, *by Emile Antoine Baward, c. 1885, depicts the last Templar grand master, Jacques de Molay, being burned at the stake on the island of Paris.*

In 1127, after nine years in the Holy Land, most of the founding knights of the Order returned to Europe, and in January 1128, at a Church council in Troyes, the Templars were officially recognized as a religious-military order—an acknowledgment that was due mainly to their patron, Bernard of Clairvaux, who was originally a follower of the Roman Catholic Carthusian Order and later was instrumental in establishing the Cistercian Order. This rapid rise in their stature indeed suggests that the knights discovered something of tremendous religious and historical significance.

The Templars were sworn to poverty, chastity, and obedience. They enjoyed virtual autonomy due to a papal bull issued by Pope Innocent II in 1139 stating that the Templars would owe allegiance to no one other than the pope himself. One result of this decree was that over the next two decades, throughout Europe, younger sons of noble families flocked to join the order's ranks. And because a man forfeited all his possessions, including his land, on admission to the order, Templar holdings proliferated.[3]

Within a mere twenty-four years of the Council of Troyes, the Templars held substantial estates in most of Europe, the Holy Land, and points east. By the mid-thirteenth century, the Templars had become powerful enough to play a role in high-level diplomacy between nobles and monarchs throughout the Western world and the Holy Land. The Order's political activities were not, however, confined to the Christian world. It forged close links with Muslim rulers and commanded respect from Saracen leaders that far exceeded that accorded any other Europeans.

At the same time, the Templars created and established the institution of modern banking and, in effect, became the bankers for every throne in Europe and for various Muslim potentates as well. But the Templars did not trade in money alone. From their ongoing relations with Islamic and Judaic culture, they came to learn of and accept new areas of knowledge, including the sciences. As a result, the Templars controlled a veritable monopoly on the best and most advanced technology of their age and contributed to the development of surveying, mapmaking, road building, and navigation.

The Order possessed its own seaports, shipyards, and fleet, both commercial and military, with their major fleet based in La Rochelle, France (see fig. 1.2). It is said that the Templars also possessed the finest map library of their time, including a number of rare portolan maps of unknown origin—likely those found beneath the Temple of Solomon. The Order also maintained its own hospitals with its own physicians and surgeons who apparently understood, among many other concepts, the properties of antibiotics. Unfortunately, in 1185, during this time of advancement, King Baudouin IV of Jerusalem died. One immediate consequence was that in July 1187, Gérard de Ridefort, grand master of the Temple, in part because of personal vanity, lost Jerusalem and most of the Holy Land to the Saracens.

After this defeat, the Templars retreated to the south of France, specifically to the Languedoc, the principality of the heretical Cathars. Because many wealthy landowners who were either Cathars themselves or sympathetic to the Cathar beliefs had donated vast tracts of land to the Order, the Templars felt that perhaps the Languedoc could become their New Jerusalem. The region promoted religious tolerance, and as a

Fig. 1.2. The Templar Maritime Fleet, early-fifteenth-century woodcut, artist unknown.
Note that the Templar fleet sailed independently under the Templar cross,
displayed prominently on its sails, and not under the banner of church or state.

direct result, Greek, Arabic, Hebrew, and the ancient esoteric tradition
of the Kabbalah were enthusiastically studied. Not unlike the Roman
Empire, however, complacency and decadence set in among the leaders
of the Cathars, and by 1208 the Church had become increasingly threatened by the Cathar heresy.

Under direct orders of Pope Innocent III, a holy crusade—now
known as the Albigensian Crusade—was waged against the Cathars
with the full cooperation of the French throne. In 1209 a northern
army led by Simon de Montfort invaded the Languedoc, and during
the next forty years, approximately thirty thousand Cathars were
killed. Although initiated by the pope, this episode of genocide (the
only truthful way to describe it) is best remembered for the fanaticism
of a Spanish monk named Dominic Guzman, who created the tortures
of the Holy Inquisition.

By 1243, the Albigensian Crusade had leveled all major Cathar
towns and forts in the region except for a handful of isolated strong-
holds. Chief among these was the remote mountain citadel of Montségur. In March 1244, after fighting for some months against all odds,
the fortress finally surrendered, and the Cathar heresy ceased to exist,
at least officially, in the south of France. Because the Cathars were

known to be wealthy, rumors spread of a fantastic treasure kept hidden at Montségur, but nothing of consequence was ever found in the fallen fortress.

For the next sixty-three years, the Templars, who had previously been somewhat allied with the "heretical" Cathars, continued to live in peace, but at dawn on Friday, October 13, 1307, King Philippe IV of France decreed that all members of the Order be placed under arrest and all their possessions in France be seized.[3] Grand Master Jacques de Molay was arrested and Templar properties throughout France were confiscated. Subsequently, a number of Templar priories and other holdings were awarded to an order known as the Knights of St. John—the Hospitallers—mandated by the pope. Interestingly, according to the researcher John J. Robinson, the English Peasants' Revolt of June 7, 1381, led by Wat Tyler, was actually organized and carried out by the English Freemasons as retaliation against the Hospitallers. But who were these seeming rival of the Templars, formally known as the Knights of the Order of the Hospital of St. John of Jerusalem? According to history, in 1099 many Crusaders joined the Brotherhood of St. John, which later became the religious order of the Knights of the Order of St. John of Jerusalem. This order participated in all Crusades waged during the next two hundred years, after which they were forced to retire first to Cyprus and later to the island of Rhodes. In 1523 the Hospitallers were forced to withdraw a third time, to the island of Candia, the modern Crete, where they remained for seven years. Then, in 1530, the emperor Charles V of Spain gave the island of Malta to the order. Thus, the Hospitallers became known as the Knights of Malta for the next two hundred and fifty years, until, in 1798, Malta was captured by Napoleon and the order was finally dispersed.

After confiscation and redistribution of the Templar holdings in 1307, Philippe's primary interest, the Order's immense "hidden" wealth, was never found, and added to the mystery of the Cathar treasure was the whereabouts of the fabulous treasure of the Templars.

It is said that with his last breath, after seven years of captivity and torture, Jacques de Molay recanted his confession and called upon his persecutors, Pope Clement and King Philippe, to join him within the year before the court of God to account for their own sins.[4] By the end of the year both Clement and Phillipe were dead and the mystique and arcane knowledge surrounding the Templars had grown to epic proportions, as had the legend of their secret treasure, which was said to have vanished from the port of La Rochelle under the cloak of darkness on the now famous Friday, October 13, 1307, along with eighteen galleys filled with knights.

Could it be that the Cathar treasure so sought after by both Church and state after the demise of that sect was part of the same treasure that disappeared with the Templar fleet from the port of La Rochelle? Templar historians now agree that at least some of those eighteen Templar galleys sailed to Scotland, Portugal, or Scandinavia. It is also possible that a number of the galleys made their way directly across the Atlantic to already established settlements in the New World. As their earlier history has shown, the Templars were wise enough to ensure that not all of their eggs were in one basket.

Under the Rose

One of the world's oldest symbols, signifying confidentiality and secrecy, is the rose (*rosa* in Latin, *rhodon* in Greek). Surprisingly, roses are native to only the Northern Hemisphere, yet they have flourished from the earliest times, even before human time. Excavations in Europe have uncovered thirty-five-million-year-old fossilized rose flowers and hips, and petrified rose wreaths have been unearthed from ancient Egyptian tombs.[5]

In Greek mythology, Aphrodite (the Roman Venus), the goddess of love, is said to have created the rose.[6] In Rome it became the symbol of love and beauty. Cupid added to the flower the symbolism of secrecy when he offered a rose to Harpocrates, the god of silence, in order to hush up Venus's amorous escapades.[7] Roman dining room ceilings were decorated with roses, reminding guests to keep secret what had been said during dinner and leading to the term *sub rosa*, "under the rose," which refers to discretion and confidentiality.

Like the meanings of the cross, those of the rose can be paradoxical. It is at the same time a symbol of purity and passion, heavenly perfection and earthly emotion, virginity and fertility, life and death.[8] The rose is also representative of the blood of Adonis and of Christ. Early

Christians saw the five wounds of Christ in the five petals of the *rosa sancta*. In its Christian interpretation it has become symbolic of transmutation—taking food from the earth and transforming it into a beautiful, fragrant, "divine" flower—and, through the idea of the rose garden, is emblematic of Paradise. During the Renaissance the emblem of the rose garden came to represent human love and lovers, but at the same time the religious Marian symbolism of the rose was popularized by the devotion of the rosary.[9]

Numerologically, the rose represents the number five because the wild rose has five petals and the petals on all roses exist in multiples of five. Geometrically, the rose corresponds to the arcane symbols of the pentagon and the pentagram, which was the symbol of the school of the Pythagorean brotherhood.[10] Because of its association with the number five, the rose has also been linked to the five senses and, in an absolute sense, to the expanding awareness of being through the development of the senses.[11]

During the Middle Ages, the theme of the rose garden developed from the the literature of courtly love, in which the rose often appeared as a symbol of the beloved lady. Later, the influence of the Song of Songs led to the rose symbolizing the mystical union between Christ and his church, or between God and each of his people.[12] Because the Virgin Mary was honored as the model of union with God, the rose became a privileged symbol of the union between Christ and Mary. The image of Mary holding a rose rather than a scepter appears in many of the greatest examples of thirteenth-century art. The image of Mary in a rose garden or under a rose arbor or before a tapestry of roses also appears in the work of many artists of the Middle Ages.[13] (See fig. 1.3.)

The rose, the queen of flowers, was evidently a privileged symbol for the Virgin Mary, queen of heaven and earth. This type of Marian symbolism is much in evidence in Dante's description of Paradise. In chapter 23, verses 71–75 of *Paradiso,* Dante's guide, Beatrice, invites him to contemplate among the heavenly inhabitants the beauty of Mary, the Mother of God: "Why are you so enamored of my face that you do not turn your gaze to the beautiful garden which blossoms under the radiance of Christ? There is the rose in which the Divine word became flesh: here are the lilies whose perfume guides you in the right ways." Fasci-

Fig. 1.3. The Mary Garden, thirteenth century, artist unknown. The first recorded Mary garden was created by the Irish saint Fiacre in the seventh century. Reproduced courtesy of the Staatliche Museum, Berlin.

nating examples of this symbolism can also be found throughout Gothic cathedrals and especially in their rose windows, the circular, stained-glass windows that enhance the three entrances to these churches. Coincidentally, the Knights Templar were the financiers behind the construction of the Gothic cathedrals and rose windows across France, including the Cathedral of Chartres and its famous rose window.[14] The "text" behind these immense, intricate works of colored glass is said to be the revelation of the world of salvation offered by God to the lost human race through the Hebrew Bible and Christian scriptures. Christ is most often at the center of these rose windows, where he is usually portrayed either sitting in judgment or in the mystery of his Incarnation.

For all the traditional rose symbolism associated with the Virgin Mary, however, many recent books now explain the importance of that other Mary—Mary Magdalene, who may have stolen the heart of Jesus—to provide a secret symbolism to the image of the rose. According to the authors of *Holy Blood, Holy Grail*, the name Notre Dame de Lumière is in fact a direct reference to Mary Magdalene. They hint that even the earliest Notre Dame churches in France are dedicated to the Magdalene, not the Virgin Mary. The authors seem also to identify Mary Magdalene with the Meridian, the ancient longitudinal line established as the starting point of a grid that spans the earth, and claim that within a modern context, she may have been the progenitor of a bloodline from her "husband" Jesus, which became the central hypothesis of their book.

The notion of a series of longitudinal meridians spanning the globe is not a new concept, as began to be suggested in the introduction to this book, but to associate it with Mary Magdalene implies both an ancient and a secret connection. It offers that through the union of Jesus and Mary, the bloodline of ancient kings, including the House of David and Tribe of Benjamin, continues to this day, but also that there has been perpetuated an ancient knowledge which, among other things, allowed the highest of initiates to establish their relative position on the earth's surface. In a time when the Church was promoting the concept that the earth was flat, this information represented pure power in terms of trade and natural resources. Needless to say, the holders of such knowledge would very quickly realize the necessity to veil it in layers of esoterica and religious symbolism that outwardly fell under the sanction of the Church.

A perfect example of this hidden double meaning is the veneration afforded to Ste. Roseline de Villeneuve les Arcs, a Carthusian nun who died on January 17, 1329, and continues to be associated with a "rose miracle": She was apparently so saintly that her body remained uncorrupted after her death. King Louis is said to have checked whether she was still alive by putting a needle through her eye, which is reminiscent of the circumstances of the untimely death of Dagobert II, the last Merovingian king (who was lanced in the eye in a hunting "accident"). When she was alive, Roseline was a person of noble lineage who apparently had frequent visions. When asked the best way to get to heaven, she replied: "To know oneself."[15]

Ste. Roseline's feast day is January 17, an important date also for the Merovingians because it marks the day that Dagobert's son, Sigebert IV, escaped an assassination attempt, thus enabling the line of Merovingian kings to continue. Some authorities have suggested that the saint's name itself—Roseline—symbolizes the Merovingian bloodline. As any reader of *The Da Vinci Code* can tell you, the Roseline is a direct reference to the ancient meridian that is marked within the Chapel of St. Sulpice in Paris by a golden north–south line. Intriguingly, January 17 is also the feast day of St. Sulpice, or Sulpicius Severus, the biographer of St. Martin of Tours, who was frequently associated with places of sacred toponymical significance as well as with pagan tree cults. The Roman Sulpicius Severus, an aristocrat of France's Aquitaine region, was intended for an administrative career and educated in the classical manner. After the early death of his wife, he renounced his career and entered the monastic life. Sulpicius wrote a world history, *Chronicorum Libri duo,* or *Historia sacra,* which extends from the creation of the world to A.D. 400. It is surprising, however, that although St. Sulpice is at least outwardly a Christian icon, Sulpicius Severus omitted the historical events recorded in the New Testament.

During the past three decades, the Order of St. Sulpice has been linked to the location of a great treasure or secret. In addition, through conversations with the authors of *Holy Blood, Holy Grail,* Pierre Plantard de St. Clair, a past grand master of the modern Priory of Sion, made reference on many occasions to lines of longitude or meridians said to lead to the site of immense treasure, perhaps to where the earthly remains of Jesus were hidden.[16]

The Roseline Chapel

Following this central theme of the ancient meridian or roseline leads directly to Rosslyn Chapel, the ancestral home of the Scottish St. Clairs, or Sinclairs, located fifteen miles south of Edinburgh. In earlier times, this area was named Roslin, an amalgamation of the Celtic words *ros,* meaning "ridge" or "promontory," and *lin,* or "waterfall."[17] There is, however, a deeper explanation of the origin of the name Roslin: It comes directly from Roseline, which symbolizes a bloodline of immense significance that has perpetuated ancient knowledge handed down to or rediscovered by the original nine knights who excavated beneath the Temple of Solomon in Jerusalem following the First Crusade. As such, it has also been suggested that the Sinclairs were descended from the Jesus Roseline lineage—the "true vine."

Alternatively, speculation has only just begun that the chapel falls on an ancient ley line—a roseline—within a geometric grid pattern that crisscrosses the world. Ley lines, also known as dragon lines, are straight lines or trackways passing over and through the landscape. Throughout Europe, ley lines appear to carry earth energy or an electromagnetic force and are marked by landmarks including standing stones, megaliths, earthworks such as barrows and mounds, and holy wells. The signature of the chapel's founder, Sir William Sinclair, on a prominent charter suggests this very theory: His reads "St. Clair of Roselin." This confirms that since the earliest times, Rosslyn was considered an energy point and spiritual center.

The chapel construction was initiated in 1446, 144 years after the dissolution of the Templar Order in 1312. Its building required immense effort and was personally orchestrated by Sir William St. Clair, the third and last St. Clair, earl of Orkney. It took forty years for the chapel to be completed and many claim that it represents part of what was intended to be a much larger building. It exists as a unique "arcanum in stone," with symbolism in every carving. With imagery in its carvings ranging from pagan to biblical, the chapel reflects a profusion of Celtic and nature themes, including the predominant Green Man, an image found in a number of ancient Eastern temples as well.

One of the most fascinating aspects of Rosslyn Chapel is the engrailed-cross window marking the western entrance to the building (see fig. 1.4). The engrailed cross, the emblem found on the Sinclair coat of arms, consists of four arms that refer to the four rivers of Eden or, with their scalloped edges, to the scales of the dragon of wisdom.[18] The dragon or sea serpent—the shamir—depicted on Prince Henry Sinclair's coat of arms has always represented the Celts' ultimate symbol of sovereignty. Curiously, during the nineteenth century, the fourth earl of Rosslyn placed around the chapel railings that were surmounted by the St. Clair heraldic engrailed cross, the arms of which were overlaid with a single rose at their point of intersection. This entire image thus symbolizes the Crucified Rose—that is, Jesus on the cross.

Among the Celtic imagery carved in the stone of the chapel, it is possible to find a large number of Masonic-related images as well, including those on the famed Apprentice Pillar (see fig. 1.5, page 20).

Fig. 1.4. The western entrance to Rosslyn Chapel. Note the engrailed cross (with its scaled or scalloped edges) found within the rose window above the west-entrance door. Photograph by William F. Mann.

Fig. 1.5. The Apprentice Pillar in Rosslyn Chapel. Legend has it that the carver of the pillar, an apprentice mason, was murdered by his master, who flew into a rage upon returning from a pilgrimage to the Holy Land and witnessing the beauty of the finished carving. Photograph by William F. Mann.

As for the positioning of the chapel, its location is due precisely to the surrounding natural environment and the locale's earlier association with pagan ritual. Within the adjacent glen of the river Esk, for instance, there are caves in which Bronze Age artifacts have been found and that contain a number of Pictish carvings. In the numerous excavations that have occurred surrounding the chapel over the years, findings such as pottery shards have suggested the worship of Mithras, who was the Persian god of light and truth, later to become the Roman god of the sun.

Father Richard Augustine Hay (b. 1661) wrote one of the best-known sources on Rosslyn Chapel and the St. Clair family in 1700. In it, he describes how the founder, Sir William, personally inspected each and every carving in draft form before allowing the masons to carve it in stone. These stonemasons were said to have come from the craft guilds of "other regions" and "foreign kingdoms," lending credence to the importance of Rosslyn as a great spiritual center. The fact that Sir William personally approved the design for each carving demonstrates that he likely intended the chapel to remain a permanent record not only of ancient Masonic ritual, but also of the secret voyage that had taken place in 1398 by Sir William's grandfather Prince Henry Sinclair.

The Scottish Sinclairs have also been inextricably linked with the fugitive Knights Templar—some of those men in the eighteen boats that left La Rochelle—who arrived on the shores of western Scotland following their 1307 flight from France and who purportedly won the day for Robert I, the Bruce, during the Battle of Bannockburn in 1314. The Sinclairs also acted as hereditary grand masters of the Masonic Order in Scotland until 1736, when Sir William Sinclair, in a clever maneuver, renounced his hereditary position and was immediately elected the first grand master in the Scottish Grand Lodge of Speculative Masons. In part, this transpired because the Sinclair family had been hereditary guardians of Scotland's holy relics—which also gives greater credence to the notion that the Templar treasure was spirited to Rosslyn, at least on a temporary basis, until it could be secreted away to the New World.

The subject of a number of documentaries and books, Rosslyn Chapel is thought to hold a number of secrets. For years many have speculated on what, if anything, was hidden there: Suggested are the Ark of the Covenant, the mummified head of Christ, the Holy Grail, a Black Madonna, the Mandylion (the image of Jesus' face on the shroud of Veronica), the lost scrolls from the Temple of Jerusalem, and, of course, the treasure of the Knights Templar. What many have failed to realize, however, is that the chapel itself is a testimony of faith in stone, a monument to a transatlantic voyage that has remained veiled in secrecy for more than six hundred years.

It is certainly possible that under the supreme guardianship of Henry Sinclair, earl of Norway and prince of Scotland, along with a trusted inner circle of Knights Templar, the ultimate treasure of the Temple was spirited away to what at that time was considered a secret refuge—a "rose" settlement—in Nova Scotia, or New Scotland. The ultimate purpose behind this daring and dramatic adventure was not only the need to establish a refuge for members of the Holy Bloodline and its guardians, the Knights Templar, but also to reactivate a series of ancient longitudinal meridians, or roselines, through the inland movement of the Holy Bloodline to strategic "rose" positions across the New World.

Prince Henry Sinclair

In order to understand Prince Henry Sinclair, "a man worthy of immortal record," as he is described in the *Zeno Narrative*, we must first understand the history immediately leading up to his life and times. During the earliest part of the fourteenth century, Scotland was constantly attacked by the English king Edward I. Beginning with the Battle of Rosslyn in 1303, the outnumbered Scots decisively beat the English in three separate engagements. In 1314, Edward, intent upon revenge, marched north with a highly trained army to meet the Scots at Bannockburn. The Scots won the battle, due largely to the intervention of the Knights Templar on the side of King Robert the Bruce, assisted by Sir William Sinclair and his two sons, William and Henry. In appreciation of the role played by the Templars at the Battle of Bannockburn and in an effort to disguise the presence of the Templars within his kingdom, Robert the Bruce created the Royal Sovereign Order of Scotland. His successor, King David II of Scotland, also appointed William Sinclair the grand master of the Crafts and Guilds of Scotland, which became a hereditary position.[19]

Young Henry Sinclair, born in 1345 and named after an ancestor, Henri de Saint-Clair, an original Knight Templar who served with Godfroi de Bouillon when Jerusalem was secured during the First Crusade, was only thirteen years old when his father died in battle and he became the young Henry Sinclair, lord of Rosslyn. He was highly educated, trained in military matters, and spoke both French and Latin. His first wife, granddaughter of the king of Sweden and Norway, died while she was still very young. Henry then married Janet Halyburton, of Dirleton, and fathered thirteen children over a period of twenty years. Throughout his lifetime he came to be known as Henry the Holy because of his upholding of Christian virtues.[20] Following the hereditary line, Prince Henry Sinclair became the grand master of the Crafts and Guilds of Scotland as well as a Knight Templar. Subsequently, King David II rewarded him with the title Lord Sinclair and the position of lord chief justice of Scotland after a successful raid into England. When he was only twenty-four years old, Sinclair was installed as the earl of Orkney and lord of Shetland, which included rule of the Faeroe, Orkney, and Shetland Islands. Sinclair actually held this appointment under King Hakon VI of Norway, for Norway had ruled the islands since the ninth century. In response to his obligation to the Norse king to maintain control of all of the islands, Henry then constructed Kirkwall Castle as his headquarters in Orkney.[21] At the same time, he oversaw the building of a fleet of ships to provide trade across the Norwegian Sea and to patrol the waterways. This proved to be of immense strategic importance, for Norway was hard-pressed to defend itself from Baltic pirates without Sinclair's assistance. Amazingly, all of this was completed before he turned thirty-five years of age.

Over the next twenty years, Henry was compelled to exercise control of trade among the islands because of the fierce independence of their people and continuous harassment from the Hanseatic League, which was composed principally of a collection of seafaring German towns. In dividing his time between his ancestral home, Rosslyn, and the Orkneys, Henry was constantly challenged to maintain the king's sovereignty over his people. In addition, because the Templar community was becoming such a thriving entity that its trading activities began to extend beyond Scotland's boundaries, he was also forever challenged to disguise the activities of these Scottish Knights Templar who fell under his control. All the while, he was also preparing for an event that he realized would require all of the skill and wisdom he had gained throughout a lifetime of service to God in accordance with the Sinclair motto—"Commit thy work to God"—which was soon to be put into play for all eternity.

The Secret Voyage

According to the historical document known as the *Zeno Narrative,* anonymously published in Venice in 1555, Prince Henry Sinclair sailed across the North Atlantic in 1398 to what was then known as Esto-tiland.[22] The author of the narrative, Antonio Zeno, was, as we have learned, a direct descendant of both Admiral Nicolo and Admiral Anto-nio Zeno, who, it appears, were ordered to sail to Scotland from Venice to provide Prince Henry with the expert navigational skills that would be required for such a journey. Historical records tell us that, unfortu-nately, Nicolo passed away prior to the actual journey. Thus the story is told that with the aid of his trusted friend and lieutenant Sir James Gunn and the Venetian admiral Antonio Zeno, Sinclair led a fleet of thirteen galleys from Scotland on April 1, 1398, to what is today Guys-borough Harbor, Nova Scotia, where they made land on June 2, 1398.[23] The *Zeno Narrative* includes what has come to be known as the Zeno Map (see fig. 1.6), which shows two castles, or settlements, positioned on both sides of a major river in the lower left-hand corner, in the land marked ESTOTILAND.

The historian Frederick J. Pohl was one of the first to connect the *Zeno Narrative* to the oral legends of the native Mi'kmaq of Nova Sco-tia relating to their sacred entity, Glooscap, the secret voyage of Prince Henry, and the Knights Templar who accompanied him. For instance, Pohl determined that there are seventeen striking similarities between Glooscap, the man-god, and Prince Henry—which is not to say that Prince Henry's identity was conflated with this Mi'kmaq entity, but rather that Henry may have assumed the Glooscap persona for his own purposes, as Henry and his followers would have realized soon after their arrival in the New World that if they were to maintain a settlement

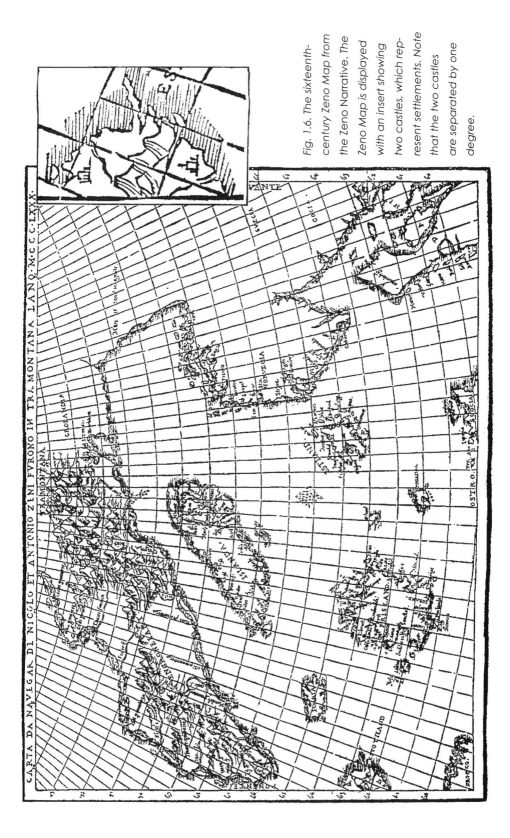

Fig. 1.6. The sixteenth-century Zeno Map from the Zeno Narrative. The Zeno Map is displayed with an insert showing two castles, which represent settlements. Note that the two castles are separated by one degree.

or to move inland in any manner, then they must have the local knowledge of the natives—especially as it related to rivers and trails, for these were the inland highways of the New World—as well as their goodwill and cooperation.

The Mi'kmaq legends describe Prince Henry's winter quarters as being in the vicinity of Cape d'Or and Cape Blomidon, both on the Bay of Fundy. From this, it is quite obvious that Sinclair would have carefully chosen both of these sites for one very specific reason: their strategic lookout positions. Each site is structured in such a way as to offer unobstructed views of both the entire Bay of Fundy and Minas Basin. At an elevation of five hundred feet above sea level in the case of the Cape D'Or promontory and 760 feet above sea level in the case of Cape Blomidon, on a clear day a person can observe from them not only the mouth of the Bay of Fundy at Grand Manan Island, but also the Northumberland Strait across the low-lying Chignecto Isthmus.

Rather intriguingly, the *Zeno Narrative* tells us that Prince Henry sent Antonio and his fleet back to the Orkneys shortly after making landfall at Guysborough Harbor and retained only a number of smaller, flat-bottomed oar boats. This suggests that Prince Henry knew exactly where he was going from his landing position—as though once on land, he knew of the signs that would direct him to a previously established settlement, one possibly initiated by the Vikings or Celts.

Whatever his reasons for reducing his numbers at this point, the tidal Shubenacadie River, one of Nova Scotia's longest waterways (appearing to split mainland Nova Scotia in two) and at present a popular site for exciting white-water rafting, was to the fine military strategist Prince Henry, and no doubt to those who came before him, a seemingly impregnable defense. A settlement located along the Shubenacadie River would be accessible only to those who possessed the knowledge to "ride the tide" (see fig. 1.7).

As previously noted, one odd element within Rosslyn Chapel is the carvings depicting maize, aloe, *Sassafras albidum* (sassafras tree), *Trillium grandiflorum* (wood lily), and *Quercus nigra* (black oak), which are all Native American plants (the last three being confined to the Carolinian Forest Region) that were unknown in Europe at the time of the chapel's construction. It is therefore speculated that these carvings

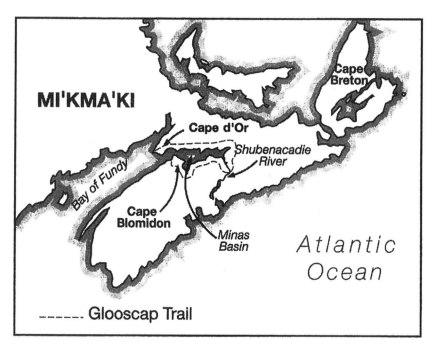

Fig. 1.7. A general map of Nova Scotia highlighting areas attributed to the Mi'kmaq legend of Glooscap. The Glooscap Trail is centered on the Shubenacadie River.

were based upon drawings or actual samples of North American plants that Antonio or others brought back to Europe after leaving Prince Henry and his crew. In addition, the numerous strange cube-shaped carvings projecting from the chapel's ceiling and covered with Templar symbols may represent the chests that were initially distributed among the thirteen galleys of Prince Henry's fleet to both serve as ballast and yet hold the treasure of the Templars during its transport to the New World (see fig. 1.8, page 29).

Green Oaks, Nova Scotia

In *The Knights Templar in the New World,* it was revealed how a "secret" shown to me by my great-uncle Frederic George Mann, a past supreme grand master of the Knights Templar of Canada, allowed me to relate the two main principles of Masonry—sacred geometry and moral allegory—

to the landscape of Nova Scotia, resulting in the discovery of perhaps one of the most important of the lost Templar colonies. On the 1545 Caspar Vopell map of the coast of Nova Scotia, this community is represented by the drawing of a bust of a Templar Knight and the legend *Agricolae pro Seu. C. d. labrador,* which could be interpreted literally as "Farms (or farmers) for the Lord of the Cape of Laborers."* (See fig. 1.9.)

At the modern community of Green Oaks, Nova Scotia, located directly east of the Shubenacadie River and south of a promontory known locally as Anthony's Nose, I discovered archaeological evidence confirming that a Celtic agricultural settlement existed there even prior to Prince Henry's time. As a result, I theorized that upon landing in the New World, Prince Henry Sinclair either knew exactly where he was going, by virtue of his awareness of the coordinate position (latitude and longitude) of the abandoned colony or through his uncannily accurate maps showing him exactly where the settlement was located, or he had to conduct a series of initiations reflecting Masonic ritual, a series of degrees, which started on the south shore of Nova Scotia at the enigmatic Oak Island. One of the many "instructions" or clues for the Masonic initiate in order to complete this journey is that he follow the nose of one of the medieval Templar patron saints, St. Anthony. As I discovered through my journey, the cape or promontory known as Anthony's Nose, positioned at the "headland" of the Minas Basin, is the nose that belongs to the head of a symbolic Green Man positioned at the same location.

How is it that there might have been nonnative settlements in this area long before the time of Prince Henry? The area around Green Oaks is rich in metallic minerals such as copper, gold, and titanium. While most historians attribute the immense quantities of gold and copper

---

*Michael Anderson Bradley, *Holy Grail Across the Atlantic* (Toronto: Hounslow Press, 1998), 213. Of equal importance to Bradley is the Gastaldi map, which first appeared in the Venice Ptolemy in 1548, three years after the Vopell map, but which may have been drawn as early as 1539. On this map are the place-names "p=refuge," "Larcadia," "Angouleme," "Flora," and "Le Paradis." Bradley logically put together the progression of these names to form the message: "The Flower of Angouleme has found a refuge in the Paradise of Arcadia." Of special note is the map's reference to Norumbega, which calls the region of Nova Scotia "Terra de Norumbega" (Land of Norumbega). The land of Norumbega played an important part not only in the discovery of the New Jerusalem, but also in illustrating that Prince Henry Sinclair followed in the footsteps of his Norman ancestors. See chapter 2, page 61, for more information on Norumbega.

Fig. 1.8. A Rosslyn cube, an example of one of the many cube-shaped carvings extending from the ceiling of Rosslyn Chapel. Photograph by William F. Mann.

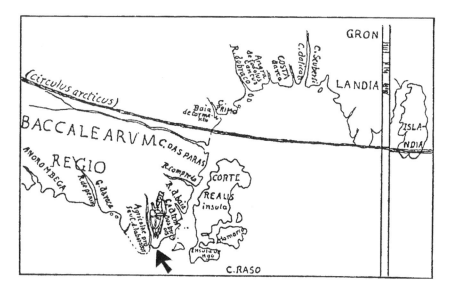

Fig. 1.9. The 1545 Caspar Vopell map. Note the illustration of the Templar knight from the waist up, east of what appears to be a major river, at a location corresponding to modern-day Green Oaks, Nova Scotia.

possessed by the medieval Knights Templar to their activities in Europe and particularly the Middle East, in reality the activities of the Templars—specifically their building endeavors, which included cathedrals, preceptories, and farms—would have required more gold or copper than was available in all of Europe.

Moreover, it has been established that during the building of the original Temple of Solomon, the vessels of Kings Hiram and Solomon were at sea for forty-two days before reaching their secret gold mines. Thus, North America appears as likely a candidate as any for the location of King Solomon's mines and the land of Ophir and for the Templars' secret source of gold and copper.[24]

In his book *America B.C.*, Barry Fell contends that over three thousand years ago a band of roving Celtic mariners crossed the North Atlantic to discover and subsequently colonize North America. Fell found support for his theory in the hundreds of inscriptions discovered among stone ruins during an archaeological survey of New Hampshire, Vermont, and other Eastern Seaboard states. From these inscriptions he systematically traces the remnants of a North American Celtic civilization throughout the New World as well as evidence of Egyptian hieroglyphs and Iberian-Punic script. In most cases, evidence of pre-Christian exploration and habitation in the Americas corresponds to the geological patterns underlying the Appalachian and Allegheny Mountain chains, which run from Nova Scotia to Louisiana.[25]

As noted by the authors Tim Wallace-Murphy and Marilyn Hopkins in their recently published *Templars in America: From the Crusades to the New World*, American archaeologists estimate that over half a million tons of copper were removed from the now abandoned mine shafts lining the north shore of Lake Superior, yet only a tiny portion of it has been located in burial mounds and other archaeological sites in continental America.[26] Samuel de Champlain's diaries talk about his search for the "old copper mines" near Minas Basin during his 1604 and 1608 explorations of the area. The diaries also speak to the discovery of an old Christian cross of wood that stood atop one of the many promontories adjacent to Minas Basin.[27]

It therefore seems likely that if the Templars had reestablished mining activities in the Green Oaks area—even throughout the entire northeastern seaboard, for that matter—they would surely have veiled these operations in esoteric ritual recognizable only to those who were "on the square." In other words, the true reason behind the mysterious legends and myths of the New World would become known only to those who were well versed in Masonic ritual. What makes the theory of Templar mining activity in the New World all the more possible is that a sizable deposit of titanium and other rare earth metals has recently been discovered along the shoreline of the Shubenacadie River. An important fact to consider with this discovery is that during the First and Second Crusades, the Templars possessed the most advanced steelmaking abilities in the world. Historians have repeatedly identified this advanced art as probably the most important technological reason for the superiority of the Templars over the Saracens, until the Saracens were able to counter with their development of the more refined and resilient Damascus steel.

When titanium is combined with elements such as iron and manganese, it creates what is known as light blue steel, a steel that is lighter yet stronger than any other. If the Templars did indeed possess an unlimited supply of these metals, as well as the knowledge to forge such steel, it would go a long way toward explaining why the Green Oaks site was so significant. A unique quality regarding titanium is that unless it is forged in the right combination with other metals such as iron, it has a tendency to become very brittle and shatter, which we will reflect on later in this chapter.

Beyond its obvious material riches in the form of metals, recent geological tests at the Green Oaks site confirm that a fault line runs directly through the property, suggesting that it is an area of potential underground energy, which the more learned among the Templars would be capable of divining. Much like the site of Rosslyn Chapel, that of Green Oaks has been revered for thousands of years by those native to the area because of its natural energy. That the point of land directly opposite the Green Oaks site on the western bank of the Shubenacadie River is still known as Rose Point suggests that this land served as the north point of a compass rose of some sort, providing both guidance and protection to those who passed through the Royal Arch.

In *The Knights Templar in the New World*, it was demonstrated how geometry, including the Pythagorean theorem, could be applied across mainland Nova Scotia in the form of the Seal of Solomon/Jewel of the Royal Arch (see fig. 1.10) and how from this Green Oaks, with its European white oak signposts, could be determined to be the mirror image of Oak Island, with its red oak signposts.[28] In addition, we discovered that the personal seal of Prince Henry Sinclair, now in the possession of his direct descendant Niven Sinclair, indeed showed two oak trees flanking an engrailed cross. This coincidental evidence suggests that prior to the development of the chronometer in 1773 by John Harrison, there were ways to determine specific longitudinal positions on earth: Within the Sinclair seal was the concept that a meridian lay between the two rose settlements located in Nova Scotia when the first French settlers arrived with Champlain in the early 1600s. (One oak tree represents Oak Island and the other represents Green Oaks, with the engrailed or scalloped line between them symbolizing an ancient meridian or energy ley line.) Further, it is possible that the Templars rediscovered this meridian knowledge—or it was handed down over the centuries within certain inner circles or secret societies.

If Green Oaks was a Celtic earth fort long before the arrival of the Templars and, subsequently, the French/Acadian settlers, it is quite likely that there was a level of knowledge and understanding practiced among the Celts at this site relating to the tracking of the sun, moon, and stars. It was the Druids, of course, who are believed to have constituted the priest caste or educated class among the Gauls or Celts, studying verse, natural philosophy, astronomy, and the lore of the gods. The earliest-known records of the Druids come from the third century B.C., although Julius Caesar provides the principle source of information concerning them. Suppressed by the Romans, the Celts survived in pre-Christian Ireland as poets, historians, and judges. There is even some suggestion that the Celtic Druid was a lateral survival of an ancient Indo-European priesthood.

Significantly, considering the prevalence of the word *oak* in our study (Green Oaks, Oak Island, the presence of white and red oak signposts at these Templar sites), a reference to ancient meridians can be found in the Celtic etymological history of this word. The Celtic word *duir* means literally "oak," but also implies "door," "right-handedness," and even "divinity." The root of the word *oak (ochs)*, then, has come to represent something that is right, to the right, or at the right hand of a figure or an element of an ancient mystery.

We should not be surprised to find that remnants of four stone circles have been uncovered at Green Oaks, but it remains to be proved that the actual motions of the sun and the moon are reflected in the structure of these circles, although the Green Oaks site uncannily fits the description provided in Thomas Pennant's *Voyage to the Hebrides* (see the epigraph on page vi).[29] Pennant declares in this passage that in the plain of Tormore on the isle of Arran there are the remains of four circles and that by their sequestered situation, this seems to have been sacred ground. Apparently, these circles were formed for religious purposes, with the largest, situated to the south, serving as an altar for sacrifices to the immortal gods.

Prior to the eighteenth century, the only known method of establishing longitude was by timing an eclipse of either the sun or the moon. This method was not without its complications, however. It first required predicting when an eclipse was going to occur, and then required two parties

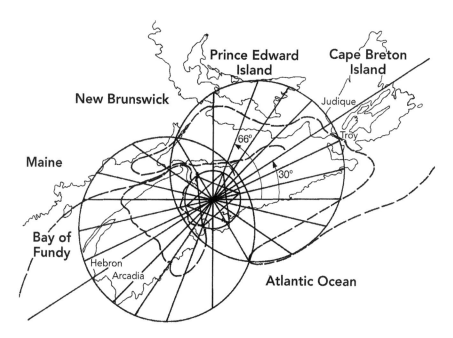

Fig. 1.10. Application of the Jewel of the Royal Arch across mainland Nova Scotia. Note how this application of sacred geometry in Nova Scotia reveals strong geographic relationships among areas that suggest a pre-Christian connection.

who were oriented east–west to record simultaneously the moment of the eclipse in local time. Then, these two individuals had to compare the hour of eclipse observed from their respective locations and multiply by 15 to convert time into an arc between the "primary station" and the other location (1 hour of time = 15 degrees of longitude). The result was the longitude west of the the primary station.

If the primary or base station was located at Brodgar on the Orkney Islands at a modern-day longitude of 3 degrees 17 minutes west and the second station was located at a modern-day longitude of 63 degrees 17 minutes west, and an eclipse of the sun or moon was recorded locally at 8:00 A.M. at Brodgar and at noon at Green Oaks, the longitude west of the base station is 60 degrees west.

Calculating the difference in longitude, then, required the ability to predict an eclipse and to accurately record local time, which would lead to the possibility that there were ground almanacs of some sort positioned throughout the world—that is, the mysterious megalithic rings, circles, and other prehistoric monuments and ruins found all over the known world, including both North and South America. Increasingly, individuals or groups such as the New England Antiquities Research Association (NEARA) are discovering in New England stone circles, dolmens, underground complexes, mine shafts, stone walls, petroglyphs, and other evidence of ancient civilization that seem to have supported advancement in metalworking, astronomical charting, and habitation well beyond what we at first thought possible. In their book *Uriel's Machine,* Christopher Knight and Robert Lomas offer powerful evidence that the purpose of the great megalithic sites in western Europe, which date to a time long before the Egyptian pyramids, was to build an international network of sophisticated astronomical observatories that provided accurate calendars and could measure the diameter of the planet and predict eclipses of the sun and moon years in advance.[30]

Stonehenge is certainly the most celebrated of all stone circles, but within the British Isles alone there are over nine hundred stone rings still in existence. These monuments may just indicate the mysterious motivation of the Neolithic, Bronze Age people and, some say, the Celts who built them throughout northern and western Europe over the many centuries from 4000 B.C. to 1500 B.C. It was the retired Scottish engineer Professor Alexander Thom who first surveyed many of the stone circles and rings and proposed that they were used to pinpoint exact days of various solstices and predict both solar and lunar eclipses. Thom determined that Temple Wood, in Argyll, Scotland, was used to make precise observations of northern and southern moonsets at the major standstill (a sort of "non-movement" of the moon that occurs roughly every 19.5 years).[31]

This very simple explanation for the thousands of megalithic sites positioned throughout the world certainly raises a fascinating idea: A specific society or societies were able to establish their relative positions around the globe in terms of both latitude and longitude and therefore, through the simplest geometry, were able to map these positions. From the perspective of worldwide trade, this ability would have represented absolute power.

Ancient Maps

Charles Hapgood, as recounted in his *Maps of the Ancient Sea Kings*, spent many years examining the earliest portolan maps (maps used mainly by sailors and bearing distinctive wind roses that give compass bearings and sailing instructions) for signs of information about the earth regardless of what was presumed to have been known at the time the maps were made. Some of these maps have been copied and recopied through the centuries from vanished originals that were once kept in the ancient library at Alexandria. These originals seem to have demonstrated startlingly accurate knowledge of lands that were as yet undiscovered (according to history as we have learned it) when the original and even the copies were made—including North and South America and Antarctica.*

One such portolan map showing startling and inexplicable accuracy is the so-called Piri Re'is map (see fig. 1.11). Painted on parchment and

---

*Bradley, *Holy Grail Across the Atlantic*, 95. Much of Bradley's general information concerning portolan charts relies heavily on *Maps of the Ancient Sea Kings: Evidence of Advanced Civilization in the Ice Age,* by Charles H. Hapgood, who arrived at his conclusions after an exhaustive search through hundreds of early maps and the replotting of significant samples onto a modern projection. According to Hapgood, these maps constitute the first hard evidence that advanced peoples existed before all traditionally recognized groups.

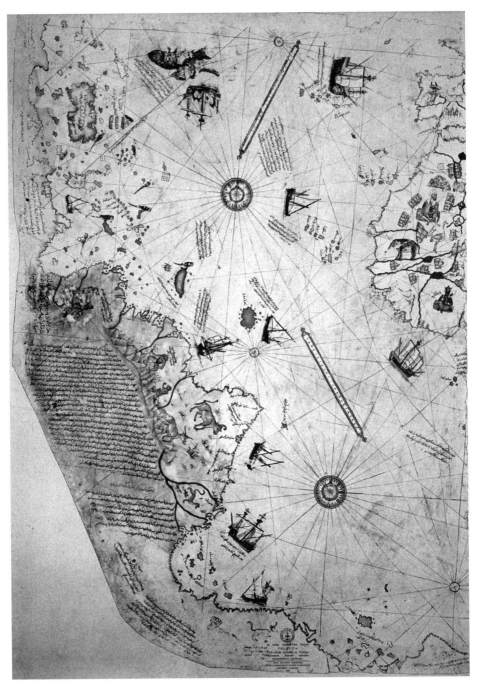

Fig. 1.11. The sixteenth-century Piri Re'is map. Reproduced from Maps of the Ancient Sea Kings, by Charles H. Hapgood, with permission from Adventures Unlimited Press.

dated 919 A.H. (in the Islamic calendar), which corresponds to 1513 C.E.,[32] it is signed by a Turkish navy admiral named Piri Ibn Haji Memmed, who is considered to be its author. It is thought to have been assembled from a set of twenty maps drawn in the time of Alexander the Great at around 322 B.C.E. Based on a larger equidistant azimuthal projection, it shows the American continents more accurately than any map drawn two hundred years later. The Piri Re'is map is most notable for the detailed notations provided by its author regarding the source of its information. The complete map includes the continents of Africa and Asia and, according to Piri Re'is himself, was intended to be a map "of the seven seas."[33] The other striking feature about it is the extraordinary level of detail in the coasts and interiors of South America. Although the scale is somewhat off, a long, high mountain range is shown as the source of the rivers flowing to the eastern coast of South America. These mountains have proved to be the Guiana and Brazilian Highlands.

Some of the other mysterious maps drawn in the fifteenth century and before also show the Bering Strait linking Asia and America and details such as river deltas that appear much shorter than they do today, islands in the Aegean that haven't been above sea level since the rise in sea level at the end of the last ice age, and huge glaciers covering Britain and Scandinavia. Long dismissed as attempts by cartographers to fill in empty spaces, some of the details on the old maps have been startling indeed when they have been found to correlate with modern knowledge of the changes in the earth's geography and topography since the last ice ages.

Traces of an ancient knowledge found within these maps were first identified in 1929 by Captain Arlington H. Mallery, a retired U.S. Navy officer, who suggested that the Piri Re'is map was based upon much older charts, which, among other regions, showed a part of Antarctica.* It was Mallery who first realized that the depiction of the Antarctic coastline must have been drawn before the present-day Antarctic ice cap covered the coasts of Queen Maud Land. This, of course, baffled him, for Antarctica was not discovered until the nineteenth century and was largely unexplored until the middle of the twentieth century.

---

*Ibid., 72–77. Hapgood's evidence indicates that some ancient peoples explored the coasts of Antarctica when they were free of ice. It is clear that these groups possessed a navigational instrument that was far superior to anything used by later peoples.

Following Mallery's discovery, Hapgood set out to prove that the portolan maps were based in antiquity. The conclusion he reached was that a civilization with sophisticated seafaring and mapping skills surveyed the entire earth in the ancient past, thereby leaving to humankind a tremendous treasure trove of charts that have been copied by hand throughout many generations.

Hapgood proved that the Piri Re'is map was plotted out in plane geometry containing latitudes and longitudes at right angles in a traditional grid (see fig. 1.12)—yet it was obviously copied from an earlier map that was projected using spherical trigonometry.[34] It seems that not only did the ancient mapmakers know that the earth was round, but that they also had knowledge of its true circumference to within fifty nautical miles. Hapgood also demonstrated that because the earth is round and the portolan design was apparently based on a flat projection, parallel meridians on the map would deviate progressively from true north the farther they were removed from the center of the map. The portolan design, however, ingeniously compensated for this by using different north points for each section of the overall map, which strongly suggests that this map was developed over a long period of time.

Very simply, in order to construct a portolan map, the ancient mapmaker first selected a center point and then drew a circle around it. He then bisected the circle four times, drawing sixteen lines from the center to the perimeter at angles of 22.5 degrees.[35] Having done this, he could construct a square by connecting the point where every fifth radius met the circle's perimeter—in other words, he created a square within the circle, the same geometric method employed by William Sinclair in his design for Rosslyn Chapel and by Thomas Jefferson in his design for Monticello. This square within the circle would result in the first of many quadrants on a flat plane, which allowed a section of distances and bearings earlier established at sea by the intrepid mariner to be transcribed onto the relevant quadrants.[36]

These bearings appear on many of the portolan maps like radiating spokes on a wheel, reproducing the pattern of the mariner's compass. Many of them are depicted as a compass "rose," with the "spokes" spaced to produce either sixteen or thirty-two equal parts. The thirty-two points represented winds that could blow a ship to a certain destination. When conventional compasses were introduced, the number of points was retained but they were said to represent directions.

Hapgood also determined that the Piri Re'is map was drawn on a polar equidistant projection, similar to the azimuthal equidistant projection maps constructed by the U.S. Air Force during World War II

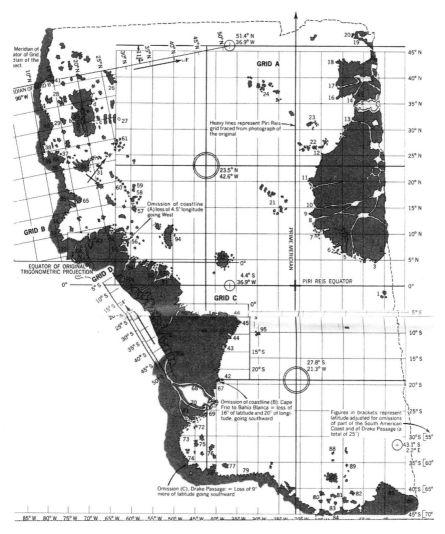

Fig. 1.12. The grid composition of the Piri Re'is map. For a full listing of the ninety-five places that correspond to their correct latitudinal/longitudinal positions, please refer to Hapgood's Maps of the Ancient Sea Kings. *Reproduced with the permission of Adventures Unlimited Press.*

(see fig. 1.13). One of the best known of these maps was centered on Cairo, Egypt, because an important U.S. air base was located there at the time.[37] What Hapgood concluded from this discovery was that the original portolan mapmaker, confronted by a spherical projection he did

AZIMUTHAL EQUIDISTANT PROJECTION
CENTERED NEAR
CAIRO

Fig. 1.13. An azimuthal equidistant projection map of the world based on Cairo, Egypt (U.S. Air Force). Reproduced from Maps of the Ancient Sea Kings, *by Charles H. Hapgood, with permission of Adventures Unlimited Press.*

not understand, had to translate his geographical data in terms of a flat surface. The finished map was therefore based on the principle that two landmasses being equidistant from a center point would fall on the same concentric ring.

Following this basic underlying geometric principle, the same azimuthal equidistant map has been overlaid with a series of rings relating to the Templar meridians, each separated by eight degrees (see fig. 1.14). The result is truly startling: Oak Island, in Nova Scotia, corresponds to the major port of Recife, Brazil, which is located in the southern hemisphere; Oak Park, Chicago, corresponds to Charleston, South Carolina; and Mexico City corresponds to Lima, Peru. Significantly, an axis or radius traced from Cairo to Nova Scotia and on through New York, Philadelphia, Washington, and New Orleans provides a straight line between the port of La Rochelle, France, and the south shore of Nova Scotia. If the Templar fleet that disappeared on Friday, October 13, 1307, had indeed possessed portolan maps of this nature, they would have known that by traveling in a straight line across the Atlantic Ocean they could reach an established refuge in the New World. According to the established traditions of a number of secret societies, in all likelihood some of the booty uncovered by the original nine Knights Templar under the Temple of Solomon was in the form of diagrams like these portolan maps, which exhibited a mathematical basis unknown to the medieval world.

But how could such accurate maps have been assembled in ancient times? As we have seen, there existed ancient knowledge that could have led to these accurate representations. In *The Golden Thread of Time,* the author and inventor Crichton E. M. Miller has demonstrated quite effectively how a simple construction resembling an ancient Celtic cross can be used to measure the angle of the sun and then, through the application of simple mathematics, can lead to a position anywhere on the earth's surface to within thirty nautical miles or .5 degree.[38] In fact, Miller's device was so successful in determining latitude and longitude that he was granted UK patent number 2344887 in November 2000 for the surveying and navigation instrument that proved his theory.

Indeed, the ancient Celts very well might have possessed the means to allow the ancient mariner to fix longitudinal position at sea and on

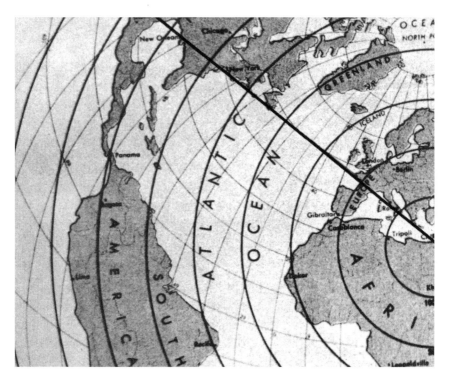

Fig. 1.14. A section of a map of the world based on an azimuthal equidistant projection, provided for comparision to the Piri Re'is map of 1513

land. This, in turn, suggests that Prince Henry Sinclair, one of a series of "visitors" to the New World near Green Oaks, knew precisely where he was going when he landed with his band of Templars.

The Westford Knight

Based on his interpretation of the Mi'kmaq legends, Frederick Pohl has speculated that Sinclair sailed away from Nova Scotia in the spring of 1399 toward what is now known as New England, where he explored the coast. No one knows, however, whether this New England visit was a short stopover before returning to Orkney or to Green Oaks, or whether the detour to the south holds greater significance in Sinclair's New World travels. Perhaps this trip was a reconnaissance for the time when the inhabitants of the Green Oaks settlement would move inland; perhaps Prince Henry Sinclair never did return to Scotland across the Atlantic but instead moved inland with portions of the Templar treasure, understanding that a series of ancient roselines lay to the west. Regardless of his intentions, Sinclair seems to have experienced a significant event during this sojourn: The trip proved fatal to one of his band, for the effigy of a fourteenth-century knight found on a rock ledge located at Westford, Massachusetts, carries a broken sword, the symbol of death.[39]

Following the discovery of this effigy in 1954, Frank Glynn, then president of the Connecticut Archaeological Society, and later Frederick Pohl visited Westford and made detailed drawings of the figure (see fig. 1.15). Both were able to determine the elements in the coat of arms on the knight's shield: a crescent, a five-pointed star, and a buckle above a masted ship. Although both were unaware of the significance of this coat of arms, it would prove to be representative of the Gunn clan, of which Sir James Gunn, Sinclair's most trusted knight, was a member.[40]

Glynn's drawing of the figure clearly reveals a medieval knight and shows the effigy to have incorporated both man-made and natural markings. Where colored streaks, patches, and parallel glacial scratches in the hard gneiss could serve his purpose, the figure's creator accepted them, and while many investigators fail to agree on a definitive likeness of the knight, they all agree that several of the Mi'kmaq Indians who had guided Prince Henry Sinclair to the south were witnesses to the death of this important person. The following passages from the *Legends of the Micmacs,* compiled by Silas Rand, suggest that the knight's name was indeed Gunn, or *kuhkw,* as pronounced in Mi'kmaq:

> He came from the east; went away toward the west. There he is still tented; and two important personages are near him, who are called Kuhkw and Coolpujot . . .
>
> *Kukhw* means "earthquake"; this mighty personage can pass along under the surface of the ground . . . One of these seven visitors was wonderfully enamoured of a fine country; and expressed a desire to remain there; and to live long; whereupon, at Glooscap's direction, Earthquake took him and stood him up and he became a cedar-tree. Seeds producing all the cedar-groves that exist in New Brunswick, Nova Scotia, and elsewhere . . .

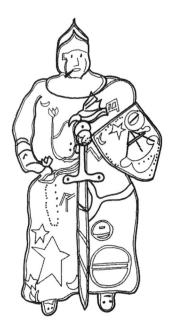

Fig. 1.15. Frank Glynn's drawing of the Westford Knight

The other men started and reached home in a short time . . .

The next day they prepared a festival, and all four are feasted and sumptuously entertained. They are then taken to the top of a hill which is very high and difficult of access. The ground is rocky, broken, and totally unfit for cultivation. On the very apex of this hill, where the sun would shine from morning until night, they halt; and Glooscap takes the man who had desired to live for a long time, clasps him round the loins, lifts him from the ground, and then puts him down again, passing his clasped hands upon the man's head, and giving him a twist or two as he moves his hands upwards, to transform him into an old gnarled cedar-tree, with limbs growing out rough and ugly all the way from the bottom. "There," he says to the cedar-tree, "I cannot say exactly how long you will live—the Great Spirit alone can tell that. But I think you will not be likely to be disturbed for a good while, as no one can have any object in cutting you down . . . I think you will stand there for a good long while . . ."[41]

What may be most intriguing about this whole episode is that investigators have failed to question the obvious: Is there any clue to be found in the design of the Westford Knight, as he is called? Yes, it has been determined from some of the markings on the figure that its model was a member of the Gunn clan, but what of all the other strange markings that are seen on its surface? What can we make of the fact determined from the Mi'kmaq legend that this man was likely Sinclair's right-hand man when it came to underground exploration and mining (see page 24)? Perhaps we can determine, from the sun, moon, and eclipse symbols carved in the effigy, that Sir James was an initiate of the ancient ways of astronomy and the old understanding of the establishment of longitudinal meridians. Perhaps the Westford Knight, in its place at 72 degrees west of the Greenwich Meridian, is positioned along one such roseline. What effect did the Westford Knight's death have on Sinclair's Green Oaks settlement? And in direct reference to the legend, who exactly did "Earthquake" (Gunn) bury under a cedar, and where was this tree located?

We might consider for a moment that the natural striations in the rock of the effigy were used to represent an underlying map depicting the latitude and longitude of inland rose settlements. This possibility may appear far-fetched at first, but perhaps not after considering the symbolism found within the effigy itself. In fig. 1.16, we can discern the pattern of north–south roselines effectively delineated by the knight's sword and the piercing of his eye and foot (itself an interesting detail in that Sir James supposedly died of a snakebite). Also provided on the diagram are the relative geographical features and longitudinal/latitudinal degrees of separation found within the grid. If we consider that the Green Oaks settlement, at about 64 degrees west longitude in modern terms, was positioned in relation to one of the first roselines established in the New World, then an ancient pattern of "8 degrees of separation" could be determined from this starting point. The number 8 has not been insignificant through time: $8 \times 8 = 64$, the number of squares on a chess board; $8 \times 9 = 72$, the number of right angles within the Seal of Solomon; $8 \times 10 = 80$, with 8 suggesting infinity and beyond. Add to this significant north–south arrangement the pattern of latitudinal positioning delineated by the angle of the knight's shield and we may begin to discern that the knight is definitely a map carved in stone. Note

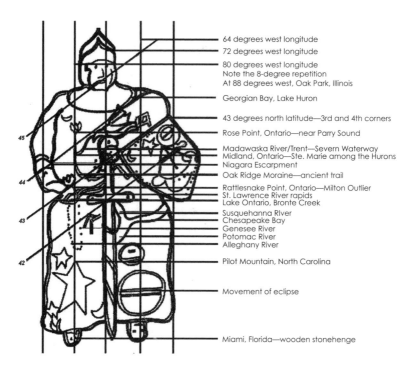

64 degrees west longitude
72 degrees west longitude
80 degrees west longitude
Note the 8-degree repetition
At 88 degrees west, Oak Park, Illinois

Georgian Bay, Lake Huron

43 degrees north latitude—3rd and 4th corners
Rose Point, Ontario—near Parry Sound

Madawaska River/Trent—Severn Waterway
Midland, Ontario—Ste. Marie among the Hurons
Niagara Escarpment
Oak Ridge Moraine—ancient trail

Rattlesnake Point, Ontario—Milton Outlier
St. Lawrence River rapids
Lake Ontario, Bronte Creek

Susquehanna River
Chesapeake Bay
Genesee River
Potomac River
Alleghany River

Pilot Mountain, North Carolina

Movement of eclipse

Miami, Florida—wooden stonehenge

Fig. 1.16. The pattern of north–south roselines delineated on the Westford Knight. These are revealed through the various alignments defined by the knight's elements. Original drawing by William F. Mann.

the 43 degrees north latitude established through the third and fourth quadrant of the shield on the effigy. What better marker would there be for those who followed in Prince Henry's footsteps and were given the "eyes" to read what remained unfathomable to the noninitiate?

If we compare those features highlighted on the effigy in fig. 1.16 to the relative features of eastern North America as shown in a modern atlas, a startling pattern begins to emerge. Speculating further, we can recognize that the knight's right hand contains both a rosary and a rose and that a rose is also positioned over his right chest. Speculating even further, might these relative positions be the sites where inland rose settlements awaited Prince Henry and his trusted entourage and where chests or caches of certain significance would be deposited for recovery in the future? Could the inclusion of the rosary and the rose suggest a veneration of both the Virgin Mary and Mary Magdalene? In comparing the "map" or grid on the effigy to an actual geographical grid reference map of eastern North America, we can also recognize that an important settlement (Montreal) is positioned at the pommel of the sword, signified on the effigy by the depiction of a dove of peace. We will learn more about these specific settlements in later chapters, but of course, if they were to be considered as "temples" of a sort in honor of the Holy Bloodline and of God, it would be necessary that treasure or relics of a holy nature be buried in order to consecrate these "temples."

Earlier we learned of the bond that Prince Henry no doubt encouraged and sought out between the Mi'kmaq and him and his followers. Some theorize that he brought with him to the New World three of his daughters, and that to cement the bond between the natives and the Templars, several marriages occurred between the two groups, including the marriage of these three daughters to three Mi'kmaq chiefs. We could further speculate from a local Mi'kmaq legend that tells of the vanished Mi'kmaq tribe that once lived along the Shubenacadie River: Might this tribe, if it included mixed European and Mi'kmaq (now known as Métis) blood, have moved inland with Prince Henry, aiding him in his travels along the ancient native waterways and trails to be found there? This may appear more reasonable when we consider that the Mi'kmaq were one of fifty-six nations comprising the greater Algonquin Nation, which extended from the eastern seaboard inland to approximately the roseline defined by the Westford Knight's right hand. The Algonquin or Wabanaki Confederation, which included the Malisett, Passamaquoddy, and Abenaki peoples as well as the powerful Huron Nation, extended as far south as Cape Hatteras on the coast of North Carolina and as far north as the Ottawa River in what is now the province of Ontario—the area that is roughly contained within the carved effigy of the Westford Knight.

Despite all our speculation, however, the veil of secrecy remained in place over the New World and its foreign visitors in the fourteenth and fifteenth centuries. It seems significant that we can find no additional rumors or clues in the myths and legends of the Algonquin Nation or in the discovery of caches or ruins relating to Prince Henry's purported or possible inland settlements. The truth is that the Templars were forever on the run simply because they possessed something of infinite value. Because of this, they were constantly on guard and likely covered their tracks through any cunning means at their disposal. Surely, one of the best methods of concealment is to blend into the native population in both manner and deed. Yet given that they possessed a military and religious outlook that was distinctly European, they would not have completely trusted their native companions, and certain of their manners and dress would have been difficult to disguise. Ultimately, those who arrived in later centuries erased any final remnants of these early settlers, assuming as their own the very foundations of the first Templar settlements and building upon them in their own ways. As we will see, this is exactly what occurred during the founding of the great city of Montreal.

Of course, it now appears that a great deal of the Templars' activity in the New World also took place underground, beyond the prying eyes of those around them. The Templars likely took advantage of the existing waterways and ancient trails that ran inland from the eastern seaboard better to conceal their activities. In addition, they possessed the advantage of being able to communicate in languages that would have appeared foreign and unintelligible to the natives they encountered—a further means of "disguise." But one of their greatest means of secrecy was that the natives passed down their stories orally, committing them to memory as they moved between generations. To aid the process of memorization and communication, the natives used a sophisticated system of symbols. The Mi'kmaq, in fact, developed a hieroglyphic form of language whose origin poses questions about earlier contact with Europe and North Africa that no one can as yet satisfactorily answer.[42] It is possible that this highly complex pictographic system not only allowed communication between two very diverse cultures and aided the memorization of an oral history, but also contained hidden symbolism or underlying themes relating to the Knights Templar, the Merovingian dynasty, and the guardianship of ancient knowledge—information that would remain locked and secret to "outsiders" but would be obvious to the initiate who recognized that time presented no boundaries.

The Books of Hours

The late fourteenth and early fifteenth centuries were a turbulent time of unrest and strife in France. Yet there lived during this period one of the greatest patrons in the history of art, Jean, duc du Berry, whose lavish and imaginative support made possible the illustration of two of the most exquisite illuminated Middle Age manuscripts known today: the *Tres Belles Heures* and the *Tres Riches Heures*.[43] These manuscripts are exceptional for two reasons: Their imagery is remarkable for its historical accuracy and detail and their illuminations contain some important—and disguised—information relating to roselines.

The Books of Hours, generally intended for private use, were the most popular devotional books of the later Middle Ages. They were collections of text for each liturgical hour of the day—hence their name. Usually preceding this text is a calendar followed by the Hours of the Cross, of the Holy Ghost, and of the Passion. These were placed between extracts from the gospels, various prayers and daily devotions, the Penitential Psalms, the Litany of Saints, and Masses for certain holy days.

Jean du Berry was not entirely satisfied with any of the existing Books of Hours and therefore commissioned the most famous contemporary artists—André Beauneveu, Jacquemart de Hesdin, and Paul de Limbourg and his two brothers—to illustrate new editions of these devotional books. Although the *Tres Riches Heures* is considered the most beautiful of all of the duke's Books of Hours, he owned others that had been executed specifically for members of his family: The *Heures de Jeanne d'Evreux* was illuminated by Jean Pucelle and the so-called *Heures de Savoie* was begun in Pucelle's workshop and completed during the reign of Charles V.

One significant miniature found in the *Tres Belles Heures* introduces Psalm 44, known as "The Mystic Marriage between Christ and the Church" (see fig. 1.17): "Hearken, O daughter, and see, and incline thy ear: and forget thy people and thy father's house. And the king shall greatly desire thy beauty . . . All the glory of the king's daughter is within in golden borders clothed round about with varieties." Most fascinating about the illumination accompanying this text is that it depicts Christ holding a red book and leaning in a rather intimate fashion toward a woman who is quite pregnant. Outwardly, this woman is representative of the Virgin Mary as the Church. But Christ is depicted as a grown man here—how can Mary still be pregnant? A group of saintly figures, halos shining against a delicately squared background, participate in the spiritual marriage but at the same time appear to be partaking in some kind of gossip, as though whispering secrets about what is about to occur.

The *Tres Belles Heures* essentially depicts the twelve months of the year and the outdoor activities related to each. One of the most interesting symbolic illuminations is found in the month of May (see fig. 1.18). Traditionally, May Day, a pagan holiday that honored and promoted fertility and marked the beginning of the growing season, was the scene for this month. This particular painting shows the more courtly aspects of the holiday, depicting three distinct yet related royal women riding their horses. Atop their muscular horses they appear as the symbolism of royal virginity and breeding, with each lady bedecked in green, the color of fertility, and crowns of laurel and other greenery. With the creation of this image occurring in the same era as Sinclair's voyage, could these be

Fig. 1.17. The Mystic Marriage between Christ and the Church, Psalm 44 in the Tres Belles Heures, commissioned by Jean du Berry and painted by the Limbourg brothers. Note that the Virgin Mary is depicted as pregnant at a time when Christ is depicted as a grown man. Reproduced courtesy of the Musée Condé, Chantilly, France.

Fig. 1.18. A depiction of May in the Tres Belles Heures, commissioned by Jean du Berry and painted by the Limbourg brothers. The symbolism of the three sisters, all dressed in green and riding majestic horses, relates directly to fertility and the rites of spring. Reproduced courtesy of the Musée Condé, Chantilly, France.

symbolic of the sisters of the Holy Bloodline who traveled to the New World with Prince Henry Sinclair?

The color green relates back to the knightly Order of St. Lazarus, formed during the Crusades. While in Palestine and during the first two centuries following their retreat to Europe, the members of the order marked themselves with a simple cross of green fabric sewn to the front of their robes or tunics and the left side of their mantle. It was in all likelihood at the beginning of the twelfth century that the Hospitaliers of St. Lazarus adopted this badge to differentiate themselves from the warrior-monks of the Order of the Knights of the Temple, who wore a red cross on a white mantle, and the Hospitallers of St. John, who wore a white cross on a black mantle that later became the familiar eight-pointed figure known as the cross of Malta.[44]

A papal bull issued by Pope Innocent VIII in 1489 joined the Orders of St. Lazarus and St. John of Jerusalem. After more than half a century of passive resistance, in 1557 the Order of St. Lazarus agreed to be led by grand masters belonging to the Order of St. John. In 1608, King Henry IV decided to join the Order of Our Lady of Mount Carmel—the Carmelites—to the Order of St. Lazarus. Of course, the raising of Lazarus, as described in the Gospel of John, speaks of the healing powers or mysteries of Christ. Apparently the headquarters of St. Lazarus in the thirteenth century were near Orleans, suggesting that Jean du Berry knew a great deal about what lay in the secret rose garden of courtly love, which was established in the New World by Prince Henry Sinclair.

Good King René

It is René d'Anjou, grand-nephew of the duc du Berry, who has in all probability provided the greatest wealth of material relating to Prince Henry Sinclair's activities in the New World. Born in 1408, René d'Anjou was not only a major contributor to the formation of the Renaissance academies, but was also one of the first champions of the idea of Arcadia, that pristine, idyllic place of peace and bounty and beauty.

Royal duke, titular king, artist, and poet, René (known as Good King René) was intelligent, attractive, sensitive, tolerant, and fatalistic, and saw himself as a chivalric knight in the tradition of the Grail and Arthurian romances. His father was Louis II, duke of Anjou and Provence, and his mother was Yolande of Aragon. His first wife, Isabelle, was the ten-year-old daughter of Charles II of Lorraine and Marguerite of Bavaria. At the time of René's marriage, Charles, the dauphin of France, was married to René's sister Marie and had been living at the Angevin court for five years. By the time René was twenty, in 1429, he and Isabelle had four children: Louis, Yolande, Jean, and Marguerite, who became queen of England after marrying Henry VI as part of truce negotiations after the Hundred Years War (the Wars of the Roses).[45]

In 1419, his grand-uncle Cardinal Louis, duke of Bar, adopted him as inheritor of the duchy of Bar, which he assumed after his grand-uncle's death in 1430. In November 1434, Duke Louis III of Anjou, René's elder brother, died while campaigning for Giovanna II of Naples. As a result, René inherited Anjou and Provence and claims to the kingdoms of Naples, Sicily, and Jerusalem, all confirmed by Giovanna on her death in 1435. But although René held the title of king of Jerusalem, he never exercised his authority.[46]

In 1449, René staged a series of "plays" known as *pas d'armes*. One of the most famous, *The Pas d'Armes of the Shepherdess*, features an Arcadian shepherdess presiding over a tournament of knights whose identities represent conflicting values and ideas. For his second wife, Jeanne de Laval, whom he married following the death of Isabelle in 1453, he wrote *Regnault et Jeanneton*, a pastoral ode of ten thousand verses that presents a debate on love between a shepherd and a shepherdess, with a pilgrim wayfarer serving as arbiter. René also wrote *Le Cavalier Coeur d'Amour*, a beautifully illustrated satire on courtly love.[47]

In René's writing, the theme of an Arcadian underground stream, often symbolized by a fountain or a tombstone, appears to relate to the "underground" esoteric tradition of Pythagorean, gnostic, Kabbalistic, and Hermetic thought. But the imagery might also refer to very specific factual information—perhaps to a "secret," such as an unacknowledged, and thus "subterranean," bloodline or, more concretely, to a labyrinth of settlements that existed in the New World/Arcadia during the fifteenth and sixteenth centuries.

This concept of a "subterranean" bloodline that René incorporated into his writing suggests that certain members of nobility were predestined to marry other identified bloodlines both for political purposes and to keep the "stock" strong and healthy. René's own bloodline, which included the House of Lorraine, is a prime example of a controlled mix of heraldic and genealogical purity.[48] The same can be said for that branch of the Sinclair family descended directly from one of the original nine knights, Henri de Saint-Clair.

Probably the most famous of all of René's literary works is the allegorical tale *Le Couer d'amours espris* (The Heart Smitten with Love). Modeled on the previously published *Roman de la rose,* it represents a return to earlier knightly poetry involving the theme of a quest for the Holy Grail in which a "green" knight and his attendant/apprentice try to free a damsel in distress through a number of gallant deeds. One of the more famous illustrations from this work is *La Fontaine de fortune,* depicting the knight posed in reflection near a magical fountain while his attendant rests near the duo's two horses.

It is said to be an illustration of the concept of the underground stream of esoteric thought, including the theme of Arcadia. The researchers Richard Andrews and Paul Schellenberger, in *The Tomb of God—The Body of Jesus and the Solution to a 2000-Year-Old Mystery,* claim that this work by René d'Anjou is one of the first—perhaps the first—to attempt to preserve the most secret of secrets (knowledge of the Holy Bloodline and that this bloodline possessed ancient knowledge) by means of occult art.[49] But even though Andrews and Schellenberger have realized the significance of this painting in terms of its underlying geometric composition, they have failed to grasp the rose symbolism that pervades it.

In figure 1.19 we can see that the tree trunk, the knight's lance, and the right foreleg of the horse are positioned in such a way as to approximate a tripod, an ancient symbol of the Olympian god Apollo and of secret societies in general. But the tripod is also a surveying instrument—and here it may represent such an instrument that was used to determine a roseline, with the tree trunk itself serving as the western meridian. Further, although many scholars claim the painting depicts the time of sunrise, there is the faint hint that an eclipse is occurring (see page 33). Another

Fig. 1.19. The illustration La Fontaine de fortune *from René d'Anjou's* Couer d'amours espris. *Reproduced courtesy of the National Gallery, London.*

clue related to meridians is the fountain—or source of the "underground stream"—located between the two green oak trees that stand parallel to each other, thus establishing a third meridian, which in this case may be positioned somewhere in the Atlantic Ocean.

René's connections to the craft of surveying continue in the symbol that he adopted as his personal emblem: the cross of Lorraine, a double-armed cross that is the modern-day symbol of the Knights Templar of Canada. This was also the emblem adopted by Charles de Gaulle and the Free French forces during World War II. Andrews and Schellenberger believe the two bars in the cross indicate that, rather than being the cross of the Crucifixion, it is the cross staff, an early surveying device for measuring angles to determine altitudes and bearings. These authors believe that the cross of Lorraine is "symbolic of surveying, and thus of the concealment of the Secret and the preservation of the knowledge of its location by means of triangulation and the establishment of the meridian and parallel of the Site."[50] Andrews and Schellenberger relate this belief to a location in the south of France, but, as we will see, a series of ancient meridians also lies across the Atlantic Ocean in the New World.

As for the apprentice in the painting, he appears almost suspended in a trance at the base of the oak tree and at the feet of his horse. Interestingly, upon looking closely at the saddle of one of the horses, we can detect what look almost like wings, suggesting Pegasus, the "horse of God" that allowed mere humans to fly to the sun. In addition, this horse's head seems to be severed from its body by the tilted lance, suggestive of a connection to the ancient Celtic practice of burying a horse's head in a field in order to ensure fertility.

All of this can be linked to the earliest Grail legends that tell of Arthur being not dead but instead transported, sleeping, to the Isle of Avalon until the time when he can be awakened. It can also be tied to the Mi'kmaq legends that speak of the "man who desired to live a long time" and was therefore buried at the base of an "ever-green" tree. Significantly, at the site of Green Oaks in Nova Scotia, a capstone has been discovered showing a carved tripod—and buried just beneath this stone was the skull of a horse (fig. 1.20).

Fig. 1.20. The capstone and horse's skull discovered at Green Oaks. Photograph by William F. Mann.

Where the search for the Holy Grail is concerned, it is easy to see symbolism everywhere, even where none exists, but the significance of René's painting cannot be dismissed. René d'Anjou was a man of learning and influence in several courts and among the nobility of France and throughout the rest of Europe. Because of this and by way of his marriages, he may well have been privy to all kinds of court rumors relating to the secret activities of the Templars in the New World. As such, René's role in establishing an esoteric elite among certain ruling dynasties should not be underestimated. With René's death on July 10, 1480, there came the notion of the sleeping white knight or king who fell silent for a time, awaiting the dawn of a New Jerusalem that would be reflective of an earlier age of chivalry, the rose, and the quest for the Holy Grail.

2

THE LOST
TEMPLAR COLONIES

In examining the rediscovery and exploration of the New World by the Knights Templar during the fourteenth and fifteenth centuries in chapter 1, readers may discern a lack of reference to the role of Christopher Columbus, who, history tells us, made his journey of discovery in 1492. But we now know that long before the time of Columbus, the New World not only was visited by the Vikings and Irish, but may also have been "discovered" by pre-Christian mariners such as the Egyptians, Phoenicians, Carthaginians, Irish Celts, and Celtic Iberians from North Africa and Iberia. In fact, solid archaeological evidence uncovered in excavations such as the one conducted at l'Anse-aux-Meadows in Newfoundland has confirmed that pre-Columbian, transatlantic exploration and settlement occurred on a regular basis.[1] There is even current speculation that ancient Hebrews from the Holy Land, black Africans from the southern Sahara, Mycenaeans, Greeks, Romans, and even the Chinese had all crossed the Atlantic over a period of at least one thousand years before 1492.[2]

In addition to our understanding that Columbus was not the first to arrive here from a faraway land are the developing theories about Columbus himself. One of the most revealing books on this particular subject is Michael Bradley's *The Columbus Conspiracy*. In it the author speculates that Columbus was in fact a double agent for the Grail bloodline and therefore purposely led the Spaniards away from the lost inland colonies located in the north of the American landmass.* Interestingly, it seems that the wife of Columbus was a direct descendant of the Sinclair line through the Drummond family, and some say that Columbus himself was once in the employ of Good King René and that he had earlier sailed to Iceland. It has even been speculated that Columbus either stumbled upon or was given outright a number of old Templar maps that showed the New World lying to the west of Europe.

Whatever Columbus's role may have been in the "discovery" of America, between 1398 and approximately 1550 the Grail refugees and their descendants in the north of the New World probed inland along a number of major river routes that eventually converged in the Great Lakes. In support of this theory of exploration, evidence of seemingly Grail-related activity has been found throughout Nova Scotia, New Brunswick, Quebec, Ontario, Maine, New York State, New Hampshire, Vermont, and Pennsylvania. In addition, as we have seen in chapter 1, there are a number of plausible reasons as to why Prince Henry Sinclair and his inner circle, the natives who accompanied them, and their descendants might have moved toward the Great Lakes via such inland waterways as the St. John, White, Hudson, Susquehanna, Connecticut, Allegheny, and Genesee Rivers.[3]

We can also assume that these refugees possessed an infinite secret that related to the direct descendants of the Holy Bloodline, and some believe that they also guarded a physical treasure of great wealth and significance. As the refugees themselves were no doubt aware, both of these possessions would naturally lead to investigation and advances by agents of several European dynasties and the Church, who would have dearly loved to get their hands on the treasure and to obliterate

---

*Michael Bradley, *The Columbus Conspiracy,* 4–16. Another recent book, *The Columbus Myth,* by Ian Wilson, supports the claim that Bristol mariners, expelled from Iceland and searching for a new supply of cod, rediscovered Newfoundland some twelve years before Columbus's arrival in the New World. Wilson attempts to demonstrate that Bristol fishermen preceded by a decade to the shores of America not only Columbus but also John Cabot. With regard to knowledge of Templar meridians and the related probability that there was a good deal of pre-Christian exploration of North America, it seems moot to discuss any "discovery" around 1492. Significant in Wilson's book is the historical account he presents of Cabot's supposed voyage(s), which, like those of Columbus and Champlain, are full of strange contradictions.

all signs of earlier Grail occupation in the New World to prevent any descendants of the House of David from laying claim to any European monarchy. Resulting from this was a significant amount of intrigue and deflection that occurred during the early part of the sixteenth century along the eastern seaboard of the New World, which itself must have taken on a certain aura to the aboriginal nations of this region. Ultimately these intrigues required that individual native tribes or whole nations choose sides.

Aside from a desire to escape the grasping hands of European nobility and the Church, there was a simpler reason for the movement inland of the "lost" Templar refugees: Because they counted important and wealthy people among their number, they were in need of maintaining a certain Old World lifestyle. This in conjunction with their need to constantly be prepared for European attack by maintaining a considerable standard of weaponry meant that they must constantly search farther inland for rich deposits of readily accessible metals and enough fertile land to sustain their ever-growing colonies. These ideas are explored in depth in Michael Bradley's *Grail Knights of North America* and in *Swords at Sunset*,[4] which he wrote with Joelle Lauriol.

It was the Canadian Shield, extending as far south as New Hampshire and Vermont and encompassing the Great Lakes, that offered a more-than-suitable area for agriculture. It is also a region with a seemingly unlimited abundance of metals such as copper and iron ore as well as the rare earth metals titanium and manganese. The significance of these deposits is that they were readily accessible to either the crude open-pit or surface mining that was typical of medieval technology.[5] Perhaps not so coincidentally, many of these deposits are found along some of the ancient roselines in the New World—areas that the natives themselves had a long and ancient practice of relating to spiritual energy.

The Templars were certainly ingrained with a European military mentality and likely approached every reconnaissance, excursion, and settlement with a strategic flair that was the result of the lessons of three centuries of constant battle. They also possessed perhaps the finest combination of agricultural, mining and smelting, milling, forestry, navigation, astronomical, animal husbandry, and stonemasonry skills available anywhere, which no doubt allowed them to construct towers and fortified settlements and practice agriculture in a fashion that would have seemed foreign to the natives of that time.

Norumbega

The idea of a series of holy refuges or secret settlements in pre-Columbian North America centers on a plot that most historians do not address, yet from a strategic point of view, the plan makes sense: The Templar refugees, aware of the possibility of pursuit, knew they would forever be fighting a rearguard action. Their strategy, therefore, must have been to have an inland settlement prepared and waiting for them whenever foreign sails were spied on the horizon. Like the knights on a chessboard, they could continually leapfrog to farther-inland sanctuaries until that time when they would be either absorbed into frontier life or obliterated from history.

Of course, even if the lines of communication between the Old World and the New were intermittent at best, rumors of New World colonies must have made their way back to the ports of Europe. Stories and myths would surely have passed among the Portuguese, English, and Basque fishermen who plied their trade just off the eastern seaboard on the Grand Banks during the fifteenth and sixteenth centuries. From his own records, we know that in 1497 John Cabot (originally Giovanni Caboto, from Genoa), while on a mission for the English sovereign Henry VII, mentioned the sighting of a number of foreign fishing boats and temporary camps along the banks of Newfoundland. Following the coast using information he apparently gleaned from the fishermen of Bristol, Cabot was one of the first to report the whereabouts of the Lost City of Norumbega.[6]

Norumbega is supposed to have been a city fifteen miles up a river and appears as such on Cornelius Van Wytfliet's map of 1597 (fig. 2.1), entitled "Norumbega and Virginia." The city is shown at 45 degrees north and 315 degrees east (at this time longitude was measured east from the Azores). Interestingly, the latitude and longitude readings add up to 360 degrees. Was this a clue that Norumbega was considered to rest at the end of the earth or beyond the north wind? Similar to the

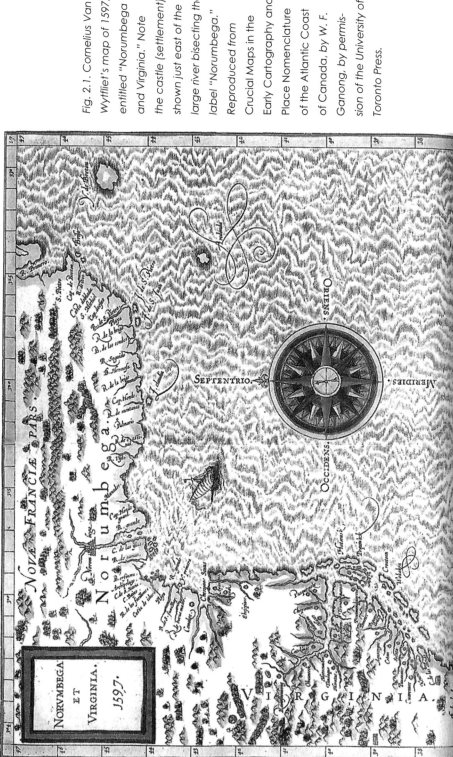

Fig. 2.1. Cornelius Van Wytfliet's map of 1597, entitled "Norumbega and Virginia." Note the castle (settlement) shown just east of the large river bisecting the label "Norumbega." Reproduced from *Crucial Maps in the Early Cartography and Place Nomenclature of the Atlantic Coast of Canada*, by W. F. Ganong, by permission of the University of Toronto Press.

supposed location of Norumbega, the Green Oaks settlement is positioned at 45 degrees 15 minutes north latitude.

As for the source of the name Norumbega, Father Sebastian Rasle, a French priest and missionary among the Wabnaki Indians of Maine during the eighteenth century, thought he had found its source in the Wabnaki word Aranmbegh,* which he translated as "at the water's head" (though more recent scholars have favored "at the clay inlet.")[7] Others have traced Norumbega to the Mi'kmaq Nolumbeka, which is said to mean "a succession of falls and still waters," or to Nalambigik, "pool of still water," or to Norman Villa.[8] It appears clear, however, that Norman Villa and Norumbega were two different places. The usual theory is that the latter was the name of a river, and many have associated Norman Villa with one of the legendary Seven Lost Cities.

The legend of the Seven Lost Cities began in eighth-century Spain, where legend holds that in the year 711 C.E., when the North African Moors descended upon the Visigoths, seven Portuguese bishops managed to escape by ship with a considerable number of their flock.[9] Somewhere in the Atlantic Ocean they eventually reached an island on which they established seven cities.

New World Maps

Along with Cornelius Van Wytfliet's map, there are other maps relating to the exploration of the New World. The La Cosa map, dated to 1500 C.E., is the first map that indisputably shows America, including discoveries made apparently by the English, for the northern coastline is decorated with no fewer than five English flags.

There is general agreement among most historians that La Cosa himself must have received detailed information on the reputed discoveries made by John Cabot. An interesting question is whether this map derived merely from Cabot's voyage of 1497 or there exists another

---

*Raymond H. Ramsay, *No Longer on the Map* (New York: Ballantine, 1973), 173. Although many books present cartographic evidence concerning medieval mapping, this section relies most heavily on Ramsay's in-depth studies of many of the earliest Ptolemy maps. In distinct contrast to the accuracy demonstrated by the Zeno and earlier portolan maps, the Ptolemy maps appear to have been based more on mariner tales and rumors than on actual discovery and cartographic skill.

hidden map with unique data from more mysterious voyages in an earlier era such as that of Prince Henry Sinclair.* If La Cosa's map does indeed represent the 1497 Cabot voyage, then it incidentally provides the strongest possible evidence that Cabot's landfall was not Newfoundland, but instead was much farther south on the North American coast.†

Many other maps offer highly suggestive information: The Gastaldi map of 1548 places Tierra de Nurumberg at 315 degrees longitude while L'Arcadia is positioned at 45 degrees latitude. Zaltieri's map of 1566, although it does not give latitudes or longitudes, has attracted a considerable amount of attention from modern institutions such as Harvard because of its remarkable representation of the entire continent of North America. This map, like many others of the same era, speaks to a *taina*—a "refuge"—somewhere along the eastern seaboard.

A significant development in cartography that would have New World implications was the 1666 establishment of the Paris Meridian, the original European marker of longitudinal measurement—the prime meridian—that was replaced in 1884 by the British Greenwich Meridian, despite repeated opposition from the French. In contrast, Norumbega was repeatedly located 45 degrees west of the Azores Meridian by Flemish and Venetian cartographers. This argument over prime meridians is significant to our study in that throughout the centuries, European countries strove to establish the mysterious lost colony or land of Norum-

---

*Andrew Sinclair, *The Sword and the Grail: The Story of the Grail, the Templars, and the True Discovery of America.* Sinclair traces the St. Clair name back to the More family of Viking and Norman ancestry. It seems that on the Epte River, Rolf Rognvald, of the powerful More family, concluded the Treaty of St. Clair in 911, when King Charles the Simple married Rolf's daughter and was converted to Christianity, taking the name St. Clair (meaning "holy light"). The river Epte runs in the north of France in what was once the duchy of Normandy, which also included the southern states of the Lowlands. It is an area that was at one time claimed by the Merovingian dynasty, which counted in its ancestry Byzantine emperors and empresses of the Eastern Roman Empire. All of this means that perhaps the Flemish, Scots, Norse, French, and even the leaders of the Holy Roman Empire can lay claim to Sinclair's explorations.

†Of the voyage of John Cabot, who, under the flag of England's King Henry VII, reputedly sailed from the West Country port of Bristol to North America in 1497, there survives no journal, no biography, and no document in his handwriting. Yet Cabot was hailed as a conquering explorer when, in 1756, the British required a claim to the New World.

bega as their own. Many other intriguing clues gathered from sixteenth-century maps are cited in *The Knights Templar in the New World*.[10]

The Newport Tower

Given the military thinking of the fifteenth and sixteenth centuries, it makes sense that nations establishing colonies or undertaking exploration would build lookouts in order not only to defend waterways leading to settlements, but also to act as beacons—either lighthouses or perhaps even astronomical observatories. This leads us directly to the enigmatic Newport Tower (see fig. 2.2).

Located in Touro Park at the central waterway entrance to Narragansett Bay in Newport, Rhode Island, the Newport Tower may well be the single most enigmatic structure in the United States today.* Many historians and scholars have written extensively about its probable builders and agree on only one point: Native Americans did not erect it.

The tower is a cylindrical structure made of granite fieldstone mortared with limestone. It has eight round columns or pillars connected by eight round arches, suggesting a Romanesque style. Much like Gothic cathedrals, however, there are only three principal windows above the arches. The first window, positioned approximately seventy feet above the ground, faces east, toward Easton Point. The second window faces the Atlantic Ocean due south, and the third window faces west toward Newport Harbor and the entrance to Narragansett Bay. It has been determined that the first and fifth columns (measured clockwise) are situated in a north–south line oriented by the North Star. Inside, the tower has seven small niches and a so-called fireplace built into the wall on the first floor. At the top of each column on the

---

*Bradley, *Holy Grail Across the Atlantic*, 45–79. Bradley notes that the ruins at New Ross are generally similar in type of construction and style to the famous Newport Tower in Rhode Island. In mentioning the Newport Tower, however, Bradley introduces a controversy that crops up throughout his book, as well as those of many others. The Newport Tower was apparently constructed prior to the founding of Newport in 1639. Yet conventional historians are unable to concede that the Newport Tower must have been built prior to any colonial period. Countering this, however, Barry Fell, in *America B.C.*, and Salvatore Michael Trento, in *The Search for Lost America*, present evidence of precolonial European settlement in North America.

Fig. 2.2. The Newport Tower. Photograph by William F. Mann.

inner side, between the arches, there are triangular "sockets" for the wooden beams that provide a solid foundation for a first floor suspended some sixty feet above the ground.

The late James P. Whittall Jr., during the time when he was archaeological director of the Early Sites Research Center in Massachusetts, conducted a number of in-depth studies of the tower and the area surrounding it.[11] It was his belief that it was constructed in the Norman Romanesque style inspired by the Church of the Holy Sepulchre in Jerusalem, the structure built in 330 C.E. and said to contain the tomb of Christ. It is known that the Templars worshipped at the round altar of the Church of the Holy Sepulchre and, upon returning to France from the Crusades, introduced round and octagonal churches to most of Europe. Whittall was one of the first to determine that based upon measurements and the study of features such as arches, windows, niches, beam holes, keystones, mortar, and the orientation of openings, its likely the tower was constructed between 1150 and 1400.

Over the years the construction of the tower has been attributed to a virtual who's who in medieval and early colonial construction, including the Templars, the Norse, the Irish, the Portuguese, and even the colonial governor Benedict Arnold. Yet never have the Cistercians—who may have accompanied Prince Henry on his journeys—received any credit for this building in spite of their obvious relationship with the Templars and similar knowledge base. The Templars and Cistercians were known to have been connected through their religious beliefs, business acumen, and engineering skills. Over time, in fact, the Cistercian order developed a virtual monopoly on mining and milling operations, became experts in the construction of waterworks, and, because of both of these skill bases, controlled commerce. What is more revealing is that within two hundred years of the establishment of the Cistercian order, at a time when the Templars were being forced to move underground to survive, the whole of Europe from Norway to Portugal was blanketed with Cistercian monasteries and convents.

Exhibiting many of the construction techniques employed by the builders of the Newport Tower, the *lavabo* enclosed a Cistercian monastery's main water source.[12] This round or octagonal structure usually had an open arcade on the first floor with an enclosed second story. Although only a few of lavabos have survived, they are rarely considered interesting enough to be mentioned by architectural historians. One of these structures can be found at the Cistercian monastery of Valmagne, near Montpellier in the south of France.

It has been speculated that the second floor of the lavabo was used for more than the monks' daily wash ritual. As their days and nights were passed in silent obedience to the rules of the order, their routine was broken only by the Sabbath, the fixed and movable feast days, and the culminating celebration of Christian faith at Easter. Fixing the exact date of Easter became an obsession with medieval churchmen, yet in order to determine its calendar day, it was necessary first to know the exact length of the year. The true length of the year had confounded calendar makers since the earliest efforts to tally the seasons, however, and this confusion only became more acute with attempts to make solar and lunar cycles coincide. The direct result of their need to sort out this mathematical knot was an astronomy called *computus*. It flourished from the time of Charlemagne through the thirteenth century, was based on classical and Arabic models, and eventually found its way into remote abbeys and parish churches throughout Christendom.

In *Astronomies and Cultures in Early Medieval Europe,* the author Stephen McCluskey outlines techniques used in astronomical observation by monks trained in the arts.[13] McCluskey explains that medieval monks were shown how to use the windows and rooflines of the abbey's buildings as accurate guides in tracking the moon and the stars in their canonical timekeeping. A prime example of this application is found in a pocket-sized eleventh-century liturgical cantata discovered in a French monastery. It includes descriptions of observing the changing azimuth for stars over the buildings of the monastic enclosure in order to determine the time for nocturnal prayers. A similar volume describing ways to tell time by observing the sun and stars as they appear at various windows can still be found in the library of the Cistercian abbey at Villiers-en-Brabant.

To prove this use for such structures, a noted astronomy professor from Rhode Island, William Penhallow, undertook a comparison between the round churches on Bornholm in Scandinavia and the Newport Tower, searching for common astronomical sight lines.[14] He found startling correlations between the Old and New World structures and determined that from within both the Bornholm churches and the Newport Tower there is an array of possible alignments for viewing celestial events, particularly the rising and setting of the sun at solstice and equinox and the positions of the major and minor lunar standstills. The accuracy of these predictions was demonstrated on December 25, 1996, when Douglas Schwartz and James Egan conducted a Christmas vigil within the Newport Tower to photograph the minor lunar standstill with the rising full moon shining through two of the tower's three windows. This northern rising alignment is one of the moon's eight cardinal turning points on its eighteen-and-a-half-year cycle through the sky. Intrigued by the Christmas lunar display, Egan, a professional photographer, began routinely to photograph the tower both inside and out during critical astronomical occurrences. As it happens, not only are Penhallow's conclusions accurate, but Egan has also documented a wide range of more than coincidental astronomically related shadow patterns and sunlight projections defined by the tower's architecture.

As we have seen, many coordinate positions are relative in some way. The Newport Tower, situated at 41 degrees 27 minutes north latitude on the highest point of the peninsula that forms the city of Newport, is located in an approximate four-degree latitudinal separation from the community of Green Oaks in Nova Scotia, adjusting for the fact that the distance between longitudinal positions diminishes the closer we travel to either the North Pole or the South Pole. In terms of longitudinal position, the tower is located at 71 degrees 17 minutes, exactly eight degrees west of Green Oaks, which is located at 63 degrees 17 minutes. Once we have established a third point due east from the tower, the relative positions of Green Oaks and the Newport Tower allow us to construct a right triangle and apply the Pythagorean theorem to determine the distance and bearings between the two land points. With this information, the learned initiate would be able to construct a relatively accurate portolan map of the coastline between the Newport Tower and Green Oaks, Nova Scotia (see fig. 2.3).

We find that the Newport Tower appears on two maps predating the colonial era by more than a half century. Giovanni da Verrazano mapped the area in approximately 1524 and listed the tower on his map and in his logs as Norman Villa. Within his log notes he described the native people who lived near the tower as "white European-Amer-Norse," apparently because of their fair hair and skin.[15] Mercator's World Map of 1569 also shows the exact location of the tower and labels the area around it NORUMBEGA.

The beauty of the site of the Newport Tower is that directly to the east and south there lies nothing but the Atlantic Ocean. At night, a

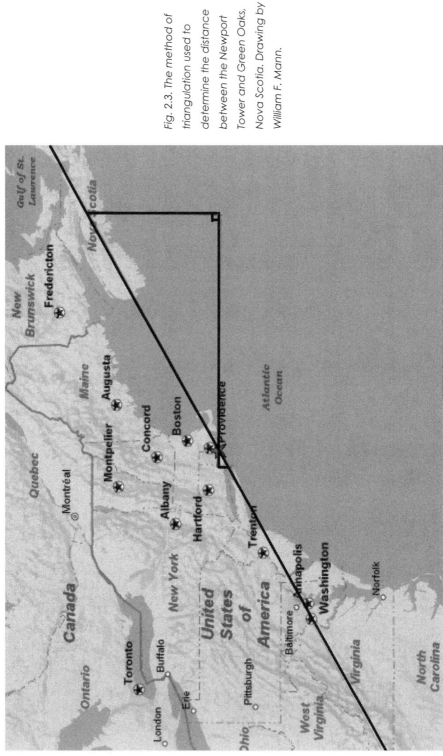

Fig. 2.3. The method of triangulation used to determine the distance between the Newport Tower and Green Oaks, Nova Scotia. Drawing by William F. Mann.

small sliver of firelight coming from the interior of the tower must have been visible for more than twenty nautical miles—but only to those who knew enough to approach the coastline on a true east–west or north–south bearing!

This brings us to the concept of *latitude sailing*—that is, sailing north or south to the latitude of a destination, then sailing east or west until the exact destination is reached. It appears that Cabot chose to follow 45 degrees north latitude, for it is said that he first made for the French port of Bordeaux (latitude 45 degrees 35 minutes north latitude) and then sailed west.

Given this, Cabot's first landfall may have been as far south as Maine, in which case Maine would have been his "mainland" and Nova Scotia his Isle of the Seven Cities. But the more favored view is that he arrived somewhere east of Nova Scotia's most southerly point, worked his way northeast along the coast, and then headed back to Bristol. Coincidentally, like Nova Scotia's Bay of Fundy, Bristol has one of the highest tidal ranges in the world, with its spring tides reaching forty feet. Also coincidentally, La Rochelle—the port from which the Templar fleet disappeared on October 13, 1307—is located at 46 degrees 15 minutes north latitude, approximately one degree latitude north of Green Oaks.

During medieval times, the magnetic deviation of any compass could range from one to three degrees on average, which means that if we were sailing two thousand nautical miles across the Atlantic Ocean using latitude sailing, we might think we were sailing due west when actually we were sailing somewhat southwest and could end up in a location that was one degree south of our destination.

Early Portuguese and French Exploration

During the early part of this century, Professor Edmund Dellebarre, of Brown University, began to unscramble a collection of petroglyphs found on what is called the Dighton Rock (fig. 2.4), a large boulder poking above the high-water mark in Assonet Bay on the Taunton River upstream from Fall River, Massachusetts. This detailed study has subsequently led to a theory that members of the noble Cortereal family

Fig. 2.4. Dighton Rock in Assonet Bay on the Taunton River. The original photograph was taken on December 2, 1918, for Edmund Burke Dellabarre. Reproduced from The Recent History of Dighton Rock, *vol. 20 (The Colonial Society of Massachusetts, 1919).*

of Portugal were responsible for the building of the Newport Tower.[16] According to this theory, Miguel Cortereal was shipwrecked in 1501 or 1502 while searching for his lost brother Gaspar in Narragansett Bay. As a result, he and his remaining crew built the tower as a beacon to alert long-awaited rescuers from home.

Gaspar Cortereal, a member of the Portuguese Order of Templars (renamed the Order of the Knights of Christ in 1320 to avoid persecution by the Catholic Church), was one of the first of a new breed of European explorers whose sails were emblazoned with the cross of the Knights Templar. The king of Portugal himself became grand master of the new Knights of Christ, and later Henry the Navigator (1394–1460) became grand master. This order furnished the financial resources, manpower, and religious training for the the earliest Portuguese navigational expeditions and missionary establishments around the world. The Portuguese Templars were also builders, erecting six castles (Almoural, Idanha, Monsanto, Pombal, Zêzere, and the famous Tomar) in a style similar to the round and octagonal churches they had encountered in the Near East.

In the year 1500, with three caravels and a commission from Portuguese King Emanuel to take possession of whatever he might find, Cortereal attempted to follow the old Viking route to Vinland, then south along Newfoundland and Nova Scotia and perhaps into the Gulf of Maine. He was not, however, venturing into uncharted northern waters, for in 1472 or 1473, his father, Jao Vaz Cortereal, represented the Portuguese crown in a joint venture with Danish interests that were sponsored by the Danish king Christian I.[17] Danes Deitrik Pining and Hans Pothurst led the expedition with the Norwegian Jon Skolp as navigator. It appears that after visiting Greenland and Iceland, they crossed over to Labrador, but were then forced to return to Denmark because of bad weather. It seems reasonable to guess that both father and son Cortereal were attempting to follow in Prince Henry's footsteps, which led from one northern island to another, but we may wonder from whom they received their background information. It seems the Portuguese Templars had teamed up with their Scandinavian counterparts in order to share information, much like the Zenos had been sent to team up with Prince Henry Sinclair and his Scottish Templars nearly a century before.

The notion that the Portuguese Templars possessed both ancient navigational knowledge and maps from earlier "secret" sources in the Middle East is supported by the intrigue and final negotiations that led to the Treaty of Tordesillas and the establishment of the Line of Demarcation (another New World meridian): Between 1492 and 1494, Pope Alexander VI arbitrated between Spain and Portugal, who happened to be the two greatest sea powers loyal to the Church. The Line of Demarcation was adjusted several times but eventually came to run through the easternmost parts of North and South America (see fig. 2.5), with Portugal gaining control of everything east of this line and Spain everything west. The result is that Portugal received, in the northern hemisphere, the known area surrounding Newfoundland, with its rich Grand Banks and, in the southern hemisphere, Brazil with its rich timber. Given that supposedly no one knew of the New World settlements that already existed in Nova Scotia and New England at this time, both of these areas were included within the sphere of Portuguese possession.

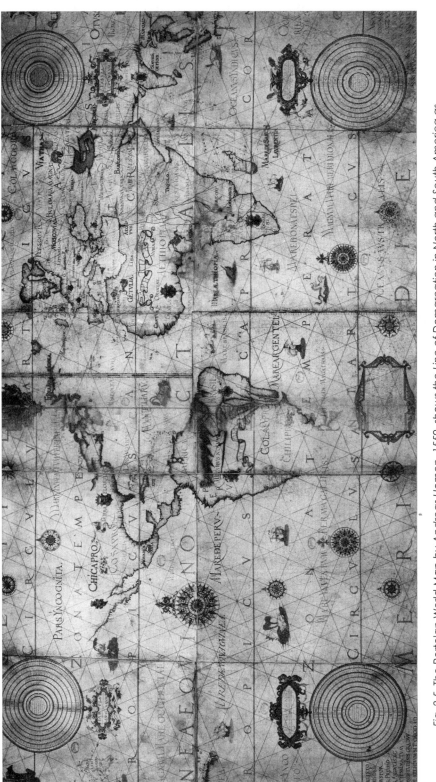

Fig. 2.5. The Portolan World Map by Andreas Homen, 1559, shows the Line of Demarcation in North and South America as negotiated in the Treaty of Tordesillas between Spain and Portugal. Reproduced courtesy of the Bibliotèque Nationale, Paris.

Gaspar's first trip took him to land at 50 degrees latitude and his second trip carried him farther north. Like Prince Henry, during this second voyage he sent home two of his ships, but he and his flagship never returned to Portugal. The following year Gaspar's brother Miguel, also a member of the Order of Knights of Christ, journeyed west with three caravels in search of his lost brother. After arriving safely in the New World, the three ships arranged an August rendezvous before heading in different directions in search of the remnants of Gaspar's previous expedition. Rather curiously, two of the three ships met at the appointed time and place, but Miguel's vessel never appeared and was never heard from again.[18]

Then in 1917 Edmund Dellebarre revealed the discovery of the Dighton Rock showing the date 1511, some Latin letters including MIG–L, and an outline of the Portuguese Templar cross. This discovery allowed for the possibility of the presence of the Cortereals near Narragansett Bay in the early years of the sixteenth century. The theory contends that either Gaspar or Miguel and his respective crew were shipwrecked and built the Newport Tower as a watchtower and signal tower while they waited for rescuers from across the sea. Beyond the possible construction of the tower, perhaps there is a more mysterious aspect to the disappearance of the two men: Perhaps both Gaspar and Miguel had in their possession some secret Templar knowledge that compelled them to move inland following any number of rivers that flow northwest from the Atlantic.

We do know that the eastern coastline of what is now the United States remained largely unexplored for another twenty-four years after these two expeditions. The Spanish had officially discovered Florida and the English and Portuguese had officially discovered Newfoundland, but the area between these two locations was still a blank spot on the map. It was King Francis I of France who finally decided to send out an expedition to specifically investigate the area that lay between the two claims. Because the expedition was to be backed by wealthy Italian bankers and merchants living in Lyons, the king chose the Florentine Giovanni da Verrazano to lead the foray. The year for the voyage is identified as either 1524 or 1525.

Verrazano's Voyage

Verrazano, who had moved to Dieppe, France, to pursue a maritime career, was provided with four ships, but two of them were shipwrecked shortly after departing and a third was sent home carrying a number of prizes from privateering on the Spanish coast. The flagship, *La Dauphine,* was actually the only ship that made the Atlantic crossing. This vessel measured one hundred tons and had a fifty-man crew, including Verrazano's mapmaker brother Girolamo da Verrazano. It was his 1529 world map that was one of the first to show Verrazano's discoveries, including the Newport Tower.

Verrazano set out from Madeira on January 17 and touched land on or around March 1 at what is now Cape Fear, North Carolina. From there he sailed south to an unknown point near present-day Charleston, but noting in his log that he was afraid of running into the Spanish, he sailed north again and anchored not far from his original landfall. In an elaborate letter to the king, he described every aspect of his transatlantic voyage, including a somewhat long-winded dissertation on latitude and longitude, part of which reads:

> It remains for me to tell Your Majesty of the progress of this voyage as regards Cosmography. As I said earlier, we departed from the aforementioned rocks which lie at the limit of the Occident as the ancients knew it, and in the meridian of the Fortunate Islands, at a latitude of 32 degrees north from the Equator in our hemisphere, we sailed westward until we first found land at 1,200 leagues— which is equal to 4,800 miles, counting four miles to a league in accordance with the maritime practice of naval experts: geometrically, according to the ratio of three plus 1½ times one seventh [3 3/14] of the diameter to the circumference, that is, 92 and 54,164/47,233 degrees. This is correct. For, since the chord [diameter] of an arc of the greatest circle is 114 6/11 degrees, and the chord [diameter] of the parallel of 34 degrees where we first found land, according to the same ratio, is 95 and 233/450 degrees, then the circumference of the whole circle is 300 and 713/1,575 degrees; allowing 62½ miles for each degree (which most of those who have experimented confirm as the distance on earth correspond-

ing to the proportion of the sky), this should give us 188,759 and 31/126 miles, divided into 360 parts, which would come to 52 and 989/9,072 miles each . . . [19]

This notation certainly disproves the notion that the maritime explorers of the sixteenth century were merely sailing "by the seat of their pants." Verrazano obviously had some knowledge of a longitudinal science that was derived from the "ancients," as he himself says. It also suggests that Verrazano practiced latitude sailing and somehow missed the specific landfall he was expecting to reach. The area around the entrance to Charleston Harbor, located at 32 degrees 30 minutes, is certainly distinctive, as is Cape Fear to the north, at 33 degrees 50 minutes. It appears as though Verrazano was looking for a particular headland that had previously been mapped and noted, as though he knew that he had to start his journey north along the eastern coastline from a previously identified latitude. Interestingly, if Verrazano had deviated north from 32 degrees north latitude, then he would most likely have run into or at least sighted Bermuda, also located at 32 degrees 30 minutes. Curiously, he fails to mention even the sighting of this landmass.

Sailing in a northeasterly direction along the coast from Cape Fear, he first reached the Outer Banks of North Carolina. Here he mistakenly believed that the sea to the west of the banks—Pimlico Sound—was the Pacific Ocean. North America thus appeared to him to be little more than a rather long, extremely narrow isthmus. This mistake led mapmakers, beginning with Maggiolo and Girolamo, to show North America as almost completely divided in two, with its two pieces connected by a narrow piece of land on the east coast. It would take more than a century for this "Sea of Verrazano" to disappear from maps altogether.

Significantly for our story, farther north he came to a beautiful place that he called Arcadia (perhaps what is now known as Virginia Beach). Sailing farther still, he missed the distinctive entrance to the Chesapeake Bay and to the Delaware Bay because he wanted to keep away from the coast out of fear of the natives. He eventually came upon what we now know to be New York Harbor, where he anchored in the narrows that would later acquire his name (as would the bridge that spanned them). Given that he did not allow himself the luxury of hugging the coastline (a common practice in navigation), Verrazano's path suggests that he followed a distinctive compass bearing until he virtually had to run into land. Given that all of this travel occurred in early spring, when there is quite a threat of storms off the eastern seaboard, Verrazano's path farther from the coast would no doubt make it difficult to find shelter. Still, he stayed his course.

Once he shifted his direction to the east because the land itself spreads in that direction, Verrazano continued until he came upon Block Island and reached Narragansett Bay. It was here that for once he decided to break habit and anchor near the coast. After making contact with the local natives, the Wampanoags, who apparently were friendlier than most of the other tribes he encountered, he was shown the present-day sheltered harbor of Newport. Here he stayed for two weeks waiting, we are told, for better weather conditions. During this time the crew spent all of their time trading with the natives.

After departing the harbor, Verrazano sailed northeast, missing the Bay of Fundy and most of Nova Scotia altogether before reaching Newfoundland. Because this region had already been explored, he headed for France and, after a fast Atlantic crossing, reached Dieppe on July 8. In his *Lost Colony of the Templars,* Steven Sora has devoted an entire book to what he perceives to be Verrazano's discovery of the remnants of Prince Henry Sinclair's New World colony, namely the Newport Tower and the Wampanoag. Yet there is now substantial new evidence, presented in Michael Bradley's *Swords at Sunset,* suggesting that the Grail refugees had by this time moved inland, perhaps as a direct result of earlier warnings from their fellow Knights Templar, the Cortereals. We can recall that while the Cortereals were sailing under the Templar flag, Verrazano was being directly commissioned by the French king.

Verrazano himself made two more voyages, one in 1527 and the other in 1528. Apparently, during the 1527 voyage, Verrazano's crew mutinied and ordered him to return to France, but it is said that he took advantage of the crew's navigational incompetence to reach Brazil, where, now pacified because of the natural riches Brazil offered, the crew cut a red wood then called brazilwood (from which the name for the place may have originated). Upon returning to France, all was forgiven, for the backers of the voyage made a substantial profit from the sale of this exotic wood.

According to Verrazano's official biographer, his brother, the map-maker Girolamo, in 1528 Giovanni again crossed the Atlantic, this time landing in Florida and following the chain of the Lesser Antilles. It seems that by this time he had overcome his fear of the Spanish. Yet he still anchored a fair distance away from the shore, which proved fatal for the navigator in this instance. While Giromalo remained on the main vessel, Giovanni headed toward shore in a small boat to meet with the natives—who were the cannibalistic Caribs. They killed Verrazano and ate him in view of his brother. Thus ended Verrazano's chapter in the quest for whatever New World Holy Grail could be found. Next in line in the search was the Frenchman Jacques Cartier.

Cartier and Hochelaga

Jacques Cartier was, it is said, the first European to navigate, map, and attempt to settle in the northern St. Lawrence region of the New World. He sailed to this area three times and his extensive records of each voyage are among the first reliable and detailed documents of European exploration in North America. His was the first official penetration of North America and provided major changes in the cartographic representation of the continent by Europeans.

Born in Saint-Malo, France, in either 1491 or 1493, Cartier came to be considered one of the very best sea captains in Europe. Some historians believe he may have accompanied Verrazano on his New World explorations in 1524. On March 19, 1534, Cartier was assigned by the king the mission of "undertaking the voyage of this kingdom to the New Lands to discover certain islands and countries where there are said to be great quantities of gold and other riches" and to try to find a passage to Cathay (China).[20] Does this reference to gold and other riches relate to the discoveries of Columbus or to information concerning existing "rose" settlements in the northern lands?

There is no doubt that Jacques Cartier was already familiar with the sea route that he took in 1534. On April 20, he began his journey with two ships, the *Emerillon* and the *Petite Hermine,* and a crew of sixty-one, and twenty days later he reached Newfoundland. From the Baie des Châteaux (Strait of Belle Isle), Cartier tacked to southern Newfoundland, along the way coming upon the islands that he named the Magdalen. He then set course for present-day Prince Edward Island, thinking it was the mainland. According to his own logs, Cartier then moved on to Chaleur Bay (named Bay of Heat because of the hot summer weather), where, on July 7, he encountered some Mi'kmaq and Iroquois,[21] who seemed quite accepting of his arrival. It is important to note that the Iroquois and Mi'kmaq lived in peace at this time; the Mi'kmaq Nation was confined to the area of present-day Nova Scotia, Prince Edward Island, and New Brunswick, while Iroquois villages dominated the St. Lawrence area from Gaspé to Lake Ontario. Cartier's talks with the Indians were accompanied by trading—recorded as the first acts of trade between the French and the Indians.

Soon after this exchange, Cartier decided to head north toward Gaspé Bay and the mouth of what is now known as the St. Lawrence River. This is rather odd given that he was supposedly following information provided only from Verrazano's voyages—yet we know that Verrazano never explored the Gaspé region. It may demonstrate that the natives provided Cartier with information relating to several villages located along the large river.

On August 10, the feast day of St. Lawrence, the explorer gave the saint's name to a little bay on the northeastern coastline. Cartographers later applied it to what Cartier first recorded as the "great river of Hochelaga and route to Canada" leading to the interior of the continent, a waterway "so long that no man has seen its end."[22] Sailing along the river to the Iroquois village of Stadacona (near the present site of Quebec City), the ships passed what would later be known as Anticosti Island and the mouth of the Saguenay River. Cartier established his headquarters on the St. Croix (St. Charles) River, and five days later boarded the *Emerillon* to travel to the larger settlement of Hochelaga (present-day Montreal Island). Leaving his ship in Lake St. Pierre, he proceeded in a small craft to the Iroquois village, arriving on October 2. Hochelaga, Cartier noted, contained nearly two thousand people, and given the mountain that dominated both the island and the village, he renamed the settlement Mont Réal (now Mont Royal), in honor of the French king.

The inhabitants of Hochelaga told Cartier many tales of wealthy kingdoms upriver such as Seguna and the Saguenay. The people of these mysterious kingdoms apparently dressed themselves in cloth, like Cartier himself did, and they wore ropes of gold around their necks and had plenty of precious stones.[23] The explorer also learned that the country of Canada extended much farther west and was enclosed by immense lakes and guarded by waterfalls of great height. Most of all, the natives made it clear that in the west there were copper, gold, and silver and the same metals that had been used to make the weapons carried by Cartier and his men.

If we accept Cartier's description of Hochelaga, it would appear to be the most formidable settlement at that time in North America: It stood in the midst of broad cleared fields, round and "compassed about with timber, with three courses of rampires [ramparts], one within another, framed like sharp spikes."[24] Over the guarded single entrance and in many places along the palisades as well, there was a raised platform for use in defending against attacks, with piles of stones positioned for dropping on the heads of besiegers (see fig. 2.6). Inside the walls were about fifty longhouses, each designed to accommodate a series of extended matriarchal families. The description of this construction is interesting in that prior to the late 1500s there are no recorded instances of palisades existing in the New World. Fortified villages came into existence about a century later, in the late 1600s, when the Iroquois adopted a warlike attitude toward the Algonquin Nation. Could this section of Cartier's report have been designed to encourage King Francis's hopes of further discoveries of European-type, fortified settlements? Curiously, Cartier made no mention of this place when he returned on his third voyage to the New Land. Even more curious, when Samuel de Champlain visited the same island nearly a century later, he seemed to have found nothing there at all!

During his visit to Hochelaga, Cartier climbed Mont Royal to view the distant land and sea. From the natives who accompanied him, he learned of a series of nearby mountains and great rapids on the St. Lawrence River west of the island. He named the white water the Lachine Rapids because he apparently thought that just past them lay China. Unfortunately, these rapids prevented him from continuing his route to

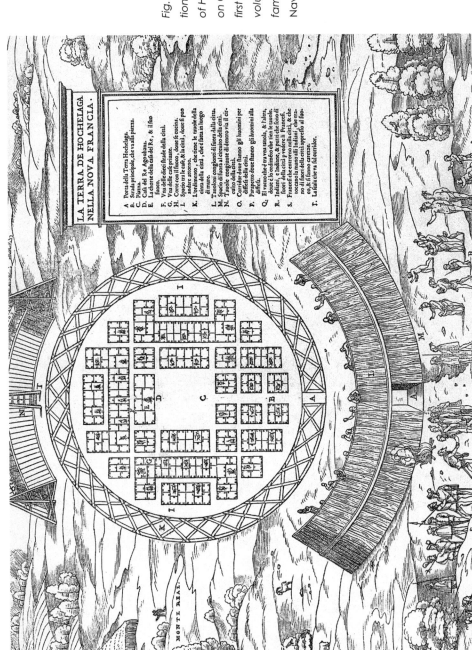

Fig. 2.6. A representation of the settlement of Hochelaga based on Cartier's description, first published in 1556 in volume 3 of Ramusio's famous collection, Delle Navigationi er viaggi.

the west; thus Cartier returned to the mouth of the St. Charles River, where he found that relations between the Iroquois and the men whom he had left behind had become somewhat strained. After a short stay during which he managed to "kidnap" two sons—Domagaya and Taignoagny—of the Iroquois chief Donnacona, Cartier returned to France with his two vessels and his two guests.

Once in France, Domagaya and Taignoagny spoke through an interpreter and told the king of the St. Lawrence River and the "Kingdom of the Saguenay." Francis was impressed. As a result, in May 1535, Cartier left on a second voyage to the New World, again in search of riches and a passage to Asia—this time in command of 110 men divided among three ships: the *Grande Hermine,* the *Petite Hermine,* and the *Emerillon.* To the relief of their father and their people, he returned Donnaconna's sons to Stadacona and left a wealth of gifts for the natives. On this voyage Cartier established St. Croix, a base on the St. Charles River, and a fort at the site of Quebec City; extensively explored the Saguenay River; and returned to the village of Hochelaga. Cartier stayed the winter in the Quebec City fort, but his crew, unprepared for a long season, became sick with scurvy. Twenty-five men died before the natives helped the Europeans regain their health by showing them how to drink a tea made from the needles of white cedar, which are rich in ascorbic acid. In the spring Cartier returned to France, this time with the Iroquois chief Donnaconna and several members of his tribe. Sadly, all of these guests except a young girl would succumb to disease and die in France in 1539.

Cartier's next voyage to Canada was delayed until 1541 due to a rather curious mixture of court intrigue and conflicting egos. On October 17, 1540, Francis I ordered the Breton navigator to return to Canada to lend weight to a colonization project of which he would be "captain general." But on January 15, 1541, Cartier was supplanted by Captain Jean-François de la Rocque, lord of Roberval and a Huguenot courtier. Roberval, who was awaiting the delivery of artillery and merchandise, authorized Cartier to leave and he departed from Saint-Malo on May 23, 1541, with seven ships, including the *Grande Hermine,* the *Petite Hermine,* the *Emerillon,* the *Saint-Brieux,* and the *Georges,* and created a new base near Cap Rouge.[25] On this trip he explored the Saguenay to its source only to find out that the river didn't lead to a larger body of water. Natives in the region harassed Cartier to the point that he left Cap Rouge after one winter. Because of dwindling supplies, most of his men were ill, and mysteriously, by the spring of 1542 Roberval still had not arrived. As it turned out, Roberval was leading across the Atlantic five vessels carrying fifteen hundred people. The crossing took more than three months—long enough to cause us to question his navigational abilities or potential motives he might have had for delaying his arrival. After leaving the St. Lawrence region, Cartier finally came upon his colleague in the harbor of St. John's, Newfoundland. Roberval ordered Cartier to return to Cap Rouge, but Cartier refused and left with his ships that night, landing in Saint-Malo in September.

Jacques Cartier never returned to Canada. As for Roberval, he continued on to the newly named Charlesbourg Royal, which he renamed France-Roi. Again, none of his group was prepared for the harsh northern climate and the bouts of scurvy. Thus, general adversity and quarreling led to the demise of Roberval's colony in 1543. Apparently, Cartier failed to tell Roberval of the native remedy for scurvy. The settlers who survived were quickly repatriated to France as soon as the ice broke in the river. Roberval himself decided to stay and to continue exploration but had limited knowledge of the area and none about the violent Lachine Rapids. In the spring he tried to sail this white water but was unsuccessful. With few remaining resources, he was forced to return to France in the summer.

Throughout his exploration, the only "treasures" Cartier found were pyrite and quartz, which he brought back to France in large quantities, thinking they were gold and diamonds, respectively. When he died in September 1557, at the age of sixty-six, he still believed that the St. Lawrence River led to China. Little did either Cartier or Roberval know that they were quite close to the location of a number of "secret" Templar settlements that flourished in the vicinity until news reached them of Cartier's inland explorations. Fortunately for the New World Templars, the natives acted as their eyes and ears in the forests and along the waterways. It comes as no surprise, then, that one of these settlements, as we will see, was established along an ancient meridian symbolized by a one-eyed owl.

The Owl's Head

A well-kept secret even within Masonic circles is the world's only out-door Masonic lodge room lying entirely in a natural setting. Called Owl's Head Lodge Room, it lies just above a modern ski resort, hidden in the clefts of the summit of Owl's Head Mountain, thirty-five hundred feet above sea level, overlooking Lake Memphremagog (which is located on the border between Vermont and Quebec at 45 degrees north). It can be accessed by only one trail, and though the sides of the mountain are almost perpendicular in places, with the aid of the ski lift for much of the journey, young and old Masons alike undertake an annual pilgrimage to the lodge every June 24.

The room itself, running true east to true west, is of sheer rock that towers more than five hundred feet. The officers' seats are of natural stone. The site was established by what many Masons claim to be a very ancient lodge located across the lake from Vermont, in Canada: At one time Golden Rule Lodge No. 5 of Stanstead, Canada, occupied a lodge room that was bisected by the boundary between Canada and the United States, with entrances on both the Vermont and the Cana-dian sides. Consequently, lodge membership consisted of men from both sides of the border. A charter was applied for and granted to the Golden Rule Lodge in 1853 by the Grand Lodge of England, and once a year on June 24, St. John's feast day, Canadian and American Masons climb the mountain and perform the 3rd degree of Masonry ritual at sunrise.[26] It is said that the ceremony conforms to ancient Masonry and that "the old customs are carried out to the letter" at a time when "the sun is at its meridian."

Many modern-day Masons may not realize that when they participate in the Owl's Head ritual, they are actually paying homage to an ancient tradition: Owl symbolism in fact can be traced back to the goddess Lil-ith, who was often depicted as having an owl's feet and wings and being accompanied by two owls. A derivation of the ancient goddess Lilith, Athena, the Greek goddess of wisdom, is accompanied by an owl that sits on her shoulder on her blind side, telling her all there is to see and know. Myth tells us that only in cooperation with the owl can Athena see the whole truth. It was the Celts who believed the owl carried the souls of the deceased into the Land of Youth, Tir nan Og, or to Avalon, the Isle of

Apples. The owl also figures prominently in a tale from *The Mabinogion,* a collection of Celtic myth and lore: Blodeuwedd is a woman crafted from nine flowers by a wise magician for the hero Gwydion, who cannot love a mortal woman. In the end, however, Blodeuwedd betrays Gwydion and, as punishment, is turned into an owl.

Many Masons insist that the owl refers to the wisdom and foresight of John the Baptist, whose birth has been celebrated on June 24 from the earliest days of the Church. It was John, as the final prophet of the Hebrew scriptures, who told the people that their true lord was near.

There remain some interesting aspects to this lodge location: Regardless of its true origin, we cannot dismiss the significance of Owl's Head Mountain as a natural astronomical observatory (it is the highest point in the vicinity), located at 45 degrees 15 minutes north latitude. In addition, its latitude corresponds rather nicely to that of Green Oaks, Nova Scotia. Finally, Lake Memphremagog and its adjacent communities, such as Magog, Stanhope, Newport, Hatley, and Stanstead (a significant Masonic center), have all been investigated by Dr. Gérard Leduc, a retired professor at Montreal's Concordia University, who has made it his mission to discover evidence that ancient settlers occupied this area prior to traditional colonial times.

We might wonder if this could be the region to which the Grail refugees fled after perhaps being warned of European exploration at the start of the sixteenth century. It is true that stone ruins exist in the relatively undisturbed backwoods along the Vermont-Quebec border.[27] Archaeological investigations and specifically carbon dating conducted by Leduc and others on cairns (stone mounds) in the area now known as Potton Township have revealed that some were built as long ago as eighteen hundred years or fifteen hundred years or as "recently" as six hundred years ago. In Vale Perkins there lies a ruined water mill with distinctive markings that have been determined to be at least six hundred years old. And although it has not been dated, a stone circle discovered by Leduc on a local farm shows all the evidence of an ancient ritual site, complete with an engraved standing stone to indicate, we may assume, the azimuth of the winter solstice sunrise.

We may imagine that Grail-related settlers remained in the Memphremagog region until they received information that outsiders were making inland probes just north of the St. Lawrence River. This general area encompassing Vermont, New Hampshire, and southern Quebec is home to the Green Mountains of Vermont and the White Mountains of New Hampshire, both the origins of a number of the rivers that flow south through Massachusetts and Connecticut to the eastern seaboard. Significantly, the Connecticut River, which enters the sea just west of the Newport Tower, has its source in Lake Connecticut, above the town of St. Johnsbury, Vermont. A short portage from this lake brings us to a number of rivers, including the St. François, that run north into the St. Lawrence Basin. Lake Champlain and the Richelieu River, which runs directly north to Montreal, can be readily accessed from the Connecticut River via the White River, which connects with the Connecticut near present-day Lebanon, New Hampshire. As such, the interlacing of these waterways would provide the perfect labyrinth of escape routes for the Grail refugees if they were threatened.

In addition, the position of the Memphremagog area is significant in relation to an ancient roseline that falls close to the modern longitude of 72 degrees west. In exact terms, the ancient meridian runs north–south at 71 degrees 57 minutes west and is positioned so that it bisects Montauk Point, on the eastern end of Long Island, New York. Currently, the Montauk Point lighthouse stands in the exact location of the meridian at 41 degrees 5 minutes north latitude, 71 degrees 57 minutes west longitude. The significance of this point lies in its relative position to both the Newport Tower and Green Oaks: The present-day Montauk Point lighthouse and the old Newport Tower fall on the same bearing from Green Oaks. We are beginning to see that these locations do not appear to have been chosen haphazardly.

And where does this roseline extend to the north? It bisects the small community of Hatley Corners, Quebec, at the latitude of 45 degrees 15 minutes north. With this in mind, we might wonder whether a hidden meaning can be found in the seemingly mundane name of Hatley Corners. There is at least a suggestion of a ley line and a number of "corners" (referring, perhaps, to the four corners of the square found within Desceliers's map; see page 90). The origin of the word *hat* is the Indo-European word *kadh*, meaning "to shelter" or "to cover." A hat, then, shelters or covers the head. In Old English the word was *hatt* and in German *hoda,* from which our word *hood* is derived. The lengthened Germanic variant is *kodh-in,* or in Old English *hedan,* meaning "to heed," "to care for," or "to protect." We might then discern that Hatley Corners is a place of shelter and protection where people can take heed of those who follow.

It is quite significant that we now have both Hatley Corners and Green Oaks falling on the same latitude as Owl's Head Mountain. Added to this is the fact that some of the most important events in the religious and political history of Quebec have occurred in Oka and St. Eustache, on the north shore of Lac des Deux Montagnes in the Lower Laurentian Mountains, located . . . at 45 degrees 15 minutes north latitude, just two degrees west of Owl's Head Mountain. It is here that the Cistercian abbey of Oka, for instance, founded by French monks in the late nineteenth century, can be found nestled in the woods overlooking the Lake of Two Mountains. Similarly, starting in 1912, Benedictine monks from France built a monastery overlooking Lake Memphremagog. The modern St. Benoit du Lac Abbey, designed by the famous architect Dom Bellot and overlooking Lake Memphremagog, is said to pay tribute to the harmony of the "surrounding natural geometric forms."[28]

We can now see a pattern emerging: Places such as Green Oaks, Nova Scotia, and Hatley Corners and Owl's Head, Quebec, are rich in gold and copper and all fall along the parallel of 45 degrees 15 minutes north latitude. Further, Green Oaks is separated by eight degrees of longitude from the Newport Tower and Montauk Point, in line with Hatley Corners, which is separated by eight degrees of longitude from Rose Point, Nova Scotia. The Newport Tower and Montauk Point are separated from each other by one degree forty minutes—the same distance that separates Hatley Corners and Owl's Head. From all of this we can discern the beginning of a larger geometric pattern that can be tested scientifically and mathematically. In addition, we may find clues to the relationships of these places and to the Grail refugees themselves in the origins of the place-names of each. Amassing this information, we learn—just as any 2nd-degree Mason would—that only through the application of the "liberal arts and sciences" can we find the true "treasure."

It would make sense that this underlying geometry developed for the eastern seaboard of North America would find its way onto maps of the era of New World exploration. Surely men such as Cartier were able to follow information related to this hidden art of navigation—information that can be found within the mysterious portolan maps discovered by the Knights Templar in the Middle East.

Desceliers's Map

The French city of Dieppe, to which Verrazano was drawn, likewise lured other astronomers, geographers, and mapmakers of the fifteenth and sixteenth centuries, many of whom arrived in order to profit from the experiences of navigators who had spent a lifetime at sea and to work in an environment that addressed in a serious and scientific spirit all matters connected with maritime exploration. Dieppe boasted something like a school of seamanship, which directly resulted in France putting forth great efforts toward establishing colonies in the New World. The city thus became the major seaport of France during the 1500s and served as headquarters for men such as Pierre Desceliers, who some have called the creator of French hydrography and whose beautiful maps are now of great historical importance.

Desceliers was one of the leading figures in the Dieppe school of cartographers that was active in the years 1530 to 1560. He produced several world maps, now very rare, with an emphasis on Jacques Cartier's exploration along the St. Lawrence River and in New France. His crowning glory was the world map or planisphere that he produced in 1550.[29] The original parchment map appears in a mid-sixteenth-century atlas compiled by an unknown from the Dieppe group of portolan mapmakers. What is immediately apparent is that Desceliers had firsthand knowledge of the New World that could have come only directly from Cartier himself.

Desceliers's planisphere (see fig. 2.7), which is made up of four parchment sheets forming a portolan world map, is beautifully illustrated with both whimsy and myth—including, of all things, images of flamingos!—yet the geographic detail is copious and quite contemporary with the knowledge of his time, as is shown by the unique elaboration of the St. Lawrence

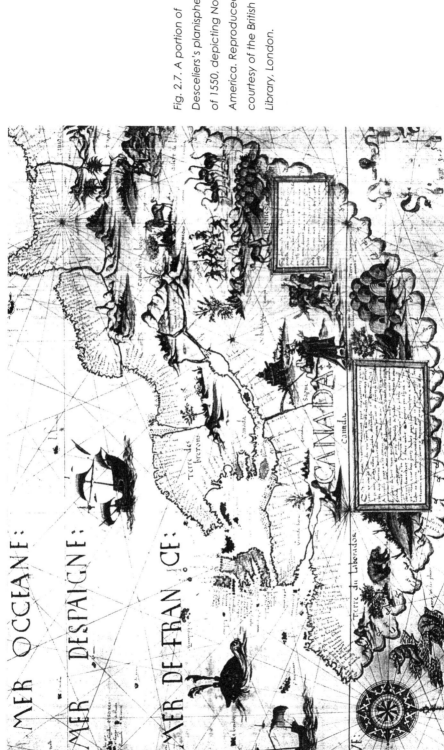

Fig. 2.7. A portion of Descelliers's planisphere of 1550, depicting North America. Reproduced courtesy of the British Library, London.

region in the north (reflecting Cartier's discoveries along the St. Lawrence) and Brazil in the south. An earlier version of this map, drawn by Desceliers in 1544, was not as polished or informative as the later version, but it does display the name Canada, which Cartier first heard from the natives in the region.[30] The word Canada originally meant "village," but Cartier misunderstood this and applied the name to the entire region.

At first glance, it appears as though the mapmaker was basing his representation on an interpretation of events as conveyed to him by Cartier, but upon further study a number of underlying strategic points relative to longitude and latitude and a resulting grid become apparent in Descaliers's work. By referring to figure 2.8, which was distilled from that portion of Desceliers's map relating to Canada, the reader will suddenly realize that whoever provided this information to Desceliers was certainly "on the square," for what first appears to be randomly drawn lines and patterns is in reality a rather sophisticated application of the esoteric "completion of the square," a balancing of east, west, north, and south.

What this means is that all locations that fall within the square have a relatively accurate coordinate position in relation not only to one another, but also to the ancient pattern of roselines that may well exist worldwide. For example, the coordinates and relating modern-day place-names of the four corners of the map are:

Port Burwell, Labrador, 60 degrees north, 63 degrees 57 minutes west

Ottawa Island, Hudson Bay, 60 degrees north, 79 degrees 57 minutes west

Charleston, South Carolina (more specifically, the Morris Island lighthouse), 32 degrees 30 minutes north, 79 degrees 57 minutes west

Bermuda (more specifically, the St. David's Island lighthouse), 32 degrees 30 minutes north, 63 degrees 57 minutes west

Amazingly, Bermuda is not represented at all on the overlying map— as though only the true initiate would be able to decipher the final point of this landfall—a real disappearing island! The same can be said for Ottawa Island, the location of which was required to establish a relative fixed

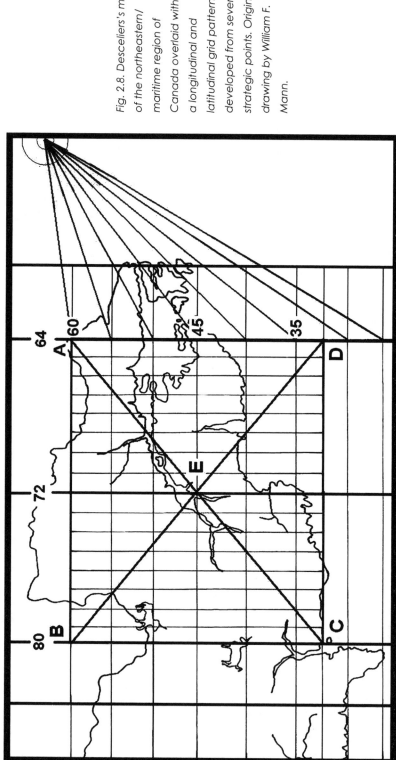

Fig. 2.8. Desceliers's map of the northeastern/maritime region of Canada overlaid with a longitudinal and latitudinal grid pattern developed from several strategic points. Original drawing by William F. Mann.

point within Hudson's Bay itself. The entrance to Hudson Bay through the later-named Hudson Strait is just north of the sixtieth parallel. Could this explain why Gaspar Cortereal first made for the fiftieth parallel to start his exploration of the New World? If he possessed an earlier map developed from the square, as speculated, he would have known to head north to fix the upper-right-hand corner of the square at Port Burwell.

As the map indicates, latitude 45 degrees 15 minutes north allows the initiate to discover the center point of the square: Hatley Corners. And by following this same latitude, it can be determined that the community of Rose Point, Ontario, lies on the square, as does Rose Point, Nova Scotia, which presents a mirror image of the Ontario Rose Point.

Assuming that the underlying grid pattern on this map is relatively accurate, we use it to align specific features along the modern-day St. Lawrence River with places mentioned in the diaries of Jacques Cartier. Stadacona matches what would be Quebec City, while Hochelaga matches Montreal Island, and is shown as such on the map. Cartier's Saguenay River to the north and the entrances to the St. François and Richelieu Rivers to the south are also identifiable. The highlighted feature at 46 degrees 18 minutes north, 73 degrees 38 minutes west on Desceliers's grid—a point that is shown to lie northwest of Montreal—is a point from which a number of radii extend. This is modern-day Mont Bellevue, though its importance on Desceliers's grid suggests that this mountain was used for something more than viewing beautiful sights. Being the highest mountain in the area, Mont Bellevue obviously provided a point of reference for surveying the countryside.

What of the illustrated vignettes and multiple symbols on the map (many of which appear in the area labeled CANADA)? The vignettes, such as that of the mines, which possibly represent the copper mines of Lake Superior to the west, seem to portray information known to be true about the unexplored country to the west of the Lachine Rapids. As the mapmaker depicted areas to the west along the St. Lawrence River, he relied on information that there were two routes into the interior of the country, both of which led to a distinct mountain range. In fact, these two routes may represent the Ottawa River to the north and the Great Lakes to the south. Regardless of the route taken, any intrepid explorer would come across the predominant mountainous feature known as the

Niagara Escarpment. Formed during a period of glaciation, this rising of land extends like a giant snake from Niagara Falls in the south to the tip of the Bruce Peninsula and Manitoulin Island in the north. Modern-day hikers travel the Bruce Trail along this ridge, which follows the same route as an ancient native trail running the full length of the escarpment north to Georgian Bay and Lake Huron. Interestingly, on the map a unicorn beside what appears to be an apple tree is featured at the top of this scene and another unicorn is located just to the south, below a group of men hunting with bows.

Of course, in medieval times the unicorn represented Jesus. The very first striking feature of the two unicorns in relation to the grid pattern taking shape here is that their eyes are bisected by longitudes, which may remind us of the story of how the Merovingian king Dagobert II met his end (see chapter 1, page 16). If you relate the positions of the two unicorns to those of the two roses found on the Westford Knight (see page 44), it could be surmised that the unicorns served as another symbol denoting the positions of two significant "rose" settlements, both along the longitudes denoted by 78 degrees 57 minutes west and the ancient 80 degrees west meridian, more accurately located at 79 degrees 57 minutes west. At this point in the story, however, if we assume that Cartier indeed did not make it past the Lachine Rapids, it is hard to say whether the positions of the unicorns are simply relative to one another or represent a true coordinate position.

Interestingly, present-day Meridian, Pennsylvania, is located at 41 degrees north, 79 degrees 57 minutes west, exactly where one of the unicorns appears on the map, and the community of Meriden, New Hampshire, is located along the 71 degrees 57 minutes west roseline at 43 degrees north latitude. The naming of these communities with derivations relating to an actual ancient meridian suggests that to this day notions remain of an "energy" grid that traverses the globe. At 50 degrees north, 78 degrees 57 minutes west (the location of one of the unicorns), there lies the significantly named Lac Longley. If we follow the play on words here, we might say that the second unicorn certainly is located at the end of a "long ley line."

Amazingly, we now have two pieces of information—one carved in stone (the Westford Knight) and one drawn on parchment—that display, through relative positioning and orientation of actual land features and places, the same information that may have come out of Prince Henry Sinclair's explorations on behalf of the Scottish Knights Templar. Another illustration on Desceliers's map may support this notion. One of the major drawings on the map is the depiction of Cartier meeting with a group of people who apparently have come from either the royal city of Saguenay or Seguna, for they are white skinned, are clothed in European dress, and possess metal weapons (see fig. 2.9). While the natives stand nearby, Cartier is shown to be introducing the inhabitants to the clergy who accompanied him on his journeys. What is fascinating about this illustration is that it depicts four women of rather noble stature. In fact, the central female figure is dressed all in red with a gold cord about her waist and a gold necklace around her neck. Is this image evidence of Cartier's fanciful imagination or is there some truth to what the natives told Cartier? We can recall that the natives told Cartier of a settlement where the residents dressed in clothing similar to that of Cartier and his men and possessed weapons made of iron. Could the most prominent European-like woman (the second from the right) be a member of the surviving Holy Bloodline and could the three women attending to her represent the three daughters of Prince Henry Sinclair?

Throughout the sixteenth century, the Sinclairs of Rosslyn were close advisers to the Scottish kings, and thus to Marie de Guise, the French regent who just happened to be René d'Anjou's granddaughter. In 1546, Marie de Guise wrote a remarkable letter to Lord William St. Clair that included the following passage: "Likewise that we shall be Leal and trew Maistres to him, his Counsill and Secret shewn to us we sall keep secret" (Likewise that we shall be loyal and a true Mistress to him, his Council and the Secret shown to us, which we shall keep secret).[31]

The question that remains to this day: What was the "secret" that was shown to her? There is some speculation that it included the whereabouts of the lost crown jewels and the Holy Rood of Scotland, purportedly a piece of the True Cross. It is doubtful, however, that such information would be referred to as "the secret," nor would it require a letter from the queen regent pledging her loyalty to St. Clair. In addition, it is somewhat mysterious that the queen regent asserts her loyalty to Lord

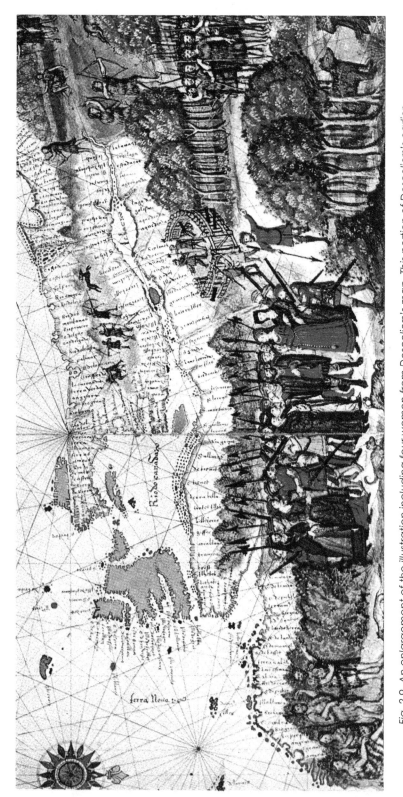

Fig. 2.9. An enlargement of the illustration including four women from Descelier's. This portion of Descelier's earlier map of 1544 depicts at the left two bearded natives.

William, rather than St. Clair pledging his loyalty to the queen regent. Recently, it has been speculated that Marie de Guise fully understood what was quietly conveyed through the illustration on Desceliers's map: Prominent members of the Holy Bloodline had sought refuge in the New World and descendants of those original refugees were alive during her time. There is no doubt that this map, drawn in 1544, would have been shown to Marie prior to her writing the letter of 1546.

There is also no doubt that the Sinclairs were held in the highest esteem, and it was they who, in turn, pledged their allegiance to the cause of the Scottish monarchy. For example, in 1556, Marie de Guise exhibited her absolute trust in William St. Clair by sending him to France to find additional support for her daughter, Mary, Queen of Scots.[32] And in 1561, Henry Sinclair, then bishop of Ross, was appointed to the Privy Council of the Queen of Scots. This allowed him to spend much of his time in Paris, where he maintained intimate contacts with the French Guise and Lorraine factions, who were making a concerted effort to displace the Valois dynasty of France. His younger brother John also became a bishop and he too was a counselor to Mary, Queen of Scots. Not surprisingly, in 1565, Bishop John Sinclair performed the marriage between Mary and Henry Stewart, Lord Darnley, at Holyrood. Needless to say, the French Guise and Lorraine factions, as well as the Stewarts, believed themselves to be of the Holy Bloodline and the Valois dynasty to be mere usurpers of the true crown.

The Lorraine and Guise factions did not have to wait long for their opportunity to claim what they viewed as rightfully theirs. The reign of Henry II was clouded by disastrous wars with Spain in which France lost the three bishoprics of Metz, Toul, and Verdun, and French armies were woefully defeated at St. Quentin and Gravelines. The death of the king in 1559 was the signal for the rise of the Guises and the pursuit of a religious policy that brought on one of the most calamitous civil wars of all time. Some historians count eight successive wars in France from 1562 to 1598, but this period can also be considered as one great civil war of thirty-six years with occasional truces. In history it is known as the Wars of Religion, involving Catholics and Protestant Huguenots. Largely because of it, all French exploration of the New World virtually ceased during this period.

The year 1598 was a memorable one in the history of France, for it witnessed the death of that "grand schemer," Philip II of Spain, who was the main supporter of the Guises, and it saw the end of the Wars of Religion and the promulgation of the Edict of Nantes by the rather adroit manipulations of Catherine de Médici. Following this long and protracted period of intrigue and infighting, a few bold spirits once more turned their thoughts to the St. Lawrence region. One of these was the Marquis de la Roche, a Breton nobleman and Huguenot who obtained from Henry IV a commission very similar to that under which Roberval had sailed. But because there was so little interest outside of the royal court for this enterprise, volunteers would not come forward and it became necessary to gather recruits from the jails. Unfortunately, the usual forlorn scenes of disease and tragedy followed. Alas, Roche was cast ashore on the Breton coast in a tempest, and was thrown into a dungeon by the king's enemy, the duke of Mercoeur, while the convicts were marooned on Sable Island.

The end of the century, however, definitely saw a new state of European affairs: The military strength of Spain had been irretrievably broken and England and the Netherlands rose as powerful competitors in the race for maritime supremacy. Before long, these two rivals would lay claim to the American coasts, looking not only to establish new settlements but also to find the remains of what now appears to be a not-so-well-kept secret: the existence of Templar colonies in the New World that in turn related to the ancient knowledge of the meridians. Outwardly, the challenge presented to France was to see if she could once again establish a lock on the New World and prevent unwanted intrusion into what was quickly becoming a giant game of chess on the giant board of the frontier territory now known as Canada. Inwardly, the French regime feared the day when a truly rightful heir to the throne would return from the New World to assume his or her crown.

3
RECORDED BEGINNINGS

By the early part of the seventeenth century, the very name Canada had become something of a joke in France, thanks to the quartz and "fool's gold" that Jacques Cartier brought back with him almost a century before. The expression "diamond of Canada" had, in fact, become a synonym for *deception* or *worthlessness*. Despite Cartier's detailed volumes describing New France and its natural wealth in furs and lumber, most French citizens were led to believe that this part of the New World was a remote, barren outpost.

In reality, Canada was about to become a secret battleground for a number of opposing forces, beginning with the Catholics and the Protestant Huguenots and ending with bitter discord between a father and son. As a backdrop to these oppositions, a deadly game of guardianship was played out among the Knights of Malta, the Knights of St. John the Hospitaliers, and the Knights Templar, each of which used Quebec City, Montreal, and the area then known as Acadia as their home base. Adding to the intrigue was the fact that many in the cast of characters acted as double or triple agents.

In seeking to understand the players and their roles—both covert and overt—it is important to grasp the complexity of alliances at the time both within France and across Europe. In France itself, the 1598 Edict of Nantes resulted in giving the Huguenots religious freedom at home and in Quebec for the following twenty-five years.[1] As a result of this religious tolerance, more than half of the fur-trading merchants in

France in the early 1600s were Huguenots, who kept as a home base the port of La Rochelle.

Adding to the difficulty of understanding the intrigue of this time is that the cast of those in power in the French government was forever changing. Of course, different heads of state had different priorities and agendas for the country. In addition, aside from the internal manipulations of those in the French court and noble families, both the English and the Dutch were signaling their intention to establish colonies in the New World. Men such as Sir Francis Drake and Henry Hudson were entering the arena and would ultimately draw in to the action the Iroquois and Algonquin Nations.[2]

In this confusing era, one man stood above the rest: Samuel de Champlain (see fig. 3.1). Through his major activities in the New World, he earned the title of Father of New France. Champlain was a gifted man—explorer, mapmaker, artist, writer, and, ultimately, governor of New France. Incredibly, from 1603 to 1635 he made twelve voyages to New France, and is credited with starting the first permanent colony in the New World at Quebec City.[3] He also became a close confidant to one of the most powerful statesmen ever to have controlled a country's destiny: Armand-Jean de Vignerot du Plessis, Cardinal Richelieu, prime minister of France.

Most of what is known about the establishment of New France, including Acadia, is due to Champlain's considerable body of writing on his voyages and explorations. The most important editions of his work are those prepared by C. H. Laverdière in 1870 and the bilingual edition of H. P. Biggar, *The Works of Samuel de Champlain,* written between 1922 and 1936. Champlain's works are the only account we have of the colonization of New France during the first quarter of the seventeenth century. As a master cartographer and artist, he embellished his works with numerous illustrated maps, the most important (and the last) being that of 1632 (see fig. 3.2, page 102). It presents everything that was outwardly known about North America at that time and, intriguingly, includes a side list of place-names not shown directly on the map.

Samuel de Champlain was born in Brouage, France, in 1570. Unfortunately, we have no authentic portrait of him and know little about his family background or youth. What we do know is that he was the son of Antoine Champlain, a mariner, and Marguerite Le Roy, and that his

Fig. 3.1. Portrait of Samuel de Champlain, artist unknown. Reproduced courtesy of the Champlain Society.

early education was entrusted to the parish priest, although both of his parents were Huguenots. Most historical accounts suggest that he was baptized a Protestant, but as of 1603 he was a Catholic.[4] From an early age, Champlain demonstrated a remarkable ability in cartography and navigation and an uncanny knack of being in the right place at the right time.

Champlain's practical abilities were probably a direct result of the fact that, as a youth, he accompanied his father on several voyages and thus became familiar with the life of a mariner. It is also known that when he was about twenty years of age he tendered his services to the Maréchal d'Aumont, one of the chief commanders of the Catholic army in the expeditions against the Huguenots. Shortly thereafter, around 1600, he probably made a voyage to the West Indies, though Champlain himself never referred to *Brief Discourse,* the account he purportedly wrote about this voyage. He supposedly owed his participation in this journey to, as Champlain later described him, "a nobleman named Don Francisco Coloma, a Knight of Malta," who was leader of the expedition.[5]

Champlain rose quickly through the ranks and around 1602 was appointed royal hydrographer by Henry IV. It was also at this time that Aymar de Clermont, sieur de Chaste, governor of Dieppe and grand

Fig. 3.2. Samuel de Champlain's map of 1632. It has proved to be intriguingly accurate regarding both latitude and longitude, remarkable (and suspicious) given that Champlain lost his astrolabe prior to completing the journey that produced this document. Reproduced courtesy of the Champlain Society.

commander of the Order of Malta, had obtained a monopoly of the fur trade from the French monarchy and was intent on establishing a trading post in New France. Henry IV had also appointed Aymar grand master of the Military and Hospitalier Order of St. Lazarus of Jerusalem.

The influential de Chaste invited Champlain to join the expedition he was sending to the New World, and thus Champlain sailed from Honfleur on March 15, 1603, under the command of François Grave Du Pont (or Pont-Grave), a Catholic nobleman who planned on following the route established by Jacques Cartier in 1535. Champlain carried no official position at this time, though he published an account of the voyage, which was the first detailed description of the St. Lawrence since Jacques Cartier's explorations. Upon arriving in the New World, Du Pont proceeded to explore part of the valley of the Saguenay River and, through trade with the natives, was led to suspect the existence of Hudson Bay. He then sailed up the St. Lawrence as far as Cartier's Hochelaga, where he found, surprisingly, that nothing was to be seen of the native people and village that Cartier had visited. We do know from Champlain's account of this first voyage that the newly named Sault-Ste.-Louis (the Lachine Rapids) remained impassable; he did confirm from guides, however, that above the rapids there were three great lakes (Erie, Huron, and Ontario) waiting to be explored.

Significantly, by the time Champlain made his first voyage, the Algonquin people had taken control of the St. Lawrence area from the Iroquois, but nothing in his account suggests a large native settlement anywhere in the Laurentian valley. When Jacques Cartier arrived in 1535, the Iroquois who lived there referred to the site of present-day Quebec City as Stadacona. When Champlain arrived, however, it was known as Quebecq, the Algonquian and Abenaki word for "the place where the river narrows."[6] Whether from this discrepancy in nomenclature from Cartier's time to theirs or for some unknown reason, the 1603 expedition ended abruptly with Du Pont and his crew sailing back to France later that same year.

Meanwhile, Aymar de Chaste had died in France and Pierre Dugua de Monts, a French nobleman and Huguenot, had become lieutenant governor of La Cadie, or Acadia. The boundaries of the territory included, in today's terms, Nova Scotia, New Brunswick, Prince Edward

Island, and part of the state of Maine. Not much is known about de Monts's earlier years other than "he had distinguished himself fighting in the cause of Henry IV during the religious wars in France."[7] Because de Chaste had died, which automatically forfeited his monopoly to the crown, de Monts was able to secure from the king a monopoly in the New France fur trade. In exchange for an exclusive ten-year trading patent, de Monts undertook to settle sixty homesteaders a year in that part of New France. From 1604 to 1607, though the search continued for a suitable permanent site, none was established. A short-lived settlement was created at Port Royal (present-day Annapolis Royal, Nova Scotia).

In 1604, Champlain sailed to Acadia with the sieur de Monts, again only in a semiofficial capacity as cartographer. Here he was given the responsibility for investigating the coast in search of an ideal location for settlement. Twice, in 1605 and 1606, Champlain's own volumes say that he explored the coastline of what is now New England, going as far south as Cape Cod.[8] In all, he journeyed over one thousand nautical miles along the Atlantic coast from Maine to Cape Cod (42 degrees 5 minutes north latitude), mapping the coastline in intimate detail (see fig. 3.3). It seems surprising, however, that Champlain could have sailed such a large area, charting most of the coast of Nova Scotia and the coast to present-day Cape Cod and Martha's Vineyard, yet no suitable site for a permanent French colony could be found. As Michael Bradley points out in the *Holy Grail across the Atlantic,* it seems as though Champlain purposely dealt in deception and misinformation.[9] Could it be that he, too, was in possession of information that earlier had a direct bearing on the explorations of Prince Henry Sinclair and on the positioning of both Norumbega and the Newport Tower?

Bradley devotes a whole chapter to the question surrounding Champlain's rather curious assertions during the mapping of Acadia.[10] As he points out, the cartographer's account of his exploration of Minas Basin is both confusing and misleading. Champlain fails to describe or include on any of his maps the Shubenacadie River, the largest tidal river in Nova Scotia, which leads directly to the abandoned settlement at Green Oaks! It is as though he was trying to discourage people from sailing into the Minas Basin area and beyond. Perhaps the explanation for his

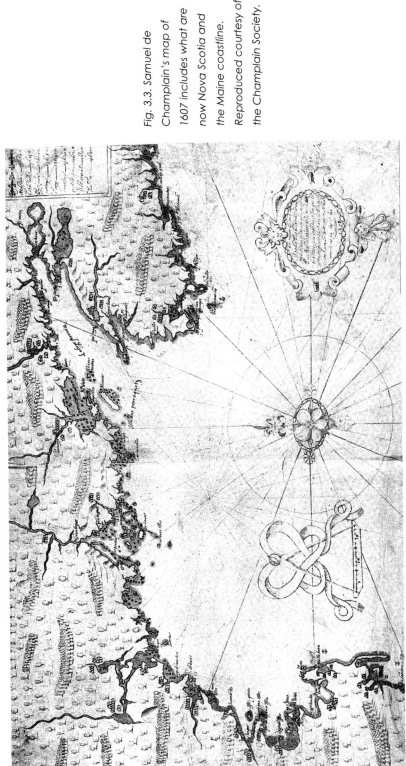

Fig. 3.3. Samuel de Champlain's map of 1607 includes what are now Nova Scotia and the Maine coastline. Reproduced courtesy of the Champlain Society.

omissions lies in Champlain's knowledge of Templar meridians and the movement inland of the Holy Bloodline.

Pierre Dugua de Monts himself could have been in on any cover-up, for he might well have been either a Knight Templar or a Knight of Malta (formerly the Knights of St. John or the Hospitallers).[11] Officially, it was said that de Monts was unable to enforce his rights along the coast of Acadia because of "Basque interlopers."[12] The story goes that because de Monts was unable to continue financially, the decision was made in 1607 to give up the settlement at Port Royal. Whatever the official reasons for abandoning the coastal settlement, it is as though an air of indecisiveness hung over the entire venture. Finally deciding on establishing a site in the St. Lawrence area instead, in 1608 de Monts sent Champlain to what is now Quebec City, from which, it was said, the fur trade with native peoples in the interior could be controlled more easily.

On July 3, 1608, Champlain founded what was to become Quebec City and immediately set about building his residence there. He also explored the Iroquois River, now called the Richelieu, which, in turn, on July 14, 1609, led him to the lake that would later bear his name. It is here we find Champlain exploring an inland waterway that directly leads to an area previously sheltering a Templar colony.

Ultimately, because Champlain had established and developed a vast trade network by forming alliances with the Algonquin Nation, he was obliged to support his allies in their traditional wars against the Iroquois, whose territory was to the south of the St. Lawrence and Lake Ontario. Unfortunately, this intervention in local politics was eventually responsible for the warlike relations that were to pit the Iroquois against the French for generations. In addition, it fostered an alliance between the Iroquois and the Dutch, who, thanks to Henry Hudson, had gained a foothold in the New World: In 1610, the Dutch began trading up the Hudson River and in 1614 established permanent trading posts in Manhattan and Orange (Albany).

At roughly the same time, in June 1606, King James I of England had granted a charter to a consortium of London entrepreneurs to explore and settle the New World. The Virginia Company received the right to hold all the land from what is now Cape Fear, North Carolina, to the St. Croix River in what is now Maine. This organization comprised two divisions: the London Company, with control over the southern part of the territory, and the Plymouth Company, controlling the northern part. In 1607, the Virginia Company sponsored the establishment of James-town, Virginia, by Captain John Smith and 144 colonists. In essence a tobacco plantation, Jamestown spawned the agricultural economy of the southern states. Later, in 1620, the Plymouth Company sponsored the Plymouth colony, which was a venture of disciplined Pilgrim plant-ers, led by Miles Standish, that gave birth to the trade and manufactur-ing economy of New England.

The story of Captain John Smith contains some intriguing details that may relate to our subject of "lost" Templar colonies in the New World: Along with serving as one of seven leaders of the new colony of Jamestown, Smith led expeditions exploring Chesapeake Bay and the New England coast, including a voyage up the Potomac River to the present-day site of Washington, D.C. On one of these trips, Smith was taken captive by the chief of the Powhatan tribe and was condemned to death. What is probably best known about this expedition is that the Indian princess Pocahontas saved Smith's life. What is not widely known is contained within an account of his encounter with the Susquehannock tribe. Captain Smith wrote that:

> 60 of those Sesquesahanocks came to the discoverers with skins, Bowes, Arrowes, Targets, Beads, Swords, and Tobacco pipes for presents. Such great and well-proportioned men are seldome seene, for they seemed like Giants to the English, yea and to the neigh-bours. . . . Some being very great as the Sesquesahamocks, oth-ers being very little as the Wighcocomocoes: but generally tall and straight, of a comely proportion, and of a colour browne, when they are of any age, but they are borne white. Their haire is gener-ally black, but few have any beards.[13]

"[B]orne white," "with . . . Swords," and "beards"? This is certainly one of the strangest documented descriptions of Amerindians. North American aboriginals had no facial hair and were not known to work metal, especially weaponry. A detailed drawing of these natives can be found in John Smith's book *A Map of Virginia*, published in 1612 (see fig. 3.4). Interestingly, in one of these illustrations, a native is shown wearing a garment that very much resembles a Masonic apron. Coincidentally, the French explorer Étienne Brulé, who had been Champlain's advance scout into the heartland of the New World, visited this same Susquehannock tribe sometime during 1613–15. Was this because the Susquehannock held strategic control of the Susquehanna River, which was a major east–west route inland to the Ohio and Allegheny River valleys and thus to the Great Lakes?

In 1611, after establishing Quebec City, Champlain sailed back to the area of Hochelaga, where he found an ideal harbor. There, facing the waterway, he built the Place Royale (royal square) around which the town of Montreal developed from 1642 . Perhaps more important, at this time he succeeded in penetrating beyond the Lachine Rapids, becoming the first European to begin exploring the full extent of the St. Lawrence River and its tributaries as a route toward the interior of the continent. In 1613, on one such journey into the interior, Champlain recorded in his journal that he had lost his astrolabe, which was probably the single most valuable item in his possession, for it allowed him to establish his latitudinal position. Despite this, he was able to produce accurate readings and maps. How this was possible has never been fully explained, but it suggests that Champlain possessed a certain knowledge beyond his skill with an astrolabe—which, incidentally, was found in 1867 and in 1989 was acquired by the Canadian Museum of Civilization from a museum in New York.

In 1614, Champlain was enticed by the natives' descriptions to make a voyage up the Ottawa River to Allumette Island. It was his initial foray along the route that eventually led him to the heart of present-day Ontario and eventually to Lake Huron in August 1615. He spent the winter of 1615–16 with the natives in what had come to be known as Huronia. In 1616, however, he made his last voyage of exploration: his return journey across Huronia (see fig. 3.5; page 110). In the years that followed, he devoted all of his efforts to establishing the settlement at Quebec, forgoing his knowledge of the strategic location of what had been the site of Hochelaga.

Despite opposition from the various merchant companies that employed him and found it profitable to be involved only in the fur trade, Champlain vowed to make Quebec the center of a powerful colony. In a

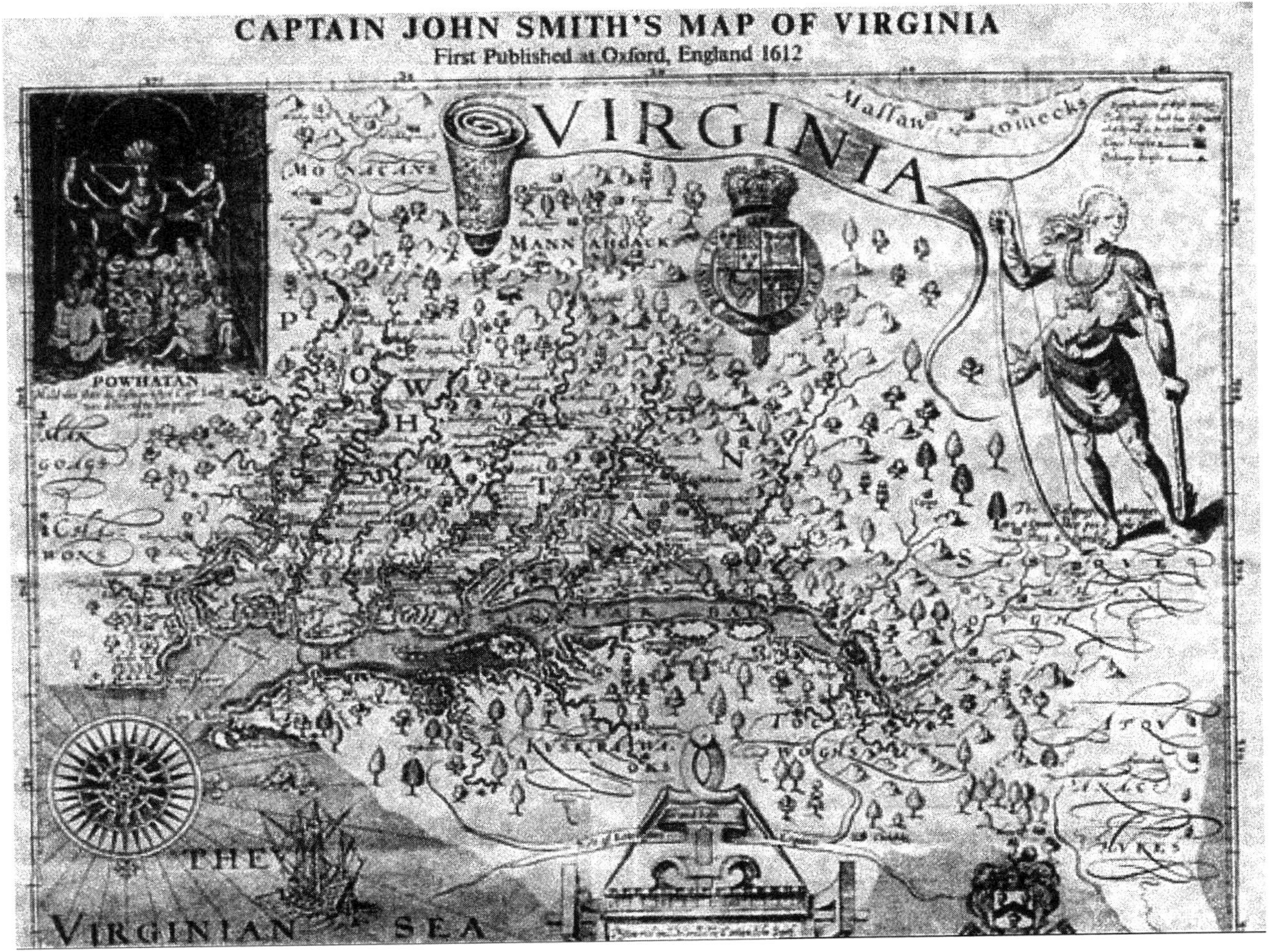

Fig. 3.4. Captain John Smith's 1612 map of Virginia, from his book A Map of Virginia, engraved by William Hole and published in London in 1624. Reproduced courtesy of the Library of Congress.

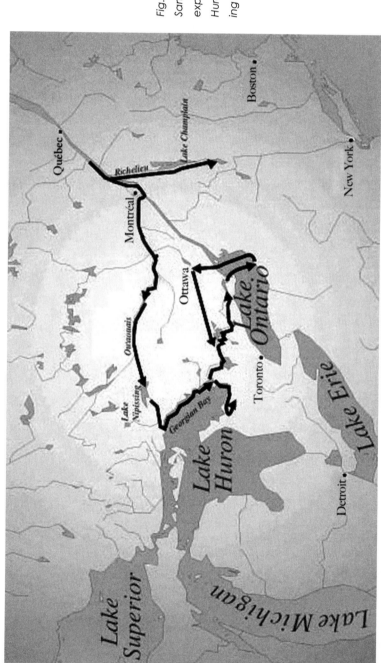

Fig. 3.5. The routes of Samuel de Champlain's explorations through Huronia. Original drawing by William F. Mann.

1618 report, he outlined to the French monarchy as well as to his initial investors the commercial, industrial, and agricultural opportunities in New France. In 1627, he himself sailed to France, where he met with the powerful cardinal Richelieu.[14] Champlain convinced the cardinal of the vast resources available in Canada. Might he also have revealed his discoveries relating to the inland movement of the Grail refugees? It appears likely, given that Champlain was the first "official" European to have gone beyond the Lachine Rapids to the western boundary of the Algonquin Nation. What he discovered during this journey or through his interaction with the natives will be revealed in later chapters.

As a result, Richelieu created the Company of One Hundred Associates and began recruiting investors interested in exploiting the commercial potential of the New World and possibly seeking out the secret Grail settlements. As a reward and to ensure his authority, Champlain was also given the title of lieutenant to the viceroy of Quebec and became the governor of the colony. Under his commission, he was required to establish a permanent colony in New France with a population of at least four thousand before 1643—a telling date when compared with Richelieu's activities on the homefront, which included the commissioning of a unique painting by Nicolas Poussin, for it almost seems that the cardinal anticipated that something momentous was going to occur by this date—something that would have an immense effect on both New and Old France. Of course, Richelieu was forever manipulating the French aristocracy and therefore saw the endless possibilities of using the New World Holy Bloodline to his favor.

Yet England's Kirke brothers, who were actually French Huguenots, foiled the plans of both Richelieu and Champlain in 1628. A year earlier, the Scottish poet William Alexander, earl of Stirling, had convinced King James I of England (formerly James VI of Scotland) to grant him territory in Acadia, which he would name New Scotland. As the newly appointed governor of Nova Scotia, Alexander created the Knights Baronet of Nova Scotia, a group of investors whose specific aim was to reclaim, by force if necessary, the land that had supposedly been "founded" by John Cabot in 1497.[15] To this end, British merchants and other investors contributed enough money to purchase and supply three warships, each of which was captained by one of the Kirke brothers: David, Louis, and Thomas.

The English plan worked far beyond the expectations of anyone involved. When the Kirkes first sailed to the New World in 1627, they were successful in winning most of Acadia and in capturing its French governor, whom they brought back to Scotland later that year. When they returned to the New World in 1628 with the intent of capturing Quebec City, to escape an oncoming storm they took refuge in Gaspé Bay, where they chanced upon the French fleet that had also sought protection there. The heavily manned and agile English ships surprised the French fleet, whose admiral had ordered the French guns lashed below deck because of the storm. The result was a complete and ruthless victory for the English. A second French fleet, commanded by Emery de Caen, unaware of the fate of the first, arrived shortly afterward in Tadoussac, on the Gaspé Peninsula. Ironically, de Caen had been sent to deliver a message that a peace treaty had been signed between the French and the English. His message unfortunately went undelivered, for the Kirkes attacked and routed this fleet, too. Quebec City was thus effectively cut off from France and any hope of supply or reinforcement.

The British commander David Kirke blockaded French supply ships and as a result, Champlain and his men nearly starved, surviving mostly on eels purchased from the Indians and on roots and wood bark. Thus, in 1628 Champlain was forced to surrender and was sent for four years to England. Following a rather intense series of negotiations involving, among others, Cardinal Richelieu himself, the Treaty of St.-Germain-en-Laye was signed in 1632, which brought Champlain back to Quebec City, much of which had been burned to the ground by the Kirkes. Richelieu, however, sent enough settlers, supplies, and laborers to begin rebuilding the colony. Before his death in 1635, Champlain had succeeded in rebuilding Quebec into a prosperous settlement and even succeeded in establishing a new trading post at Trois Rivières. At the time of his death at Quebec City on December 25, there were 150 French men and women living in the colony. Although they have never been identified, Champlain's remains were buried under the Champlain chapel adjoining Notre Dame de la Recouvrance, which may today lie under the basilica of Notre Dame de Quebec.

After Samuel de Champlain's death, Richelieu replaced him with provisory governor Marc-Antoine Bras-de-Fer de Châteaufort, who was known to be a Knight of Malta. He was soon named commander of Trois Rivières, and in the following year the king himself nominated the second official governor of New France: Charles Hualt, sieur de Montmagny, also a high-ranking commander of the Order of Malta. This seems to suggest that the Order of Malta had intended to make Quebec City and all of New France its own.[16] Indeed, in 1624 it seems there was an agreement between Champlain and the Knights of Malta to turn over New France, including Acadia and Montreal, to the order, with Champlain agreeing to establish a church in Quebec City through the Franciscan Recollets, later known as the Jesuits.

From the start, it appears that there was an ongoing rivalry between the Knights of Malta and the Jesuits, who controlled Quebec City, and the rather more nefarious group of Knights Templar, supported at this time by the Sulpicians, who controlled Montreal. From the very first day that Montreal was officially founded in 1642, the appointed governor, Paul Chomedey de Maisonneuve, who in all actions and manners was a Templar Knight, adamantly refused to take any orders from the sieur de Montmagny. Not surprisingly, the established clergy of Quebec City tried to force the women of Montreal to join the nuns in what was then seen as the capital of New France. Finally, every boat containing settlers bound for Montreal was pressed to stop in Quebec City, where it was suggested that they not continue on to Montreal.

As for Champlain himself, was he a Knight of Malta, or was he something more? It is interesting that he concentrated on the settlement of Quebec City over the development of a settlement on Montreal Island. Granted, the cliffs at Quebec City dominated the mouth of the St. Lawrence, but Montreal Island strategically provides a natural staging area to the heart of Canada. Given that Champlain was a superb military strategist, surely he would have realized the importance of controlling both points. Could his outward concentration on Quebec City have been meant to deflect other, more secretive activities that were occurring in Montreal?

Perhaps guarding such secrets was the true purpose behind de Monts's giving up on Acadia and sending Champlain to establish Quebec City. Did some information come into the possession of the Knights of Malta that confirmed that the Grail refugees had moved inland and established colonies west of the 64-degree meridian? Did the Knights of Malta and the Knights Templar have the same inner purpose? The answer to these questions may lie with the notion that Champlain strategically positioned himself to be the guardian of all that lay beyond Acadia, allowing others to discover in their own time what he already knew, evidence of which may be found in his meeting with Richelieu and in the Poussin painting that perhaps came of it, as we will see later.

Acadia

During roughly the same period, the rightful possession of the area known as Acadia was immersed in as much controversy and intrigue as was the rest of New France. This particular battle was heightened by the fact that it pitted a father against his son. By 1627, the governor of Acadia, Claude de La Tour, was in constant fear of an English attack, having received leaked information from the Scottish/English court. Unfortunately, his fears were soon realized: In the early spring of that year, the Kirke brothers attacked the south shore of Acadia, where they happened upon the governor, who had just left his son, Charles, at Cape Sable. The Kirkes kidnapped de La Tour, who cooperated and led them to the locations of a number of French settlements. To his credit, de La Tour did forgo pointing out the site of the fort at Cape Sable, where his son was living. This allowed Charles to escape capture, but Cape Sable was, in effect, the only remaining French settlement in Acadia. With the English having taken over all of the other colonies, Acadia was officially renamed New Scotland in order to attract a great number of Scottish settlers to be led by Sir William Alexander, who was appointed the king's hereditary lieutenant general of all lands and seas lying roughly between latitudes 43 degrees and 47 degrees north.[17]

Following the battle for Acadia, the three English ships returned to Scotland with Claude de La Tour, who became friends with the Kirke brothers during the crossing. Upon reaching Scotland, Claude also apparently became good friends with Sir William Alexander, pledged allegiance to England's king, and married the lady in waiting to Queen Henrietta Maria. Accepting rather quickly that Acadia now belonged to the English crown, de La Tour proposed that he and his son be given a barony in New Scotland in exchange for Charles's pledge of allegiance to King James I.

Alexander accepted these terms and offered baronies for both father and son from present-day Yarmouth to Lunenburg, Massachusetts. Charles de La Tour, however, had sadly miscalculated his son's resolve. In his father's absence, Charles had reasserted French control of all the lands around Cape Sable. He had also solidified his position with the Mi'kmaq, who still controlled most of the countryside, by marrying the daughter of one of the Mi'kmaq chiefs.

In 1630, three years after having left Acadia, Claude returned to his son's fort with what he thought was an appealing offer. But when he proposed the barony offer to his son, Charles was appalled to learn that his father had sided with the English, who had burned Port Royal and robbed his ships of their precious furs. The son would not even consider siding with the English. Claude, who had already promised the English that his son would join him, apparently had no choice but to force Charles's allegiance by attacking his fort. Two days later, unsuccessful in his attempt, Claude retreated. His ties both to the English and to his son were severed. Ultimately, bowing to formal pressure, Charles allowed his father to return to Cape Sable and live in a house that was built outside the newly constructed Fort St. Louis, named after King Louis XIII, but he never once allowed his father to enter the fort.*

Back in Europe, France and England were again at war, which resulted in a treaty returning New France and Acadia to the French. This was to be the first of many back-and-forth transactions of ownership for this area of the New World. Thus, in the summer of 1631, Charles de La Tour received word that Richelieu had decided to appoint him lieutenant governor of Acadia in return for his undying loyalty. He now found himself in a position that he had always wanted and believed that he deserved. When Acadia was returned to the French, William Alexander and the Scottish settlers were forced to leave, suggesting that a higher level of negotiations had occurred that spoke of a secret remaining in this area of the New World—a secret to which the French believed they

---

*Bradley, *Holy Grail Across the Atlantic,* 281–84. If any of Bradley's or Joan Hope's theories concerning the Stuart refugees are true, then it is possible that the castle at New Ross sheltered its last refugees in 1653. If the puritan Robert Sedgewick of Massachusetts did not destroy it out of hatred for the Stuarts, perhaps the Acadian settlers themselves did what they could to erase any obvious signs of the inland haven.

could rightly lay claim. By contrast, when the English took back New Scotland, the Acadians were left to live in peace until 1755.

There has been speculation that William Alexander was actually the "front man" or unofficial representative for the Stuart royal family, who, because of their connection to the Holy Bloodline and intermarriage with the Sinclair lineage, sought refuge in Acadia around this period. This could explain why, for some time, the English and French houses appear to have agreed simply to share Acadia/Nova Scotia. It was obvious, however, that all of Nova Scotia was extremely open to attack from a number of forces, the most prominent of which was the Protestant Puritans to the south.

Unfortunately for de La Tour, his title lasted for only one year. It was taken from him by a cousin of Richelieu, Isaac de Razilly, who had the distinction of being a founding member of the Company of One Hundred Associates. Richelieu gave Razilly not only the necessary funds to start a colony in Acadia, but the title of governor as well. In 1632, he left France with three hundred settlers and landed in La Have, on the south shore of Acadia, where he built Fort Ste. Marie de Grace. Along with him came two important men who made immense contributions to the development of Acadia: Razilly's cousin Charles de Menu d'Aulnay, a man born with title and prestige, who became a great leader in Acadia, and Nicolas Denys, rough and coarse with a background in the fishing industry. Denys could not have been more opposite from d'Aulnay in demeanor, yet he went on to establish several successful fishing and lumber businesses in Acadia, including one at Rossignol (present-day Liverpool, Nova Scotia). He also wrote a book, *A Description and Natural History of the Coasts of North America*, which contains a wealth of information concerning the early history of the region.[18]

Charles was furious when his replacement Razilly confronted him and he immediately returned to France to argue his position before Richelieu. Surprisingly, Richelieu settled the dispute over the governorship of Acadia by splitting the province into equal shares. Razilly and de La Tour, who turned out to be reasonable men, went on to share the title of governor and the fur monopoly and were granted the additional power to watch over each other's business practices. Amazingly, the two men cooperated and Acadia flourished. Charles de La Tour continued to bring people to Acadia as governor and Razilly built up his habitation in La Have. By 1635, de La Tour had moved his headquarters from Cape Sable to present-day St. John, New Brunswick, and built a fort there called Fort La Tour, allowing Razilly to have complete control of the south shore.

In 1635, Isaac de Razilly died unexpectedly, at the age of forty-eight. His brother, Claude, inherited all his titles to Acadia. Because he lived in France, however, and wanted to stay there, he put his cousin, the very same Charles de Menu d'Aulnay, in charge of Acadian affairs. Unfortunately, d'Aulnay hated de La Tour and the two men became bitter enemies who were forced to share a title in Acadia. Charles de La Tour controlled the areas of Cape Sable and St. John; d'Aulnay controlled the south shore area, including Port Royal and La Have.

Over the years, d'Aulnay and de La Tour fought bitterly over Acadia, for neither one trusted the other. They constantly attacked each other in the French courts and at their forts in Acadia. In 1641, de La Tour received word that d'Aulnay had appeared before Cardinal Richelieu in Paris to accuse him of treason. Because he could not defend himself against d'Aulnay's accusations, the court sided with the latter man's evidence and, consequently, de La Tour was ordered to give up his title and posts in Acadia. Though incensed at the accusations, in a show of good faith, de La Tour gave up Fort St. Louis to d'Aulnay because, in part, it had proved to be the hardest port to defend from attack. This half measure outraged d'Aulnay to the point that he burned the fort to the ground, even though a royal decree stated that it must be permanently occupied.

By 1642, with the help of several business associates and French nobles, d'Aulnay had destroyed de La Tour's reputation in France and had gained control over all of Acadia. Angrily, de La Tour left Acadia for Quebec City, vowing never to return. From that time, this region of New France was left to its own devices for another one hundred years. During this period, under the governorship of men like Razilly, it prospered and the population grew; the Acadians were skilled in the reclamation of the saltwater marshes that spread throughout the fertile and temperate Annapolis Valley.

During this episode, what might d'Aulnay have said to Richelieu that would have caused the cardinal to set aside all the loyalty and good-will that Charles de La Tour had demonstrated over the years—including disowning his own father in deference to the French throne? We may never know for sure, but Richelieu was the supreme puppeteer in this game, pulling the strings of every major player in the New World in the first half of the seventeenth century.

Cardinal Richelieu and the Duchesse d'Aiguillon

Even though it appeared at times that Richelieu was a wizard, one question has always remained: How did he know what was happening in New France from his palace over two thousand miles away? The answer lies not with the leaders of the various colonies that sprung up throughout the New World but rather with those admirable women who worked behind the scenes as nuns and nurses in New France, for here were the true eyes and ears of the Holy Bloodline. The one common denominator among all players in New France, including the nuns, nurses, and military and spiritual leaders, was a remarkable lady named Marie de Vignerot de Pontcourlay, marquise of Combalet and duchesse d'Aiguillon, the niece of Cardinal Richelieu.[19]

Born in Paris in 1604, Marie was first promised to the comte de Bethune, son of Sully. Being independent of mind, however, in 1620 she instead married Antoine de Route, marquis of Combalet, who was killed two years later at the siege of Montpellier. Now a childless widow, she entered the Carmelite convent in Paris, fully determined to end her days there; but after Richelieu became prime minister under Louis XIII, she responded to his request to "do the honors of the Cardinal's palace" and was appointed lady of the bedchamber to Marie de Médici, King Henry IV's widow and mother of Louis XIII.[20]

Responding to this obligation, Marie took into her hands the distribution "of his [Richelieu's] liberality and of his alms." Convinced of the vanity of worldly honors, she apparently busied herself only in distributing riches, without seeking any enjoyment from her own wealth. Through her virtue and piety, she well deserved to be described as a great Christian and a heroic woman, which is how her admirers referred to her. In his famous eulogy to the duchess, the great writer Esprit Fléchier declared, "Here was a woman whose charity was her dominant virtue."[21] She founded, endowed, or enriched the establishments of foreign missions in Paris and in Rome, the church and seminary of St. Sulpice, the hospitals of Marseilles and of Algiers, the convent of the Carmelites, the Sisters of St. Vincent de Paul, and all the religious houses of Paris. In addition, she gave fifty thousand francs for the founding of a general hospital in Paris, which she first established at La Salpetrière. Patron of St. Vincent de Paul, she was seen as the soul of charitable assemblies, of evangelical missions, and of the greater part of the institutions created by the children of St. Vincent. She was even responsible for the funding of the College des Bons-Enfants. Her charity also extended to the missions of China and she paid for the expenses of the first bishops who were sent there.

But it was the colonies of New France that received the largest share of her benefits as well as of her attention. It is said that she was the first to pique the interest of her uncle with respect to New France, leading Richelieu to be the first to send Jesuits to the New World. The Hôtel-Dieu (hospital) in Quebec was erected at her expense, and she put the Religieuses Hospitalières of Dieppe (the remnant of the Order of St. John the Hospitallers) in charge of it after providing the facility with an annual income of three thousand francs. Masses are still said daily at the hospital for both her and Richelieu, and an inscription composed by her appears above the main entrance. With Jean-Jacques Olier, she conceived the founding of Montreal and convinced the pope to approve of the Society of Notre Dame de Montreal, which was formed in Paris for this purpose.[22] Finally, it was under her patronage that the first Ursulines were sent to Quebec City.

As for Richelieu's awareness of matters in New France, what better informant network could have existed than the French regent and representatives of each and every religious order that was involved in the colonization of New France? Richelieu knew that he could handle the knights and noblemen directly, playing on their sense of duty and individual egos, as long as he could receive behind-the-scenes information from the women who were ultimately devoted to his niece—information relating to the existence of any members of the Holy Bloodline in New France. This, in turn, guaranteed that whoever won this game of chess, whether Quebec City (the Knights of Malta) or Montreal (the Knights Templar), France would ultimately reap the rewards.[23]

Because of her philanthropy, the duchesse d'Aiguillon had access to the many female orders that had taken up positions in the New World, for interestingly enough, women in the New World were accepted on the same level as their male counterparts. Marie Madelaine de Chauvigny, who has come down in history as Madame de la Peltrie, along with a novice, Marie Guyart, together established the Ursuline convent in Quebec in 1641,[24] with Guyart becoming the first superior of the order in the New World. Apparently, while in prayer she had heard the words, "You must go there and build a house for Jesus and Mary."[25] Guyart was to become known as Marie de l'Incarnation because of her pious and devoted work among the sick and disabled and is said to have written over twelve thousand letters to her female counterparts back in France.

Another celebrated woman was Jeanne Mance, the first lay missionary and nurse in America, who reached the island of Montreal on May 17, 1642. In 1645, she opened the first hospital in Montreal and in 1650 became the sole treasurer of the Société de Notre Dame de Montreal.[26] Jeanne was called the Angel of the Colony by the people she served. Under her able administration the hospital flourished, and the colony grew from forty original settlers to fifteen hundred, often in spite of overwhelming odds. More than once her courage and her talent for obtaining money, support, and volunteers saved the colony from financial ruin or destruction in Iroquois raids.

Marguerite Bourgeoys had been deeply influenced by the same Carmelite Order to which the duchess d'Aiguillon had once belonged. It was through Bourgeoys that Notre Dame de Bon Secours, the pilgrimage chapel in Montreal, was built in 1657. Here was the first religious order founded in Canada. The sisters worked among the community and some lived and taught among the native people on the slopes of Mont Royal. Among Marguerite Bourgeoys's many concerns were the *filles du roi,* the orphan girls sent from France to be the wives of settlers. She looked after them until they found husbands, and because of her efforts she came to be known affectionately as the Mother of the Colony.

For all of this involvement, it is not surprising that the duchesse d'Aiguillon was sought in marriage by princes, but she declared that it was her preference to remain a widow, for it allowed her to devote herself to her charities. When she was made duchesse d'Aiguillon, she gave twenty-two thousand livres to found a mission for instructing the poor of the duchy. She was also the enlightened patroness of the writers of her time, favoring Voltaire, Scudery, Molière, Scarron, and Corneille, to name just a few. Corneille in fact dedicated his neoclassical tragedy *Le Cid* to the duchess.[27] After the death of Richelieu, who made her his principal heir, she retired to the duchy of Petit-Luxembourg, published her uncle's works, and continued as generous benefactor to all kinds of charities until her death in 1675. One of her final acts was to have the creation of the bishopric of Quebec brought before the general assembly of the French clergy, obtaining from Cardinal Mazarin, Richelieu's successor, a pension of twelve hundred crowns for its support.

She carried out the cardinal's last request by having the church and the college of the Sorbonne completed, as well as the Hotel Richelieu, which has since been converted into the famed Bibliothèque Nationale, where, curiously, starting about 1950, material was deposited giving clues to the existence of a Holy Bloodline: genealogies of little-known families in the Pyrenees; long dissertations about the history of the Knights Templar and Knights of St. John and Malta; information on Catharism, the religious "heresy of southern France"; and many more items.

Thus, even in death, the duchess ensured that the search for the Holy Bloodline would continue. Ironically, clues to the continued existence of a Holy Bloodline were found deposited in a building originally constructed on the orders of one man, Cardinal Richelieu, who some three hundred years earlier was desperate to uncover these hints. Whether Cardinal Richelieu and the duchess went to such lengths to uncover the Holy Bloodline in order to restore it to its former glory or to destroy it completely may never be known.

Et in Arcadia Ego

One of the biggest clues to what lay in New France can be found in the famous yet enigmatic painting by the great artist Nicolas Poussin under the express instructions of Richelieu. Entitled *Et in Arcadia Ego* (also known as *Les Bergers d'Acadie* [The Shepherds of Arcadia]), it was kept in Louis XVI's private apartments at Versailles until his death.[28] Many recent scholars have tried to relate this idyllic scene in this painting to a specific location in southern France. Yet as can be seen in my book *The Knights Templar in the New World*, the painting's underlying geometry can also be applied to the landscape of Nova Scotia. Given this, it is quite possible that Richelieu provided Poussin with specific geographic information originally supplied by the explorer and cartographer Samuel de Champlain.

Art critics generally regard Nicholas Poussin as the greatest neoclassical French painter of the seventeenth century. He was born near Les Andelys in Normandy, but very little is known of his life prior to his thirtieth birthday, although it is said that his skill was recognized at a very early age. Tradition suggests that he spent most of his time in Paris studying the paintings of the Renaissance masters. His first significant commission was to illustrate Ovid's *Metamorphoses,* a series based largely on the concept of transformation, for the Italian poet Marino. But it was in Rome in 1624, that Poussin met two patrons who were to become lifelong activists on his behalf: Marcello Sacchetti and Cardinal Barberini, predecessor to Richelieu. During this period, Poussin evolved, like any other serious classical painter, into a seeker of truth and light, and in 1629, he completed his first version of *The Shepherds of Arcadia,* which now rests in Chatsworth House in Derbyshire, England.* (See fig. 3.6.)

From then until about 1633, Poussin appears to have been fixed on themes from classical mythology and ancient legend, leading him to produce such biblical scenes as *The Worship of the Golden Calf.* In 1640, he traveled to Paris on the express orders of Richelieu, and there he painted his second and most famous *The Shepherds of Arcadia,* between 1640 and 1642 (fig. 3.7, page 124). At the same time, Poussin formed a valuable friendship with Fréart de Chantelou, the French superintendent of royal battlements, from whom he received a commission for a series

---

*Lionel Fanthorpe and Patricia Fanthorpe, *The Secrets of Rennes-le-Château* (York Beach, Maine: Weiser, 1992), 59–64. When the Fanthorpes investigated the background of Poussin's painting, they uncovered a mysterious subplot related to misinformation concerning the number of paintings completed by Poussin on *The Shepherds of Arcadia* theme. The trail in this plot leads back to Shugborough Hall, Staffordshire, and the home of the Shepherd Monument and Lord Anson.

Fig. 3.6. The 1629 version of Nicolas Poussin's Et in Arcadia Ego *(also known as* The Shepherds of Arcadia*). Reproduced by permission of the Duke of Devonshire and the Chatsworth Settlement Trustees.*

Fig. 3.7. Poussin's 1640–42 version of Et in Arcadia Ego. *Notice that the shepherdess appears to be pregnant and dependent upon the young shepherd/knight for support, as though he is her guardian. Reproduced courtesy of the Louvre, Paris.*

of paintings depicting the sacraments. Poussin completed two series of these paintings during his time there.

This repetition of theme and duplication of subject may have come about from Poussin's deeply religious and moral transformation. During the 1640s, he started to choose rather amorphous mythological heroes who showed no human emotion and his style took on a rigid and austere tone. At the same time, his landscapes became geometrical and more classical. Overall, his paintings developed a subjectivity and coldness. Perhaps Poussin's health was deteriorating and he was desperately searching for the true spirit of Christ and the meaning of life. Or perhaps he knew a great deal more of the New World's mysteries and secrets than he wished to share with his public audience. Was Poussin shocked and dismayed to learn of the Holy Bloodline and Richelieu's desire to control this information? We do know that Poussin had been initiated into the French Masonic Order (a later self-portrait clearly shows him wearing a Masonic ring). Perhaps Richelieu's manipulations offended his new Masonic-inspired sense of Christian harmony and brotherly love.

Poussin did not try simply to paint the surface of his canvas. Under the stark, external, classical stillness of his later work, it is possible to see hidden Christian symbolism, specifically within the later version of *The Shepherds of Arcadia*. The woman and two men examining the tomb may represent Mary Magdalene, St. John, and St. Peter at the empty burial place of Christ on the first Easter morning. The standing figure with his arms spread may symbolize the risen Christ himself. He does wear a laurel, which hints at the crown of thorns. Also apparent is symbolic baptism in the image of the female's feet immersed in water. Could the female figure, the shepherdess, be Mary Magdalene, who anointed Christ's feet?

In the earlier, 1629 version of the painting, the shepherd standing nearest the tomb traces an inscription on it with his right hand, while a rather removed fourth figure sits off at a distance to the right of the other people in the painting. Perhaps, then, the seated figure with his back to us symbolizes the risen Christ, who had warned the Magdalene not to touch him because he had not yet attained a state of grace. Behind the tomb there looms a dark black cliff that might represent one of the pillars of the temple. The most significant difference between the two versions of the paintings is the shape and position of the tombs. The earlier version shows the tomb with its writing as more of a "scroll"; while in the later version, the tomb has taken on a specific geometric shape common to a stone sepulchre.

With his later painting, did Poussin show an inkling that the simplest geometry had to be applied to a specific location, one that he learned of during his two years in Paris through his relationships with Richelieu, Nicholas Fouquet (who was finance minister to Louis XIV), and de Chantelou?[29] It makes sense that Poussin's first version of *The Shepherds of Arcadia* was not specific in terms of geographic location. But because its theme had attracted the interest of Richelieu, who could help Poussin locate the allegory in a specific point on earth, the second painting may well have had a particular setting.

Nicolas Poussin's painting in fact transcended the classic geometry that most Renaissance masters imposed on their compositions. During the Renaissance there were two basic types of layout available to the artist.[30] The first system was based on the account of the creation given in Plato's *Timaeus,* which generally entails dividing the canvas into specific "divine" proportions. The second system derived from the older Masonic tradition, and basically employs an application of sacred geometry and a balancing or focusing of two circles into one—a completion of the square. This system seems to have survived to this day but it is often surrounded by an air of secrecy and, when used, is attributed to practitioners of magic because it incorporates the pentagram. From all accounts it would seem that Poussin constructed his paintings in conformity with the Timaean system—and indeed, conventional art historians have found evidence of this—but there is also evidence of an underlying, Masonic-geometric system in his work, as first demonstrated in *The Knights Templar in the New World.*

Not only did Poussin employ pentagonal geometry in the initial development of his painting, in keeping with the Masonic system, but he also incorporated other principles of sacred geometry such as the Golden Mean in the overall layout of his canvas. In simplest terms, the Golden Mean is the division of a unit of length into two parts so that the ratio of the shorter part to the longer part equals the ratio of the longer part to the whole length. Rather than the common "rational" ratio of 1:2, the Golden Mean works out to be 1:1.6. Using this ratio, Poussin centered his painting on the forehead of the shepherdess and on the middle or third eye of her guardian.[31] What this suggests is that Poussin quite remarkably used not only two intertwining layout systems, the classical Timaean and less common Masonic, for his composition, but also developed two relative scales within it: an outer circle and an inner circle, through the esoteric practice of "squaring of the circle."

Amazingly, if we apply what is known concerning the discoveries of those "secret agents," men such as Cartier and Champlain, who explored the New World during the sixteenth and seventeenth centuries, we can discern a third underlying pattern in Poussin's *Et in Arcadia Ego.* Minimizing the painting to illustrate the basic relationships among the four figures and positioning the painting over an accurate map of the northeastern seaboard of North America (see fig. 3.8), we can see that the western border of the painting corresponds to the extent of Champlain's explorations into

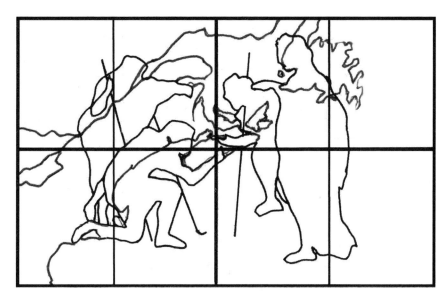

Fig. 3.8. A diagram depicting The Shepherds of Arcadia *overlying a map of New France. Note the grid pattern formed by the longitudinal meridians. Original drawing by William F. Mann.*

the heart of the New World and the entire painting seems aligned to a grid pattern that reflects the Templar meridians.

By examining this grid pattern more closely, we can discern that the center of the painting falls on the area including Green Oaks, Nova Scotia, which splits the painting horizontally at 45 degrees 15 minutes north latitude and vertically at 63 degrees 57 minutes west longitude. The importance of this location seems confirmed by the two figures in the painting who apparently are "in on the secret"—for they are pointing to the location of the "rose" settlement at Green Oaks—as opposed to the two other figures, who appear to be peering over the shoulders of the first two, trying to get a glimpse of their knowledge. Could the latter two figures, those peering over the shoulders of the other two, represent Mary Magdalene and Jesus Christ, thereby suggesting that the guardians of an ancient knowledge were instrumental in transferring the Holy Bloodline to the New World? Could the manner in which the north–south roseline splits the painting in two denote a pattern of settlement that grew to the west from the first "rose" colony established in New France at Green Oaks?

In examining the map overlaid with the painting, notice how modern-day Nova Scotia falls in the space between the figure shown kneeling and the one who appears to be bowing before him. Perhaps the kneeling figure is meant to represent St. John the Baptist, for he stares squarely at present-day St. John, New Brunswick, which had been established by La Tour prior to 1640. We can also see how Prince Edward Island and Cape Breton, when combined, create an amazing set of wings for the shepherd who is physically supporting someone who appears to be a very pregnant shepherdess. Given that this supporting figure's colors are red and white in the painting, it can be surmised that he is a symbolic representation of the Knights Templar. Could Poussin be depicting a "guardian angel" (or perhaps devil) who supports yet hides behind the veneration of the female goddess? If this is the case, it comes as no real surprise to find the goddess positioned in a manner suggesting that she came from the sea: Her feet and the lower part of her body are located in the Atlantic Ocean, recalling the tradition that the Merovingian dynasty derived from the union of a human female and a mysterious aquatic creature. That she is pregnant also suggests that descendants of the Holy Bloodline made their way across the sea to find refuge in the New World. Remember that the Merovingian female's major role was to perpetuate the royal lineage, something that is hinted at through the Duc du Berry's use of symbolism within his *Tres Belles Heures*.

Following the pattern of longitudinal meridians west of Nova Scotia, the next prominent roseline falls where the staff of the rather ephemeral, Christ-like figure intersects the latitudinal cross-section that divides the painting in half, corresponding to the kneeling figure's sight line. Here we find the area surrounding Lake Memphremagog—more specifically, Hatley Corners. It is here that evidence has been found of a second Grail colony established on the metaphorical foundation of a New Jerusalem, a new Temple of God. After all, even the Roman Catholic Church considered John the Baptist the true founder of the Christian faith. Further, we can recall that the Masons celebrate the rising of the sun at Owl's Head Mountain on June 24, the Baptist's feast day. If, as shown, the only figure in the painting with crossed legs and outstretched arms is meant to represent Christ, Poussin must be suggesting in fairly accurate geographic terms that during the 1640s, at the very least, the essence of God represented by the Christ-like figure standing cross-legged behind the kneeling figure could be found in both Quebec City and Montreal. Perhaps Prince Henry Sinclair and his Knights Templar had transported to this area something even more tangible relating to the Christ himself. Perhaps, as we speculated earlier, the Knights Templar had discovered a genealogical record of the Holy Family or even the very bones of Christ. In one way, this would explain the intrigue and guile practiced by the various factions in both New and Old France.

The borders of *The Shepherds of Arcadia* and where they fall on the map of New France support the symbolism within the painting itself. Poussin clearly could not have manipulated his composition so that the left-hand border would correspond to the Templar meridian of 80 degrees west longitude if he hadn't been supplied with an accurate map containing these meridians. Given the timing of his painting relative to the death of Champlain and of Cardinal Richelieu, it is reasonable to assume that his painting would stop at the last known roseline in the New World at that time. Further, the bottom of the painting stops approximately at the point where both Charleston Harbor and Bermuda are positioned, two geographic points of which the French inner navigational circle of the time would have been aware. We have only to recall the positioning of the two roses on the Westford Knight and the two unicorns depicted on Desceliers's map to see other manifestations of this knowledge. Like them, here lies, at the western end of Lake Ontario, the Niagara Escarpment and the great wall of limestone over which Niagara Falls tumbles. Also here is the western boundary of the Algonquin Nation, the sworn allies of Champlain and the French, and here lies the western edge of the Carolinian Forest, where the black oak and sassafras depicted at Rosslyn Chapel give way to the western prairies.[32] Finally, we must acknowledge that those who controlled the junction of the St. Lawrence and Ottawa Rivers, at Montreal, also controlled the passage to the land known as Huronia. All of this suggests that Montreal presented a sort of spiritual crossroads, and that within the outer boundaries of the settlement itself a powerful relic or talisman might be required to sanctify and protect the "gateway" into another world, into the inner sanctum of the natural temple.

Montreal

Francine Bernier has penned a fascinating book called *The Templars' Legacy in Montreal: The New Jerusalem*. Using a variety of sources, including material initially developed by Gérard Leduc, Bernier presents the rather seductive theory that Ville Marie—as Montreal was known in the early 1600s—was a Templar preceptory prior to its official founding in 1642.[33] In support of this, she puts forward a great deal of convincing evidence, including the discovery of an original foundation cornerstone with a carved Templar cross beneath the crypt of Notre Dame de Bon Secours Chapel. Founded in 1675 by the nun Marguerite Bourgeoys, the Congregation de Notre Dame, of which the chapel is part, may well have been both figuratively and physically built upon earlier Templar foundations.[34] Only two 1685 stone towers remain of the original fort that stood on this site, but tellingly, they are similar to the Masonic pillars of Joachin and Boaz, which support the Royal Arch entrance to the Temple of Solomon.

Additional evidence of the city's Templar association includes the identification of Templar crosses on some of the first maps or plans of Montreal, denoting, no doubt, the presence of earlier Templar structures. Another clue is St. Sulpice Old Seminary, established by the Compagnie du St. Sulpice in 1684 on Notre-Dame Street, right next door to Notre Dame Basilica.[35] What this suggests is that the founding Société de Notre Dame de Montréal was in fact an offshoot or subdivision of the Compagnie du (Tres) Saint-Sacrement, the legendary core of the Knights Templar. Clues also lie in the carved altars and statues still contained within the Grand Seminary Chapel of St. Sulpice. Further, it is historical record that of the eleven original members of the Société de Notre Dame de Montréal, six were members of the Compagnie du Saint Sacrement. As any reader of *Holy Blood, Holy Grail* may realize, Montreal was founded by a "rose" society that had connections with the Seminary of St. Sulpice, where the French priest Berenger Saunière is said to have deposited those providential and beneficial documents that he had discovered in Rennes-le-Château.

While we gather clues to explain the founding of the city, the subsequent battle for its ownership and control has never been completely understood. Originally, the *seignurie* of Montreal was owned partly by the Company of One Hundred Associates and partly by Jean de Lauson, attendant of the dauphin and future governor of New France. As one of the founding members of the Company of One Hundred Associates, Lauson bought the island of Montreal in 1636. In turn, he sold it to two other members of the Compagnie du Saint Sacrement: Pierre Chevrier, Baron de Fancamp, and Jerome Le Royer de La Dauversière, who eventually became executive members of the Société de Notre Dame de Montréal.[36] Who were the founding members of this influential society? None other than de La Dauversière and Jean-Jacques Olier, the founder of the French Order of St. Sulpice, whose teachings are said to be very close to the esoteric teachings of the apostle John.

Olier was the fourth of eight children of the highly devoted Jacques Olier, Count of Verneuil, and Marie Dolu, Dame d'Ivoy, of the noble du Berry family. His father, who was adviser at the Parliament of Paris and secretary to King Henry IV at the time, named Jean-Jacques after John, one of the favorite apostles of Jesus. Olier apparently based the work of his St. Sulpice church on the philosophy of St. Augustine, according to which the Church has both an exoteric teaching and a higher esoteric one that was available to an inner elite. In this way, the establishment of a New Jerusalem at Montreal could be perceived as an attempt to reinstate a more esoteric Church based on the sacred mysteries and secret teachings of Christ.[37] Was it any wonder that the earlier Franciscan Recollets named Ville Marie the Holy Colony? Ultimately, although many of the early Sulpicians were educated in France by Franciscan Recollets and Jesuits, the potential existence of a new Church based on mystic teachings brought to the forefront in the fight over New France the secret activities of the almost fanatical black-robed Jesuits.

The Black Robes

Historically, the Society of Jesus (the Jesuits) was founded in 1540 by Ignatius Loyola as the Company of Jesus. St. Ignatius was originally a Spanish Basque soldier who, along with six other Spanish and French students from the University of Paris, started what has today become the largest religious order in the Roman Catholic Church. The term Jesuit was first applied to the society in 1544, but the order's name was eventually changed to the Society of Jesus by Pope Paul III.[38] The stated objective of the Jesuits was to strengthen the Catholic faith in all lands while counteracting the spread of Protestantism. They thus became the main instruments of the Counter-Reformation movement, and it is said that the preservation of the Catholic faith in France and other countries was due largely to their efforts. As a result of their mission, starting in the fifteenth and sixteenth centuries, the Jesuits became widely known as the secret police of the Vatican as well as the schoolmasters of Europe and beyond. As such, they would have stopped at nothing to eradicate any traces of the Holy Bloodline and eliminate any body of knowledge that challenged the basic teachings of the Church.

Even though their main goal in the New World was the religious conversion of the aboriginals, they also contributed greatly to the exploration and mapping of North America. The first missionaries to arrive with Champlain at Quebec City in 1615 were four Franciscan Recollets who had traveled to the New World at the request of Cardinal Richelieu. One of the original four, Friar d'Olbeau, began his labors converting the Montagnais, who occupied the area along the Saguenay River. Another, Friar Le Caron, ascended the St. Lawrence and Ottawa Rivers to carry the faith into the heart of Huronia. Once again, we find Richelieu's hand in New France, this time under the guise of religious conversion.

The two other Recollets remained at Quebec City to look after the colonists and the neighboring Indians, all the while trying to penetrate the religious barrier surrounding Montreal. For ten years these four Franciscans made repeated journeys into the wilderness, opened schools for the young natives, and summoned recruits from France. But ultimately, the story goes, the four were unable to carry out their important work unaided and thus sought the official assistance of the Jesuits, whereupon the now infamous Father Brebeuf and Father Lallemant sailed to Canada in 1625.

One unconfirmed account places the Jesuits in Acadia as early as 1611. We do know for certain that in 1629 they were on Isle Royale—Cape Breton—where they established the first Jesuit mission and chapel at Sipo, a Mi'kmaq name for the gathering place, later renamed Fort St. Anne.[39] Later that year, a vessel left France carrying several more Jesuit missionaries, but it was shipwrecked somewhere in the vicinity of Canso and fourteen priests lost their lives. Between the years 1630 and 1632, when the English were in possession of New France, the Jesuits were forced to abandon their work and retreat to France. When the French regained control of the area in July 1632, however, they returned to St. Anne, where they continued to serve the Mi'kmaqs until 1641, when the mission at St. Anne's was closed.

Rather surprisingly, from 1632 to 1673, through their religious conversion of the Algonquin Nation, it appears the Jesuits gained control of all of New France except for the colony at Montreal. Thus, for over fifty years they were the primary source for furthering any knowledge about the Canadian frontier. Most of what we know concerning their activities can be found in the many volumes of *Relations,* a massive work that brought together the reports of the missionaries working in Canada. These priests meticulously kept French administrators informed of events that occurred in the many regions of the New World, especially around the Great Lakes and between the St. Lawrence River and Hudson Bay, where the English were making great attempts to penetrate the fur trade through the newly established Hudson's Bay Company. They were also primarily responsible for the prevention of any real penetration from the south by the Dutch and their Iroquois allies until about 1648—largely through their spiritual influence among the Hurons.

Of the many spiritual centers established by the order, the most famous is the French mission of Ste. Marie among the Hurons, located near present-day Midland, Ontario (a significant location in that, at 44 degrees 45 minutes north latitude and 79 degrees 57 minutes west longitude, it corresponds to the roseline defined by the left edge of Poussin's painting of 1640–42). Begun in 1615 by the Recollets who accompanied Champlain inland, the mission was renewed in 1634 by the arrival of three priests. In 1638 Father Lallemant arrived as the new superior and by 1639 there were thirteen fathers active among the Huron and Petun Indians. Lallemant had planned an agriculturally self-sufficient, fortified mission centrally located in Huronia, with easy access to the canoe route to Quebec. It was to serve as a retreat for other priests already in the region and ultimately became the nucleus of a Huron Christian community. The structure was dedicated to the Virgin Mary and was thus named Ste. Marie, or Notre Dame de la Conception.[40] By the late 1640s, along with their mission among the Huron (Ste. Joseph), the Jesuits at Ste. Marie also had missions to the Petun (Les Apôtres), the Nipissing (St. Esprit), the Ojibwa and Ottawa (St. Pierre), and some Algonquin bands along Georgian Bay (St. Charles).

In 1648 the Iroquois began a series of devastating attacks on the Huron and a year later on both the Huron and Petun. In these raids, five Jesuit fathers working out of the mission lost their lives, including Brebeuf and Lallemant, who succumbed to the agonizing tortures practiced by the Iroquois. The Iroquois, seeing the resolve and courage of the priests under torture, ate their hearts upon their death, which ultimately earned each of these priests the title of martyr. In the spring of 1649 the mission was withdrawn, and Ste. Marie was burned by its occupants to prevent it from falling into Iroquois hands, in which it would suffer desecration. Some of the Huron who escaped the fury of the Iroquois took refuge on Manitoulin Island and others on Île-Saint-Joseph (Christian Island) in Georgian Bay, where a new Ste. Marie was built and occupied for one year. After further defeats of the Huron and Petun and following a severe winter famine, the mission was removed to Quebec on June 10, 1650. Hence, the secret objective of the Jesuits, to find the true descendants of the Grail Refugees and the remaining Templar Treasure, would have to wait.

In 1657, the Pope placed all missionaries in New France under the jurisdiction of the archbishop of Rouen, who immediately appointed the superior of the Quebec Jesuits as his vicar general. This arrangement continued until June 1659, when Bishop François de Laval came to Quebec as the first vicar apostolic of New France, appointed by Pope Alexander VII. Laval remained in Quebec until 1662, when he returned to France, leaving the Indian missions in the care of the Jesuits. In 1663, the diocesan Seminary of Quebec was founded under the title Foreign Missions, and at this time the Jesuits restored the Iroquois missions south of Lake Ontario and founded, south of Montreal, the permanent mission of La Praierie de la Madeleine (the Priory of the Magdalene), suggesting that they had discovered something relating to the earlier Grail colony located in the Memphremagog area.

It was in this area that René Goupil and the Jesuit priest Isaac Jogues were put to death by the Mohawk in 1642 and 1646, respectively. Furthermore, this was the home of Catherine Tegakwitha, mysteriously called the Lily of Canada by Pope Leo XII. She was also known as the Genevieve of New France.[41] Interestingly, upon her natural death there the Church sought her beatification along with that of the murdered Goupil and Jogues. Pope Leo XII declared that she was born in the same village where the two men were killed, but gives no reason to consider her for martyrdom. Catherine was born in 1656, some ten years after Father Jogues was murdered. Her father, it is said, was a chief of the Turtle Clan and her mother was an Algonquin. Was perhaps the real reason for Tegakwitha being recognized by the Church that she was a known descendant of the Holy Bloodline?

The inland progress of the missions continued between 1660 and 1680, with Father Allouez penetrating as far as Lake Superior, where he founded two missions in 1665. In 1673, allying themselves with the French explorers Saint-Lusson and Cavelier de la Salle, other Jesuits took possession of the western shores of Lake Huron and two years afterward pierced the wilderness as far as Hudson Bay. In 1668 Father Marquette planted the cross at Sault Ste. Marie and in the same year set up a new mission at Chequamegon Bay near the western end of Lake Superior. When the Huron Indians that he worked among fled after several Sioux attacks, he followed them and moved the mission to the northern shore of the Straits of Mackinac, located between Lake Michigan and Lake Huron.

But it was up to newcomer Louis Joliet and the indomitable Father Jacques Marquette to penetrate inland to the next Templar meridian, discovered at 87 degrees 57 minutes west longitude. Located at present-day Oak Park, a Chicago suburb on Lake Michigan, it was here that these two Jesuit priests would confirm the existence of an ancient roseline signifying the bridge between the Great Lakes and the Mississippi River basin. Much as Champlain had found in Acadia at Green Oaks (page 32), these two men recognized that the meridians were identified by the oak trees that had been planted as signposts to direct them along the way!

Joliet and Chicago

Louis Joliet was born in 1645 in Quebec City, where he was taught at the Jesuit seminary. In 1667 he left for France, perhaps because his father was in the direct employ of the Company of One Hundred

Associates.[42] Rather surprisingly, because at first it was expected that he would train to become a Jesuit priest, while in France he studied cartography and navigation and the next year returned to New France to become a fur trader.

At this time there were rumors of a large river to the south in the New World that would, the French hoped, lead them to the Pacific. Joliet's superiors in Quebec City sent him out in search of it, and Father Jacques Marquette was chosen to be the chaplain and missionary of the expedition. In 1673, these two men and five others left on their journey to find what would be known as the mighty Mississippi. They followed Lake Michigan to Green Bay, canoed up the Fox River, crossed over to the Wisconsin, and followed that river downstream to the Mississippi. The first Indians they encountered were the Illinois, who were extremely friendly to the explorers.

As they journeyed farther down the Mississippi, they grew more and more convinced that it flowed into the Gulf of Mexico and not the Pacific, yet they pushed on until they reached almost the mouth of the Arkansas. Here friendly aboriginals told them that the sea was only ten days away, but also that they would find hostile natives ahead. The explorers also noticed that the Indians possessed Spanish trade goods—a further sign of potential conflict for them. Not wanting to be captured by the Indians or the Spanish, they decided to return to one of the Jesuit missions along the way via an easier route up the Illinois and the Chicago River to Lake Michigan.[43]

In October 1674, Marquette went back to the Illinois River, intending to live and preach among the native people there. He did not manage to reach the village that year, however, and was forced to winter near an area known to the natives as Chicagoa.[44] Arriving on the Illinois around Easter 1675, he preached to a large number of chiefs and braves, but by this time his health had deteriorated. He decided to return north, but died of dysentery before reaching the mission where he intended to spend his last days.

Meanwhile, in 1675 Joliet produced a rather remarkable map (see fig. 3.9) that depicted most of what are now the provinces of Quebec and Ontario. Intriguingly, on this map there is an annotation that suggests that Joliet was aware of least one area where the Grail refugees had

Fig. 3.9. Louis Joliet's 1675 map of what are now the provinces of Quebec and Ontario. Note in the upper-left-hand corner the phrase "les Massagé," denoting the location of the Massassauga Indians. Reproduced courtesy of the John Carter Brown Library, Providence, Rhode Island.

been absorbed into the native culture. Along the present-day longitudinal meridian of 79 degrees 57 minutes, at 45 degrees 15 minutes north latitude, near Parry Sound on the eastern shore of Georgian Bay, we find Rose Point, a natural secluded harbor hidden by Parry Island. A note by Joliet says that the Massassauga Indians were located here. Similar to the story of the lost Mi'kmaq tribe (page 46), native legend holds that a Massassauga tribe disappeared from the shores of Lake Ontario in the early part of the seventeenth century. The Huron would surely have known of the existence of this "lost" tribe but for some reason withheld this informations from the Jesuits who occupied the missions. Or did they? Could the most significant Jesuit mission in the New World, Ste. Marie among the Huron, have been dedicated not to the Virgin Mary but to Mary Magdalene and the Holy Bloodline? After all, it was positioned on the same ancient roseline.

Sadly, Joliet's journal and map of his Mississippi expedition were lost when his canoe overturned on the Montreal rapids. The only remaining record of this expedition is a short diary reputedly written by Marquette. In 1679 Joliet traveled on behalf of the same authorities up the Saguenay and Rupert Rivers to spy on the British positions around Hudson Bay,[45] and in 1694 he explored the coast of Labrador, where he visited Inuit. Again it appears as though he possessed knowledge of at least the two north corners of Desceliers's puzzle. He died in 1700, and the dominance of the Jesuits across the new frontier died with him. At this time the British began to flex their muscles to the north and south of New France. Still a mystery, after all this exploration, was what actually happened to the remnants of the Grail colonies and the Templar treasure, whatever it was.

4

NEW WORLD
FOUNDATIONS

We can recall from chapter 1 that the stonework at Rosslyn Chapel contains many Masonic images, suggesting a connection among Freemasonry, the Grail refugees, and the secret knowledge of ancient meridians in the New World, and that this evidence was due to the direct involvement of Sir William St. Clair, the third and last St. Clair, earl of Orkney and grandson of Prince Henry Sinclair, who was the founder of the Templar colony at Green Oaks, Nova Scotia, in the fourteenth century. In this chapter we examine the role of Freemasonry and secret societies in the New World and the young United States of America on the theory that the earlier Templar discovery in Jerusalem and their ultimate treasure was an ancient knowledge developed before the Great Flood—knowledge that is still preserved in Masonic ritual—and that those who controlled the New World territory would have had the ability to control as well the energy of the ancient meridians and the remaining treasure that lay along them. Our look at the role of Freemasonry begins with the Stuarts, the first kings of the United Kingdom, who were directly responsible for the dissemination of Scottish Rite Freemasonry, the prominent form of Freemasonry in the Americas to this day, and carries us through the first century of the United States of America.

Starting with James VI, the Stuart dynasty reigned in England and Scotland from 1603 to 1714, a period that saw a flourishing court culture in Britain but also great upheaval and instability, including plague, fire, and war. It was also an age of intense religious debate and radical politics between the Protestants and the Catholics, with both groups contributing equally to a bloody civil war in the mid-seventeenth century. The result of this civil war between the Royal Crown (the Cavaliers) and Parliament (the Roundheads) was a victory for Parliament and Lord Protector Oliver Cromwell and resulted in the execution of King Charles I in 1649.[1] Following this shocking event, England existed for a short time as a republic, until, by treaty, the crown was restored to Charles II (see fig. 4.1) in 1660, though in a much less powerful, more limited guise.[2]

Charles II himself held views of religious tolerance and supported the liberal arts and sciences. He founded and sponsored the Royal Society in 1660 to promote scientific research[3] and encouraged a rebuilding program that included extensive renovations to Windsor Castle, a huge but uncompleted new palace at Winchester, and the construction of the Greenwich Observatory. Charles was also a patron of the great architect Christopher Wren, who was responsible for the design and rebuilding of St Paul's Cathedral, Chelsea Hospital, and other landmarks following the Great Fire of London in 1666.

Parliament at this time was less than tolerant concerning religion—particularly Catholicism. The 1662 Act of Uniformity imposed the use of the Book of Common Prayer and insisted that the clergy subscribe to Anglican doctrine. The Test Act of 1673 excluded Roman Catholics from both Houses of Parliament. A result of the Popish Plot of 1678—so named from an allegation that Jesuit priests, the queen, and the lord treasurer were conspiring to murder the king—was the impeachment of the lord treasurer and the presentation of an Exclusion Bill that sought to exclude Charles's younger brother, James, a Roman Catholic convert, from the succession.

England's foreign policy under Charles II was characterized by a wavering balance of alliances with the French and the Dutch. In 1670, the king signed the secret Treaty of Dover, under which he declared himself a Catholic and England agreed to side with France against the Dutch. In return, Charles was to receive subsidies from the king of France that would enable him to maneuver Parliament. Political considerations kept Charles from demonstrating publicly any conversion of faith; instead, he issued a Declaration of Indulgence, which suspended the penal laws

Fig. 4.1. King Charles II of England, *painted by John Michael Wright, c. 1660–1665. Note the two pillars of the temple in the background. Reproduced courtesy of the National Portrait Gallery, London.*

against Catholics and Nonconformists. In the face of the Anglican Parliament's opposition, however, Charles was eventually forced to withdraw the Declaration in 1673.

As it became clear that Charles's marriage to Catherine of Braganza would produce no legitimate heirs (although he had a number of illegitimate children) and his Roman Catholic brother James's position as heir apparent raised the prospect of a Catholic king, the religious manipulation of James's two daughters, Anne and Mary, became of immense importance.[4] Through the intercession of a number of prominent Protestants such as Henry Compton, who later became bishop of London, the girls were required not only to attend Protestant services but also to receive Protestant religious instruction. Eventually, it was arranged that Mary wed the Dutch William of Orange (see fig. 4.2), a rabid anti-Catholic.

Just before Charles died, in 1685, he declared himself a Roman Catholic and passed the crown to his son James II. Yet on his deathbed, the king's Catholic sympathies and his continuing desire to rule without Parliament's input caused Parliament to call on William of Orange and Mary to take the throne. Following the defeat of James II at the Battle of the Boyne in 1690 by William of Orange, James returned to France, setting up a court in exile at St. Germain, where he stayed until his death in 1701. King Louis XIV, the Sun King, subsequently recognized Anne's half brother, James Francis Edward, as James III, the Prince of Wales. In England, William and Mary of Orange ruled as joint monarchs and defenders of Protestantism.[5]

Anne, Mary's sister, eventually married Prince George of Denmark, a match arranged by Charles II in secret with the sponsorship of King Louis XIV of France, who hoped for an Anglo-Danish alliance against William of Orange and the Dutch. No such alliance ever materialized, but after Mary died, followed by William in 1702, leaving no heirs, the throne passed to Anne. James III was the only challenger to the throne, but the English had already suffered under the rule of earlier Catholic Stuart monarchs and they wanted a Protestant queen this time.[6] Thus Anne became the last Stuart monarch and was the first married queen to rule England alone.

Upon her death on August 1, 1714, with no surviving children, the direct line of ascendancy was broken. Because she had been a declared Protestant and Parliament feared that, if she left no heirs, the throne might pass back into Catholic hands, the body decided before her death that her successor should be her nearest Protestant relative. This was George I, son of Sophia, who was a granddaughter of James I and a member of the German House of Hanover.

It was said that George I not only had a blood claim to the throne of David through his Stuart line of descent, but that he could also trace his

Fig. 4.2. The Dutch King William of Orange, who wed the Protestant Mary, heir to England's throne. Painted by John Michael Wright and reproduced courtesy of the National Portrait Gallery, London.

ancestry back to the Plantagenet and Norman kings. He was fifty-four when he ascended the throne, and because he realized that he had been selected only to avoid the rule of the Catholic Stuarts, he didn't even bother to learn to speak English. When the Hanoverian line took over the throne of England, the Stuart supporters were forced underground.

It was at this time that they became known as Jacobites, in honor of James (Jacob in Latin). The attempts of the Jacobites between 1708 and 1745 to restore the House of Stuart to the throne of Britain have been both historically important and the source of much romantic literary inspiration. The Jacobites may have had a false sense of optimism at the time in counting upon support from overseas and from the people of Scotland. The wealthier Lowland Scots were generally content to accept a rule that they did not truly agree with in exchange for financial prosperity. Nevertheless, the Jacobites in Scotland caused sufficient discomfort to the London government that Parliament passed a series of acts that broke up the clan system and forbade the wearing of tartan, thus changing significantly the Highland way of life.

In part because of his failure to learn the English language, George I was unpopular with the English people and was violently opposed not only by Scots Catholics, but also by a few of the old English Tories who favored the exiled James. The Catholic countries of Spain, Italy, and, of course, France also supported the Stuarts. In March 1708, King Louis of France authorized the launch of a fleet of six thousand men accompanied by the Prince of Wales and bound for the Firth of Forth in Scotland. The invasion was handicapped, however, by bad weather and a general lack of enthusiasm from the French sailors. When English ships arrived on the scene in Scotland, the fleet was prevented from landing and the invasion was aborted. James was not to make another attempt at a return to his home until the famous uprising of 1715.

The second invasion, in 1715, seemed certain to succeed even before it began. After raising the royal standard at Braemar with the support of Scots nobles, the commander of James's invasion, the earl of Mar, soon led an army of twelve thousand men. A month later he occupied Perth and Inverness and controlled part of the coast, which allowed for aid from France. South of the Tay, however, he found that most of the towns remained loyal to England's government, and the Whig lairds there began to raise forces against him. Making matters worse, in its desire to establish an alliance with England after the death of Louis, France failed to provide support. James himself arrived at Peterhead on December 22, and, discouraged to see his failing troops, departed from Montrose on February 4, 1716, leaving his supporters to fend for themselves.

The French subsequently expelled James III when the Treaty of Utrecht allied France and England. James retreated to the protection of the pope, the only one to still recognize him as king, and set up a small court in Rome. Given that he himself was a member of the Holy Bloodline, this recognition by the Vatican was in itself quite peculiar[7] in that if the Vatican recognized the divine right of the Holy Bloodline, then the Church itself would become somewhat disempowered. He found a bride in the Polish princess Clementina Sobieski. Despite being taken prisoner for a time by the emperor of Austria, she eventually escaped to join James in Rome. On December 31, 1720, she gave birth to a son, Charles Edward, who was later romanticized as Bonnie Prince Charlie (see fig. 4.3).

Bonnie Prince Charlie

Having first raised the Stuart standard at Glenfinnan in Scotland on August 19, 1745, the prince initiated what was to be referred to as the '45—the last Jacobite uprising.[8] And so, numerologically, the number 45 makes yet another appearance. It is known that the medieval Knights Templar followed such numerological beliefs, using them to inform many of their endeavors. As we have seen, the number 45 is very significant as a north latitude coordinate. The New World settlement of Green Oaks, Nova Scotia, is positioned at 45 degrees 17 minutes north latitude. As for the date August 19, 1745, we find that numerologically the numbers in the date—8 +1 + 9 + 1 + 7 +4 + 5—add up to 35, which reduces to 3 + 5, or 8, the symbol of infinity. Perhaps in his choice of date for raising his father's standard, Bonnie Prince Charlie was invoking the notion that the Stuart dynasty would live on forever.

Among Charlie's supporters were three hundred from the Macdonald Clan and seven hundred from Clan Cameron. These rebels quickly took control of Edinburgh and by September 1745 had defeated the king's army at Prestonpans. Several victories followed and Bonnie Prince Charlie's army grew in number, at one point reaching more than six thousand men. Spurred on by the victories, they crossed the border into England, where they came within 130 miles of London. Unfortunately, the English Catholics' apathy and the lack of French support plus the might of the English king's army forced the Jacobites at this time to withdraw back to Scotland.

The culminating Battle of Culloden Moor, near Inverness, was followed by a crushing defeat of the Jacobite army at the hands of the Butcher of Cumberland, William Augustus, the duke of Cumberland. The battle itself lasted for only about one hour but a widespread massacre of Scots ensued—including the murder of those not even involved in the Jacobite

Fig. 4.3. Bonnie Prince Charlie, *by Sir John Pettit, 1892. Reproduced courtesy of the Paul V. Gavin Library, Chicago.*

uprising. Thousands were killed and the Battle of Culloden went down as one of the bloodiest in Scottish history. With this, the uprising was over and Bonnie Prince Charlie became a hunted fugitive. He spent the next five months in hiding in the Highlands and outer islands of Scotland, until he was able to reach the safety of France. From the Isle of Skye, the Clan MacKinnon helped the prince make his way across the English Channel. For their part in aiding his escape, it is said that the clan received the prince's secret recipe for Drambuie!

Bonnie Prince Charlie's failed attempt to regain the Scottish and English thrones for the Stuarts had a far-reaching and long-lasting impact on Scottish culture, including Freemasonry, and resulted in further suppression of the Scots by the English. Jacobite supporters were either executed or forced to emigrate and their land was turned over to George II, who distributed it among his English supporters. The infamous Highland Clearances resulted when landowners found it more profitable to keep sheep on land that had always been used for farming. As a result, many Highlanders found themselves without a home, and thus there came a surge of Scottish emigration to the New World. Many Scots sailed to Nova Scotia and, in particular, to Cape Breton Island, where the rolling hills reminded them of their homeland.

Bonnie Prince Charlie himself spent the rest of his life in Europe, where he had many affairs and became an alcoholic. He eventually settled in Rome as the duke of Albany and died on January 31, 1788, with no heir, marking the end of the Stuart bloodline.

Alternatively, according to Laurence Gardner's *Bloodline of the Holy Grail: The Hidden Lineage of Jesus Revealed,* on April 3, 1784, Pope Pius VI annulled the marriage of Charles III and his wife Louise, supposedly for Louise's inability to produce an heir and her open involvement with a lover named Alfieri. The story continues that Charles married Marguerite Marie Therese O'Dea d'Audibert de Lussan, comtesse de Massillan, in November 1785 in Rome. The following November, Marguerite gave birth to a son, Edouard Jacques Stuardo—Edward James Stuart—who became known as Count Stuarton.[9] The Stuart bloodline, then, supposedly lived on and apparently lies with the current Prince Michael of Albany, president of the European Council of Princes, founded in 1946 and recognized by all European royal houses except the House of Windsor.

Scottish Rite Freemasonry

From this Stuart history, what we do know for certain is that during their stay in France, the Stuarts were deeply involved in the dissemination of Freemasonry. Indeed, they are generally regarded as the source of the form known as Scottish Rite Freemasonry, which promised initiation into great and profound mysteries that supposedly had been preserved and handed down in Scotland. Although in his later days he was frowned upon by both supporter and enemy, Prince Charlie was one of the main perpetuators of Scottish Freemasonry and, more specifically, of the notion that Freemasonry had developed from older Templar roots. It is known that in his later years, Charlie met with the American ambassador to France, Benjamin Franklin, and discussed such matters with him.

When the Young Pretender, as Prince Charlie came to be known, was disastrously defeated at the Battle of Culloden Moor, most of the highest-ranking Jacobite Freemasons were either imprisoned or executed. A few months later, Charles Radclyffe, a Stuart exile who had earlier assumed the title of earl of Derwentwater and was reputedly grand master of the Priory of Sion, was beheaded at the Tower of London. Most likely it was Charles Radclyffe who originally promulgated, if not entirely devised, Scottish Rite Freemasonry.[10]

During Radclyffe's time, in 1737, a prominent English Jacobite, Freemason, and Scottish tutor of Prince Charles Edward Stuart, Andrew Ramsay (known as Chevalier Ramsay), delivered what has come to be known as Ramsay's Oration.[11] It declared that Freemasonry had originated among "Crusader Knights" who had formed themselves into "lodges of St. John." Furthermore, Ramsay stated that Scotland had been instrumental in preserving Freemasonry from the Crusades to the present. Although Ramsay took pains to avoid using the word "Templar" in his pronouncement, it appears that Pope Clement XII made the connection. In 1738, approximately three hundred years after the construction of Rosslyn Chapel, Pope Clement XII (who, ironically, shared his name with the pontiff who had condemned the Knights Templar some four hundred years earlier) condemned Freemasonry on the grounds that it was descended from the medieval Knights Templar.[12]

This association raises the question as to which really came first, Freemasonry or the Knights Templar. In his oration, Ramsay referred to

Freemasonry as having been founded in remote antiquity, but said that it was renewed in the Holy Land by the Crusaders ("our ancestors"), who had united in Palestine for a noble purpose. Indeed, according to Ramsay, Freemasonry had managed to "preserve its splendour among those Scotsmen to whom the kings of France confided during many centuries the safeguard of their Royal persons."[13] If this was truly the case, the Sinclairs of Rosslyn indeed provide the missing link between the Holy Bloodline and the Templar treasure of the New World and its origins in the Old World. Most Masonic scholars, however, are not inclined to believe in this connection due to insufficient historical evidence. We can only speculate that Ramsay—who had been granted a certificate of nobility, had been made a Knight of St. Lazarus, and had been given a barony by James III—was inspired by the many references to medieval orders in the knighting ceremony.

Significantly, it was the German nobleman Baron von Hund und Altengrotkau, Karl Gotthelf, who claimed that exiled Scottish nobles in Paris, including Bonnie Prince Charlie himself, had initiated him into a Templar Masonic Order in 1742,[14] and then went even further, declaring that "every Mason is a Templar." Von Hund said that he had been authorized to reform Freemasonry by restoring it to its Templar roots. Within a form of early speculative Freemasonry known as Strict Observance, he introduced the highest degree, Knight Templar, which eventually spread throughout Europe.[15] The basic tenet of Strict Observance was that it had descended directly from the medieval Knights Templar. Those who followed it believed that if the Templar treasure was ultimately found, a rightful claim could be made to it in the name of Scottish Freemasonry and the Stuart dynasty.

In all of this history, what is most certain is that Scottish speculative Freemasonry (as distinct from traditional, craft-based operative masonry) predated English speculative Freemasonry. We know that Rosslyn Chapel, built by a Scotsman, was begun in 1440 and includes many carvings signifying the various degrees and rituals contained within Freemasonry. In 1483 the burgh of Aberdeen recorded involvment in the resolution of a dispute between six "masons of the lodge"—not "stonemasons," not "craftsmen," but "masons of the lodge." In his book *The Secret Scroll*, Andrew Sinclair even claims that at Kilwinning Lodge No. 38 at Kirkwall

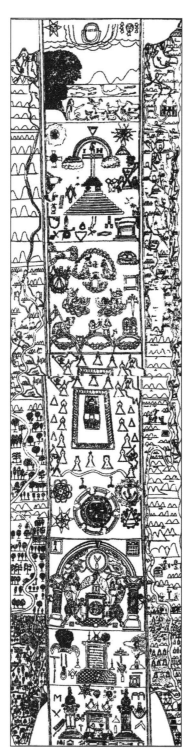

Fig. 4.4. A representation of the Kirkwall Scroll, found on the island of Orkney. Taken from Kirkwall, Kilwinning No. 38, "The Story from 1736," with the permission of the Shetland Times Limited.

on the island of Orkney there is preserved a Masonic scroll that serves as a key to all Masonic secrets.[16] (See fig. 4.4.) Although it has never been satisfactorily deciphered, the scroll has been dated to the Middle Ages. Sinclair strongly believes that the scroll is a Masonic treasure map of sorts, setting out an ancient code that offers vital clues in the quest for the Holy Grail.

Significantly, the Stuarts of Scotland made speculative Freemasonry fashionable in seventeenth-century England, with Charles II himself becoming a Freemason and patron of the Royal Society. In 1583, a William Schaw was appointed by King James VI as master of the work and warden general. In 1598 he issued the first of the now famous Schaw Statutes, which set out the duties its members owed to their lodge.[17] It dealt with such issues of operative masonry as the imposition of penalties for unsatisfactory work and prohibition of work with unqualified masons. But it is his second statute, drawn up in 1599, that is more significant for the world of speculative Freemasonry that exists to this day, for this document makes the first veiled reference to the existence of esoteric knowledge within the craft of stonemasonry. It also reveals that the Mother Lodge of Scotland, Lodge Kilwinning No. 0, existed at that time.* Schaw's regulations also required all lodges to keep recorded minutes of meetings, to meet at specific times, and to test members in the "Art of Memory."

The earliest known record of a Masonic initiation is that of John Boswell, laird of Auchenleck, who was initiated in the Lodge of Edinburgh according to the lodge minutes of June 8, 1600. While this particular lodge was operative, Boswell appears to be an example of one of the first speculative initiations, which adds weight to a case for the

---

*When the Grand Lodge of Scotland was finally formed in November 1736, the question of Kilwinning's antiquity was once again raised. Just as in the time of William Schaw, and partly because Kilwinning's minutes were missing prior to 1642, the Lodge of Edinburgh was ruled as Scotland's premier lodge, with Kilwinning running a close second. The brethren, however, were unable to adjust to this ruling, and in 1743 the lodge seceded from the Grand Lodge in Edinburgh and reverted to its former autonomous state. For the remainder of the eighteenth century, Kilwinning doggedly pursued a policy of Masonic independence and its brethren evidently enjoyed a growing mythical status that extended well beyond British shores. For the next sixty-three years, the lodge issued numbers to lodges that still bear its name, until finally, in 1806, it was persuaded to rejoin the Grand Lodge if it would agree to the concession of being granted the honorary number of 0 on the list of lodges, which they still proudly add to the name Kilwinning, "Mother Lodge of Scotland."

theory of a transition from operative masonry to speculative Freemasonry, at least in Scotland: Given that non-stonemasons, considered to be speculatives, were clearly being initiated from this time in England, some historians believe that Freemasonry was in transition at this point from pure, operative masonry to nonoperative or speculative Freemasonry. It could be argued that around this time, England copied the Scottish Masonic structure and set up an entirely speculative form of Freemasonry that bore a merely allegorical likeness to much earlier Scottish operative lodges. This view definitely has merit when we consider that a disproportionate number of early grand masters of English lodges were Scotsmen rather than Englishmen.

The earliest records of an initiation in England include that of Sir Robert Moray in 1641 and of Elias Ashmole in 1646.[18] Ashmole was a renowned author and scholar and knew great thinkers of the day such as Robert Boyle, Sir Robert Moray, Christopher Wren, and Dr. John Wilkins—the joint founders of the Royal Society, which would go on to play a major role in the birth of modern science while perpetuating an underlying fascination with more esoteric beliefs. One of the first achievements of the society was the development of a new Royal Observatory, which ultimately came to be located on the rural site of Greenwich Castle. The direct result was that the Prime Meridian of Greenwich was established under the guidance of Sir Christopher Wren in 1675, much to the chagrin of the French, who considered the Paris Meridian of 1666 to be based on a more ancient roseline.[19]

According to the Masonic historian Robert Lomas, there is a great deal of material suggesting that the Royal Society of London, which outwardly had been set up to study the mechanisms of nature, had secret Masonic origins.[20] With founding members such as Robert Boyle, Christopher Wren, and its royal patron, Charles II, it is now obvious that the two main principles of Freemasonry, sacred geometry and moral allegory, played an important part in the formation of the Royal Society. Prior to securing its royal charter in 1662, the society was known as the Invisible College and was at one time led by Sir Francis Bacon.

Bacon was a Utopian who hoped to enlighten religion and increase education and the knowledge of science and thereby create the New Jerusalem. Bacon proposed a blueprint for the new Golden Age through an allegorical novel called *The New Atlantis,* his magnum opus, published in 1627, shortly after the foundation of the English colonies in the New World. It describes the creation of a scientific institute within the American colonies along the lines of the Invisible College advocated in the Rosicrucian manifestos. Bacon expressed his views on this subject several times, claiming that the New Kingdom on Earth (Virginia) exemplified the Kingdom of Heaven. He was more explicit in a speech to Parliament when he called for the establishment of "Solomon's House" in the colonies.[21] In this clear reference to King Solomon's Temple in a New Jerusalem, Bacon stated that the founding of the colonies in Virginia in 1606 was a spiritual act as well as a political one. Even given the potential sensationalism of these views, the most enduring theory about Bacon suggests that he actually authored the works of Shakespeare and that his original manuscripts lay in a vault beneath Oak Island, Nova Scotia, where they were deposited by the earliest privateers and Freemasons, who supported Bacon's extreme hatred of the Spanish for their support of the Catholic Church and its policies.

Similarly, the problem that Hanoverian supporters had with Scottish Freemasonry was that it was associated with the Jacobite cause and, as such, posed a real threat to the stability of their own royal line. One result was that in 1717, followers of the House of Hanover, who were already speculative Freemasons, established the Grand Lodge of London, requiring all members to renounce any teachings that fell under the umbrella of Scottish Freemasonry. For the first few years, the extent of the Grand Lodge's activities was simply an annual feast during which the grand master and wardens were elected, but in 1721 other meetings were held and the Grand Lodge began to function as a regulatory body. In 1725 it was duly constituted and by 1730 it had more than a hundred lodges under its control, including one in Spain and one in India. By this time, it also published a Book of Constitutions, had begun to operate a central charity fund, and had attracted a wide spectrum of society into its lodges, including the heads of several royal houses.

In order to summarize at this point, we must ask what contributed to the rejection of Scottish Freemasonry by the English and Hanoverians. Unfortunately, the hereditary grand masters of Scottish Freemasonry, the St. Clairs (Sinclairs), had a history that was very embarrassing to English

Fig. 4.5. The ruins of Rosslyn Castle. Photograph by William F. Mann.

Freemasons: They had supported both the Houses of Guise and Lorraine against the royal House of Valois of France and had supported the crowning of Charles II against the wishes of Lord Protector Oliver Cromwell. In 1650, during the Civil War, Rosslyn Castle had paid the ultimate price for this defiance when it was destroyed by General Monk (fig. 4.5), but fortunately Cromwell, a Freemason himself, intervened and saved Rosslyn Chapel. Still, rare literary and historical treasures were destroyed by Monk's troops, who also stabled their horses in the chapel.

After its establishment, English speculative Freemasonry began to flourish, especially within the ranks of the British military. According to the authors of *The Temple and the Lodge,* after 1732 Freemasonry spread rapidly through the British army in the form of regimental field lodges. Prior to the French and Indian War, Freemasonry included in its ranks the upper echelons of British military command and administration—such prominent figures as the duke of Cumberland, the younger son of George II; General Sir John Ligonier, supreme commander of the British forces at the time; the earl of Abercorn; and the earl of Dalkeith. English Freemasonry eventually included among its members Major General Jeffery Amherst, who played a dominant role in the American Revolution and, along with the duke of Cumberland, would be infamously linked to the sacking of Havana on August 12, 1762, and to the speculation that the treasure seized there was deposited in existing vaults at Oak Island.[22]

Freemasonry spread as rapidly in British North America as it had in Europe. It was introduced into the American colonies by individual Freemasons, some of whom organized new lodges by "immemorial right." A few charters were also obtained from the Grand Lodges of England and Scotland. On June 5, 1730, the duke of Norfolk granted to a Daniel Coxe of New Jersey one of the earliest-known Masonic deputations in the American colonies, appointing Mr. Coxe provisional grand master of New York, New Jersey, and Pennsylvania and allowing him to establish lodges through his own decree. In Boston on August 31, 1733, Henry Price founded one of the earliest official colonial lodges under a charter from the Mother Grand Lodge of England. In June 1738, British Major Erasmus James Philipps returned to Annapolis Royal, Nova Scotia, from Boston with a deputation from Henry Price to form a lodge at Annapolis Royal with himself designated as the first master.[23] This was the first lodge established under the Grand Lodge of England in what is now Canada and fifth in order of precedence of lodges chartered from Massachusetts.

Meanwhile, in Europe the Freemasons were to divide yet again: In 1751, a Grand Lodge rivaling the Grand Lodge of England—The Most Ancient and Honorable Fraternity of Free and Accepted Masons—originated in Ireland. Its founding members called themselves Antients and formed their own lodge to reinstate the ancient charge erased by the English calling all Masons "to be true to God and the Holy Church."[24] The English rejection of this charge had eliminated any discrimination based upon the religious preferences of members and thus allowed followers of various faiths to be admitted. The Antients of the new Irish lodges formed, in contrast, a specifically Christian body with constitutions that contained many Christian references. Significantly, many of the lodges within the British regiments stationed in America were in fact chartered by the Grand Lodge of Ireland, which incorporated roughly the same higher degrees as those of Scottish Freemasonry.

At this time, many lodges also practiced the Royal Arch degree within the context of English Freemasonry's first three degrees. In general terms, the Royal Arch is the fourth level of knowledge that must be achieved by a 3rd-degree Master Mason if he wishes to proceed to the Knight Templar level. The Masonic Companion's Jewel of the Royal Arch is a double triangle depicting the Seal of Solomon/Star of David within a circle of gold. At the bottom is a scroll bearing the phrase *Nil nisi clavid deest* (Nothing is wanting but the key), and beneath this is the Triple Tau (three *T*s arranged perpendicularly—two lying horizontally end to end and one standing vertically in the middle, so that all three "stems" meet), which signifies God, the Temple of Jerusalem (Templum Hierosolyma), *Clavis ad thesaurum* (a key to a treasure), *Theca ubi res pretiosa deponitur* (a place where a precious thing is concealed), or *Res ipsa pretiosa* (the precious thing itself).[25] In simplest terms, the key leads to a Temple of Jerusalem where a "treasure" lies—or perhaps the wisdom and truth gained through the discovery of the Temple is, in itself, the treasure.

The result of all these machinations within the context of Freemasonry was that the English aristocracy of the eighteenth century was able to find once again a number of seemingly lost pieces of the Templar puzzle—specifically as they relate to the re-establishment of the ancient meridians—that had been hidden within the esoteric rituals of Scottish, Irish, and English Freemasonry and which suggested strongly what treasure truly lay in the New World.[26] But it was only those in the upper echelon of these fraternities who came to realize that they were the somewhat unwitting guardians of an ancient knowledge and that only through an operative application of their ritual could the New World roseline locations of the remaining Templar treasure be determined. Before the Engish could begin any controlled search for "that which was lost," however, they had to wrest from the French control of New France and break the French alliances with American natives once and for all—for the natives, Métis and Acadians together possessed the largest piece of the puzzle relating to the earlier inland explorations of Prince Henry Sinclair and his inner circle of Knights Templar.

The French and Indian War

Many American historians today see the French and Indian War as a long, drawn-out struggle from 1689 through 1763 between Britain and France for control of North America. In many ways, however, this struggle was a series of independent wars fought across both the Old and New Worlds during the same period: King William's War, from 1689 to 1697; Queen Anne's War, from 1702 to 1713; and King George's War, from 1744 to 1748, all failed to bring a settlement to the ongoing, bitter contest over religion and freedom. Regardless of what wars should or should not be linked, one thing is certain: Most of the British and French officers who fought in these wars shared a devotion to Freemasonry.

Although it took place in the American colonies, King George's War was part of a larger eighteenth-century conflict in Europe and was named for him merely because it was fought during his reign. In the European phase of the war, from 1740 to 1748, Prussia, France, and Spain were allied against Austria and England in the War of the Austrian Succession. The colonial portion of the war was fought from Canada to the Caribbean Sea, with the English against both the French and the Spanish.

While major English expeditions against Cartagena, a Spanish stronghold on the Caribbean coast of South America, and St. Augustine, on the Atlantic coast of Florida, were unsuccessful, the chief event of the war was the capture in 1745 of the French fortress of Louisbourg on Cape Breton Island by an English fleet and an army of New England colonials. This fort was built to protect the southern entrance to the Gulf of St. Lawrence and from its strategic location the French had hoped to recapture Acadia, which they had earlier lost in Queen Anne's War. In the Peace of Aix-la-Chapelle, which ended the war in 1748, Louisbourg was restored to the French. This, however, turned out to be a mere truce before the final struggle in which the French lost New France (what would be Canada) to the English in the French and Indian War. Rather coincidentally, it was just after the Peace of Aix-la-Chapelle, according to the Masonic historian Reginald Vanderbilt Harris, when the 29th Regiment of Foot, the "Fuller's," was transferred to the new settlement of Halifax and the Knight Templar degree or order was conferred for the first time on North American soil.[27]

One of the main causes of the French and Indian War was that as the British colonies became more populated and prosperous, their citizens began to look toward the rich lands across the Appalachian Mountains for new opportunities for settlement and economic growth. The French, who claimed the entire watersheds of the Mississippi and St. Lawrence Rivers, including the Great Lakes and the Ohio River Valley, had consequently become worried about British encroachments into this region. As a result, they moved to set up a series of forts, including Crown Point on Lake Champlain and forts on the Wabash, Ohio, Mississippi, and Missouri Rivers. To counter this, the British built their own forts at Oswego and Halifax and granted lands in the Ohio Valley to the Ohio Company and to adventurous traders who had set up bases in the region.

To avert war, British and French representatives met in Paris in 1750 to try to solve these territorial disputes, but no progress was made. In 1752, the marquis Duquesne was made governor general of New France with specific instructions to take possession of the Ohio Valley and to eliminate the British presence from the area. The following year, he sent troops to western Pennsylvania, where they built forts at Presque Island, near modern-day Erie, and on the Rivière-aux-Boeufs, near modern-day Waterford. At the same time, Robert Dinwiddie, lieutenant governor of Virginia, as an officer of the Ohio Company, granted land in the Ohio Valley to citizens of his colony, setting in motion the events that inevitably led to the French and Indian War.

Hearing of new French forts on the upper Allegheny River, Dinwiddie sent out a young Virginia officer, George Washington, to deliver a letter demanding that the French leave the region. Not surprisingly, the mission was a failure, but while passing through the region where the Allegheny and the Monongahela Rivers form the Ohio River, Washington noted that the point of land at the junction of the three waterways was an excellent spot for a fort. In response to Washington's suggestion, in 1754 the British started to build what would be known as Fort Prince George at this strategic location, only to be forced out by French troops.[28]

The French completed the fortification and renamed it Fort Duquesne. Washington, meanwhile, had been sent out with a contingent of troops to help establish British control in the west. When he heard of the surrender of Fort Prince George, he set up camp in an area known as Great Meadows, southeast of Fort Duquesne, and, after receiving a report that a nearby French contingent intended to attack his men, launched a preemptive strike against the French camp. This was the first engagement of the yet undeclared French and Indian War. Though Washington won the skirmish, he was soon defeated by a superior force sent from the fort, which left the French in command of the entire region west of the Allegheny Mountains.

The next year, 1755, was even more disastrous for the British in that Major General Edward Braddock was sent to America as commander in chief of the British forces here. Ignoring the warnings of the seasoned Washington, he quickly set in motion plans to capture Fort Duquesne, leading his troops west from Virginia in June. Meeting the French ten miles east of Fort Duquesne, the British were defeated, incurring heavy losses including Braddock himself, who died four days after the battle. Once again the French maintained their grip on the Ohio Valley. In the north, the British had better luck: They won a battle on Lake George and established two forts just south of the French fortification of Fort Frederick at Crown Point on Lake Champlain—Fort Edward on the Hudson River and Fort William Henry at the southern end of Lake George.

Amid this fighting—perhaps because of the bitter defeat of the British at Fort Duquesne—the British attitude toward the French Acadians, who for more than a century had peacefully inhabited the area now encompassing Nova Scotia, Prince Edward Island and New Brunswick, changed dramatically. The Acadians were largely farmers in this "heartland"

and shared the region with the Mi'kmaqs, but on July 28, 1755, they received orders that all Acadian men, women, and children were to be deported due to their refusal to sign an oath of allegiance to the king of England. The result was that thousands of Acadians were forced to move to American colonies along the middle of the coast or south to the Carolinas and Louisiana, with many perishing aboard the crowded ships before they ever saw their new homeland (fig. 4.6).[29] The normally disciplined British troops, which by this time included many Irish and Scots as well as Hessian (German) mercenaries, then torched and ransacked all of the Acadian settlements after their residents left—no doubt following the express orders of the British high command.

Aside from the political vitriol felt on both sides, perhaps there was an underlying reason for the unusual level of cruelty and destruction on the part of the British: Could members of the British government have somehow confirmed their suspicions that within the land of Acadia lay an immense and priceless treasure or the clues to its whereabouts? In torching Acadian homes, the British might have been attempting to

Fig. 4.6. The Deportation of Acadians, 1755 (artist and date unknown). Reproduced courtesy of the National Archives of Canada, Ottawa.

force the Acadians to disclose what they knew of the treasure's location; or perhaps they hoped to expose earlier settlement foundations, upon which it was presumed that the Acadians had erected their structures. Destroying homes in this way would also have obliterated any evidence of earlier Grail settlements. Folk songs of the Acadians have always told of a lost treasure. In fact, the Acadian flag depicts a gold five-pointed star on a royal blue background, suggesting that indeed a golden treasure had crossed the sea from the Old World to the New. The star is also said to represent the north star, which guided the Acadians across the sea, but an additional level of symbolism comes from the fact that the five-pointed star was a heraldic image of many of the older French families that laid claim to the Holy Bloodline.

There are two seemingly unrelated facts that support this theory. First, among the British records of the expulsion there are listed seven families from "The River of the Old Habitation." Among them is the family name Saunière[30] (the surname of the abbé of Renne-le-Château—see chapter 5, page 216). Following an extensive search of all French records, however, although this small cluster of families has been identified, no location called the River of the Old Habitation has ever been identified. It is curious that the Acadians, supposedly the first European settlers in the region, would live in a place called the *Old* Habitation.

Second, there exists a 1757 map of Acadia (see fig. 4.7) produced by the French government "to serve as a general history of the voyages" two years after the expulsion of the Acadians.[31] Given its date, it could serve no purpose other than to provide a document identifying the French settlements prior to the expulsion. The most significant aspect of the map, other than that it is based on a longitude measured from the Paris Meridian established in 1666 and shows Oak Island lying 66.6 degrees west of Paris, is that the settlement of Shubenacadie is shown to be located where present-day Green Oaks lies, rather than at the present site of Shubenacadie, which is farther to the south. This places the old village of Shubenacadie/Green Oaks at the center of all Acadia.

Despite the Acadian expulsion of 1755, it wasn't until 1756 that war was officially declared between the French and the British. Though the military activity that year and the following year was relatively inconclusive, the French generally had the upper hand, capturing both Fort

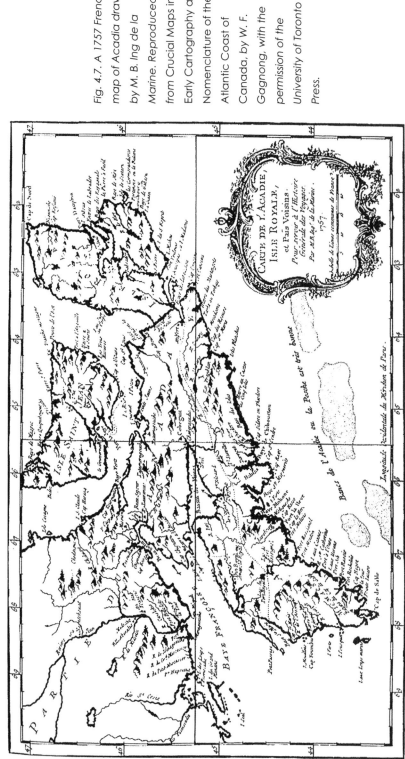

Fig. 4.7. A 1757 French map of Acadia drawn by M. B. Ing de la Marine. Reproduced from Crucial Maps in the Early Cartography and Nomenclature of the Atlantic Coast of Canada, by W. F. Gagnong, with the permission of the University of Toronto Press.

Oswego and Fort William Henry. In 1758, however, the tide began to turn in favor of the British, who employed a series of ingenious military strategies: They simultaneously launched a three-part attack on the French—against Louisbourg on the Atlantic coast, Fort Carillon on Lake Champlain, and Fort Frontenac at the eastern end of Lake Ontario.

It took most of the summer, though, before the British finally captured Louisbourg, thus establishing control of the Bay of the St. Lawrence River. While they failed in an assault on Fort Carillon, they did gain control of Lake Ontario by capturing Fort Frontenac. In July, Brigadier General John Forbes assembled a large force to move against Fort Duquesne. His success was due primarily to a meeting to establish peace between the British and the Indians of the region. When the French realized that they could no longer depend on their native allies and that their communication with Montreal was cut off with the capture of Fort Frontenac, they quickly abandoned Fort Duquesne, destroying it before they left. Forbes occupied the site and rebuilt the fortification, renaming it Fort Pitt, after England's prime minister William Pitt the Elder. For the first time, the British held control of the upper Ohio Valley.

By then the struggle in America had become part of a greater conflict in Europe known as the Seven Years' War, with Prussia and England siding against Austria and France. France and England were fighting one another in India and Europe, on the sea, and in North America.

The news in 1759 continued to be positive for the British in North America. Major General Jeffery Amherst had taken over from Abercromby as commander in chief of the British forces and he soon captured Fort Ticonderoga, Crown Point, and Fort Niagara.[32] The citadel at Quebec, the fortress originally conceived by the Knights of Malta, was the strongest one in Canada and remained under French control. It was the cornerstone of French power in North America and, as such, the British knew that if they were able to capture Quebec, the rest of the country would soon fall into their dominion. Thus in early 1759, they planned the largest attack of the war: a combined force of about nine thousand soldiers under General James Wolfe and a fleet of twenty ships under Admiral Charles Saunders. The British under General Wolfe lay siege to Quebec from June 27 until September 18, and following a decisive defeat of the French under General Montcalm on the Plains of

Abraham, the French surrendered their garrison in the city. This was the turning point of the war; a British victory was now all but certain. By the end of the year, the British had control of almost all of the French holdings in North America, other than Montreal and Detroit, and by the end of 1760, these two sites had also fallen.

Certainly, the most spectacular and most important victory in North America up to that time was the capture of Quebec City, which in all practical terms brought an end to France's power in America, though a treaty was not signed until 1763. Generals Wolfe and Montcalm, who lost their lives in the siege, share a monument outside the walls of Quebec City that marks their death in the most famous battle ever fought on Canadian soil—but though they were foes on the battlefield, they were brother Freemasons.[33]

The results of the Seven Years' War were far-reaching within North America. In 1762 France gave New Orleans and territory west of the Mississippi to Spain. England had gained a vast amount of land east of the Mississippi, what would be Canada from France, and Florida from Spain. The British flag thus flew over all the land east of the Mississippi and over Canada (see fig. 4.8)—a huge territory that became known as British North America and which, interestingly, corresponded to the confirmed ancient Templar meridians. For the future United States, the English victory ensured the use of the English language and English institutions, a Protestant majority in religion, and self-government.

The American Colonies Fight for Independence

By the early 1770s, Britain's American colonies had grown into large, prosperous communities with a strong tradition of running their own affairs. They now also had a sense of security, as the British conquest of New France had removed the threat of French invasion. This peace, however, lasted only a decade, for the American Revolution began a new episode in the history of the continent, during which the colonists learned that France had not entirely given up on the idea of wresting North America from the British. With this revolution came whispers that high-ranking British and colonial Freemasons were conspiring to ensure that the colonies would become independent in order for North

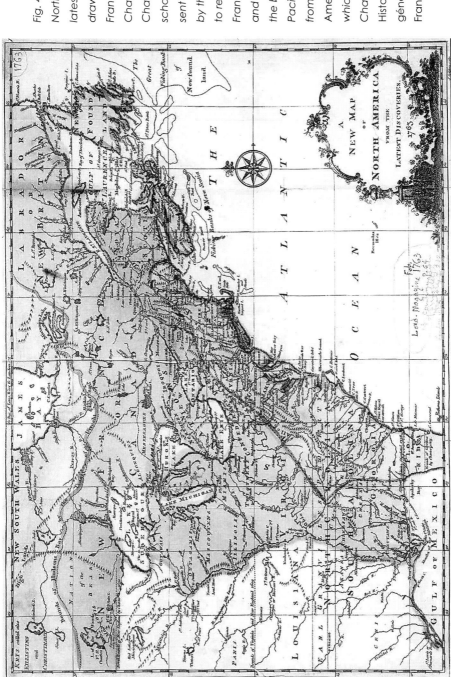

Fig. 4.8. "A New Map of North America from the latest discoveries," 1763, drawn by Pierre-François-Xavier Charlevoix. Pierre Charlevoix was a Jesuit scholar and explorer sent to America in 1720 by the duke of Orleans to record events in New France and Louisiana and to determine the best route to the Pacific. Reproduced from A Voyage to North America (Dublin, 1766), which was based on Charlevoix's earlier Histoire et description générale de la Nouvelle France (Paris, 1744).

America to remain a refuge for the Holy Bloodline and the Templar treasure.

Although volumes have been written about the American Revolution, very little has been discussed concerning the effect that the various forms of Freemasonry and its alliances had on the outcome of the conflict. It now appears that outside of what we consider to be the official history of the American Revolution, events took place to ensure that the colonies would receive outside help when they required it from such dedicated Freemasons as the Frenchmen Lafayette and d'Estaing and, intriguingly, by British Freemasons such as General Sir Guy Carleton, Sir William Howe, and Sir Jeffery Amherst. American Freemasons, too—extraordinary men such as Benjamin Franklin, George Washington, and Paul Revere—played their significant roles in the colonists' struggle for independence. There has even been speculation that the participants in the Boston Tea Party attended a Masonic meeting just prior to their act of defiance.[34]

Born in Boston in 1706, Benjamin Franklin was a man of vision, of action and invention, and, as can be seen in *Poor Richard's Almanac,* of humor. Before 1734 he had journeyed to England, and it is speculated that he was made a Mason at that time, for shortly thereafter, on June 24, 1734, he signed a petition to the Grand Lodge of Massachusetts requesting permission to form a lodge in Philadelphia. This petition was granted and he was appointed the first grand master of Pennsylvania.

In 1772, Benjamin Franklin lived for a time in France, where he was elected to the French Academy of Sciences and received honors in the academies of sciences and arts at Orleans and Lyons. As America's ambassador to France between 1776 and 1785, he participated in the initiation of Voltaire on February 7, 1778, and acted as senior deacon at the Lodge of Sorrow held on May 30, 1778, in Voltaire's memory.[35] It was at this time in Paris that Franklin's influence was instrumental in the signing of the first treaties in which France recognized the colonies as the United States of America. It is also quite possible that during this time he was initiated into a number of secretive orders of Jacobite Freemasonry, possibly through his relationship with the aging Bonnie Prince Charlie. Upon returning to the colonies, he brought these Masonic revelations with him. From this time onward, Freemasonry thrived in

America and became known as the American or Ancient Work by Freemasons elsewhere.

By 1775 lodges existed all along the Atlantic coast from Nova Scotia to the West Indies, which, during and after the Revolutionary War, began to form independent grand lodges in individual states. Virginia holds the honor of creating the first independent grand lodge at a special convention held in Williamsburg in 1778, even as the British forces still threatened the colonial capital of Jamestown a few miles away. It was at this convention that George Washington was urged to become the first grand master of a national Grand Lodge of the United States, but he refused, believing the idea was dangerous to local self-government of the Craft.

When a state of war was declared in the American colonies, Freemasons in the Continental army followed the Ancient Craft, with which many of them were already familiar from their experience in royal regiments during the French and Indian War. No fewer than ten military lodges were chartered within the patriot forces and others are known to have been active. The most notable was the American Union Lodge, which, having been organized at the siege of Boston in February 1776, soon spread throughout New York, New Jersey, and Connecticut. The lodge records still exist and list the names of more than 450 Freemasons who, after the war, scattered all over the young nation, carrying their practice of Freemasonry with them.

In the summer of 1776, New York City became the headquarters of the British army and remained so during most of the Revolutionary War, until it was evacuated on November 3, 1783, when the last units boarded ship and sailed for Halifax. But the city was not only headquarters for the high command; it was also a garrison town for a large reserve, a base for naval operations, and a sanctuary for settlers loyal to the Crown. Consequently, Freemasonry flourished there during this time, and a half dozen or more regimental lodges were very active in the city when its members were not in the field.

The practice of Freemasonry also extended to the Indians, such as the Iroquois Nation in northern New York, who were important British allies during the conflict. The Indians had originally intended to remain neutral, but Joseph Brant, who would later become a Mason, and his wife, Molly Johnston, helped persuade most of the Six Nations of Iroquois to fight for the British in order to preserve their lands. Brant, whose Indian name was Thayendagea, was the son of the chief of the Mohawk and was brought up in the household of a prominent British administration official and Freemason, Sir William Johnson.[36] Johnson had given him the name Joseph Brant, and when Brant was an adult, he fought in several battles alongside Johnson against the French during the French and Indian War.

In 1775 Brant traveled to England, where he was made a Freemason in a London lodge in 1776. He then returned to America to enlist the Mohawk in the fight against the American rebels. These Iroquois, under the command of Colonel John Butler and Brant, attacked and massacred the Americans in a number of successful raids, and prisoners were turned over to the Mohawk to be tortured. In reprisal, American troops burned most of the Six Nations' towns and cornfields in 1779. It appears that Brant himself, however, took his Masonic oaths seriously and, in a few recorded instances, released prisoners who made Masonic hand signals when they were about to be tortured. For the rest of the war, most of the Iroquois lived as refugees around Fort Niagara. After the war, Brant became a member of St. John's Lodge of Friendship No. 2 in Fort Niagara before returning to the Mohawk, who, by this time, had moved to Ohio from upstate New York.

French Involvement in the War for Independence

From 1775 on, Loyalists began leaving the American colonies for the Canadian colonies. Some sought safety but others came to join loyal militia regiments and companies of rangers, such as Butler's Rangers. From Halifax, St. John, Montreal, Niagara, and other cities and forts, these soldiers, along with their native allies and British troops, defended the Canadian colonies. From Halifax, which had become the most important British garrison and naval base in the war, the Royal Navy directed naval warfare against the rebels. Similarly, Montreal was the starting point for a British invasion of New York in 1777. When the invasion failed disastrously, France joined the war on the side of the Americans, which prompted the high commanders in Canada to fear that France might be jockeying to regain possession of Quebec. British troops were thus stationed in Quebec, Montreal, and all along the borders with the rebellious colonies.

Interestingly, France entered the American Revolution in February 1778 with only a limited military and economic alliance; the French loaned the Americans eighteen million livres and aid in the form of a fleet of ships to challenge British naval superiority. After their victory over the British at Saratoga in October 1777, the Americans believed that they could enter into an alliance with France upon equal terms,[37] asserting that France, out of self-interest, would enter the alliance hoping to upset the balance of power that Britain maintained over the nations of Europe by removing the thirteen American colonies from its control.

With this hope, the American Congress sent a diplomatic delegation to France, which included Benjamin Franklin, to negotiate a formal alliance between the two nations. Word of the delegation's success did not reach the former colonies until May 11, 1778. In the meantime, after the victory at Saratoga, some Americans believed that they could manage without an alliance with France; others questioned whether France would merely remain a secret supporter of the Revolution rather than an active participant. Regardless, many hoped for an alliance in the interest of ending the war as quickly as possible.

Yet the first French minister to America, Conrad Alexandre Gérard, saw the Americans as weak and viewed any alliance in terms of a great force assisting the weak against a common and formidable foe. Gérard subsequently asked the Americans to develop a concrete policy for peace with Great Britain, which resulted in a fiery debate in Congress over France's true goal in North America. This shook the foundations of the alliance and Gérard had to take swift action to form a political coalition that took up the cause of ending the war, all the while dedicating itself to independence. This coalition represented policies similar to those of France at the time but these were voiced by Americans in Congress, which helped to ease any mounting tensions.

Because of Gérard's lack of true understanding of the American cause, he was soon replaced by the chevalier de la Luzerne, a colonel in the French army. Luzerne's interpretation of American opposition to France's policies was quite different from that of his predecessor. Luzerne emphasized common French and American goals in the war effort, focusing on military assistance to America, yet it also appears as though Luzerne, because of his family background and his high rank in French Masonry, understood more about the unanswered question of the New World Holy Bloodline and Templar meridians. Even before Luzerne had been received by Congress, he visited Washington, with whom he discussed bringing a French expeditionary force to help fight the British as well as, perhaps, other, more secretive matters.

A direct result of Luzerne's influence in 1778 was the dispatching to America of the first French squadron, commanded by Admiral d'Estaing. Among those Frenchmen who joined the cause was the dashing twenty-three-year-old Marquis de Lafayette, who personally made possible the final victory at Yorktown.[38] France had sent one fleet of ships and five thousand troops and promised to send another ten thousand within a month. Surprisingly, sentiment relating to this quickly turned negative, with many colonists viewing the presence of French troops on American soil as a threat to independence. The American defeat at Charleston in May 1780, however, quickly changed the colonists' outlook.

The winter of 1779–80 had been an especially demoralizing one for George Washington and his army at Valley Forge after the defeats at Brandywine and Germantown. With the arrival of the French fleet and its supporting army, Washington felt that the Americans could inflict a major blow to British forces. The subsequent strategy was to pursue a joint strike with French forces on a British-held city from both land and sea. The first potential target was New York City, but it was determined that the fleet could not penetrate the harbor.

The only other possible target for such a joint strike was Newport, which is extremely interesting considering the importance of that city to the Templar meridians. In fact, Newport meant little strategically, but the thinking was that its seizure would somehow seal the alliance between the Americans and the French.[39] Did Newport itself hold a secret shared between the French and Americans? Outwardly, the Americans were anxious to see the extent of France's commitment and the French wanted to see the strength of the American forces. But for larger reasons, Newport was a key position: If it was captured, surveying crews could start to pinpoint ground coordinates there, which would be necessary to reestablish the series of ancient meridians. The American general Sullivan was to lead the ground assault with the French commander Lafayette in his company. D'Estaing was to besiege the city from the sea, but when he learned of a British convoy approaching from Halifax, he sailed out to sea to meet it. The battle that took place was indecisive, for both fleets were caught in a violent storm. The French naval forces were scattered and sailed back to Newport to give word to the ground forces that they had to sail to Boston to refit their damaged ships.

The Americans hoped that after d'Estaing arrived in Boston, he would remain in the harbor in order to allow the American merchants to open safe shipping lanes to France and the rest of Europe, but after his ships were refitted, he sailed back to Newport, where he wanted to remain until the arrival of a second squadron from France. It never arrived, however, because the British had imposed a blockade on the remainder of the navy in France. At this time, France was in essence financially powerless. Thus the French forces in Newport were the only ones available to fight against Britain in America.

French diplomats and military leaders and many Americans were counting on the arrival of the second division, however, and American officers and the citizens of Newport grew impatient as the French troops consumed valuable provisions and remained idle. Thus, both the French and Americans took to negotiations again and planned an assault. Plans never came to fruition, though, and both sides instead dispatched their armies to the Hudson River in the summer of 1780 to begin skirmishing with the British. This strategy turned out to be a great success; the American and French armies finally operated in perfect harmony, and wherever they campaigned, stories arose of the French army's superiority to the British and Hessian troops. Aiding the French and Americans in their military success was perhaps the fact that the British upper echelon, the highest-ranking officers, refused to support through every campaign the British commander in the field, Sir John Burgoyne. Apparently, Burgoyne had never become a Freemason and therefore had never become party to the conspiracy that was swirling about him![40]

Peace and the Role of Freemasonry in the First Years of America

The War of Independence effectively ended with the capture of York-town, Virginia, and the surrender of Cornwallis and his six thousand troops to Washington and the French fleet under Lafayette, who was by then a high-ranking and influential Freemason. It seems that the British high command had secretly supported their fellow Freemasons by disengaging their troops during critical conflicts, and peace negotiations between the American/French alliance and Britain soon began. France's growing troubles in the East Indies and her desire to seek conquest there, however, meant that she was no longer as concerned with North America as she once had been. Thus, while the Americans were left with a considerable debt to the French, they would not become a French colony, as some had earlier feared.

Negotiations began, and in the Treaty of Paris of 1783 Britain recognized the independence of the United States. As a result, thousands of loyalists who had stayed in the colonies during the Revolution made plans to leave the United States. About forty thousand of them, along with two thousand Iroquois, settled in Canada. In fact, so many settled in Nova Scotia that it was partitioned to form two new colonies, New Brunswick and Cape Breton (although Cape Breton again became part of Nova Scotia in 1820). The loyalists were the first large group of English-speaking settlers in Quebec, and most of them settled in what became known as the Eastern Townships, including the area around Lake Memphremagog.

During 1783, when negotiations had been concluded to determine the terms under which the American colonies were to be recognized as independent, there was a good deal of Masonic activity in the new nation. American Freemasons visited lodges in still-occupied New York City and acquired the Royal Arch and Knight Templar degrees. The former degree certainly appears to have been disseminated quite freely among the military lodges. The Knight Templar degree may not have been conferred so liberally, but as early as 1785 there were sufficient numbers in New York City for them to have a place as an escort in a Masonic procession.[41]

At the same time, mention of the Knight Templar degree showed up in the development of Masonic activity in Charleston, South Carolina. St. Andrews Lodge, in Pensacola, Florida, had been chartered by James Grant, provincial grand master for the Southern District of North America, and the lodge moved north to Charleston (surprisingly, still under British control) with military forces and accompanying civilians when Pensacola was evacuated. A certificate issued in March 1782 provides evidence of the conferral of the Knight Templar degree there and another issued in August 1783 mentions both the Royal Arch and the Knight Templar degrees.[42] These certificates provide clear evidence that during the occupation, the Royal Arch and Knight Templar degrees were introduced to both British and colonial Freemasons without discrimination, meaning that the latest information concerning the possibility of the existence of the Holy Bloodline within the wilderness of the New World would have been freely exchanged between the two factions.

Finally, on May 25, 1787, the Constitutional Convention opened in Philadelphia and devised its guiding principles of self-government. In its final form, the Constitution was the product of a variety of Masonic and non-Masonic philosophies developed by men such as George Washington, Benjamin Franklin, Edmund Randolph, John Adams, and Thomas Jefferson (whose official biography still remains rather non-committal in terms of his Masonic affiliations).[43] Of these five men, Washington, Franklin, and Randolph were known to be Masons. On September 17, 1787, the draft Constitution was signed by thirty-nine of the forty-two delegates present. At this time, the state of Maryland also ceded ten square miles of its territory to Congress to become the site of the new federal capital—the District of Columbia.

Washington was elected the first president of the United States on February 4, 1789, and John Adams was chosen as his vice president. The two were inaugurated on April 30. Adding to the solemnity of the occasion was Benjamin Franklin's death just two weeks before. The oath of office, based on Masonic ritual, was administered by the grand master of New York's Grand Lodge, Robert Livingston. On September 18, 1793, the cornerstone of the Capitol was officially laid by Washington himself, wearing full Masonic regalia, including the apron of the Grand Lodge of Maryland, under the auspices of the Blue Lodge, Scottish Rite Temple.

The Laying of the Cornerstone of the United States Capitol, September 18, 1793 (see fig. 4.9), by the noted American contemporary artist

Fig. 4.9. Washington Laying the Cornerstone of the United States Capitol, by John D. Melius. The actual date of the laying of the cornerstone was September 18, 1793. Reproduced courtesy of the Supreme Council, 33rd degree, Scottish Rite Freemasonry, USA.

John Melius, was commissioned by the Supreme Scottish Rite Council of the United States to celebrate the 1993 bicentennial of the laying of the Capitol's cornerstone and to mark the 1993 session of the Supreme Council (Mother of the World), 33rd degree. Having painstakingly researched the ceremony, the artist claims that it is the most historically accurate documented likeness of this significant event. What may most interest us here is the detail of the oak tripod placed for the purpose of laying the cornerstone. If we recall René d'Anjou's painting of 1457, *La Fontaine de fortune* (see fig. 1.19, page 55), it becomes apparent that a great deal of symbolism had been carried from d'Anjou's time to 1793, but instead of the sleeping apprentice who accompanies the knight in search of the Holy Grail, we find a carved stone signifying the foundation of a new republic. Surely, the intended suggestion was that a new Temple was being established here in the New World, following an immense struggle for freedom and the truth. Did the truth concerning the ancient meridians lie at the heart of the plan for the Capitol in Washington?

The Building of Washington, D.C.

Both the Capitol and the White House subsequently became the focal points of an elaborate geometric layout of the nation's capital city, first conceptualized by the French Freemason, soldier, and artist-architect Major Pierre-Charles l'Enfant (see fig. 4.10). But although the original design is accredited to l'Enfant, it is known that both George Washington and Thomas Jefferson had a hand in modifying the original plan in order to include a series of octagonal patterns, incorporating both the Maltese cross and the Templar cross, which are employed by Masonic Templars to this day.[44]

Although l'Enfant's designs symbolized the ideals of the freedom and independence so recently achieved by the Americans, they were undisputedly European. His original plans for the Capitol reflected the grandeur and the distinction of the Baroque landscape architecture of Paris and Versailles that strongly influenced him. L'Enfant planned for two series of broad avenues, named for the states Maryland and Pennsylvania, that would converge into circular intersections intended to complete long vistas and give direction and character to the city. L'Enfant selected two high spots—Jenkins Hill for the Congress and a second hill a mile and a half away for the President's Palace, later known as the White House—which were to be connected in a straight line by an avenue 160 feet wide. The avenue, though no longer an uninterrupted straight line because an addition to the Treasury building in 1840 effectively blocked it, became Pennsylvania Avenue.[45]

The pattern of radiating avenues in the city was filled by a gridiron matrix of streets, which were to be numbered to the east and west and lettered to the north and south—excluding J Street, which, according to a 1994 *Washington Post Magazine* article, l'Enfant omitted to avoid confusion between the letters *I* and *J*, which were indistinguishable and often interchangeable at the time.[46] Although l'Enfant's design became the basis for land sales, construction, and planning of the Capitol, President Washington fired him a year after because the Frenchman apparently had "forged ahead regardless of his orders, the budget, or landowners with prior claims."[47] Though the dismissed l'Enfant returned to France with his plans, the renowned mathematician, astronomer, and publisher Benjamin Banneker, who was assisting Commissioner Andrew

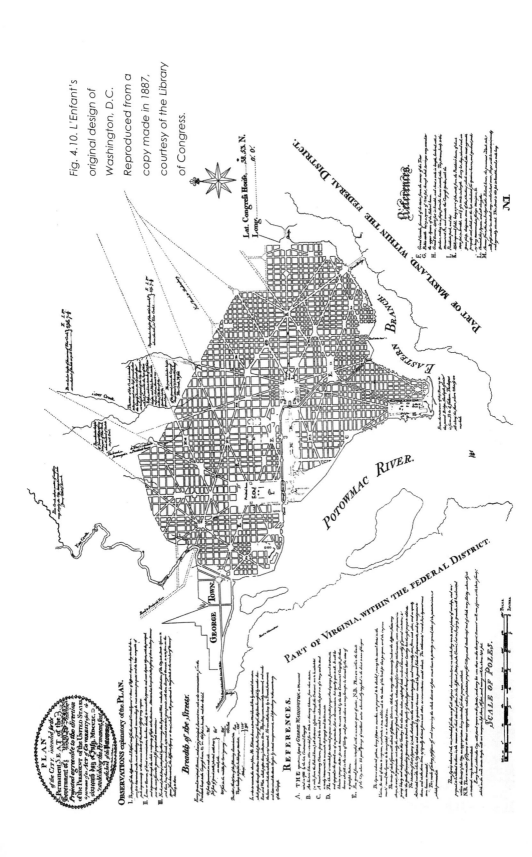

Fig. 4.10. L'Enfant's original design of Washington, D.C. Reproduced from a copy made in 1887, courtesy of the Library of Congress.

Ellicott in the survey of the site, saved the project by reproducing them in their entirety from memory.

Many modern-day anti-Masonic crusaders see a grand conspiracy in the layout of the capital. They claim that facing the Capitol from the Mall, the building can be envisioned as the top of a compass, with the left leg of the instrument represented by Pennsylvania Avenue and the right leg by Maryland Avenue. They also say that the Masonic square is found in the usual Masonic position in the center of the "temple," at the intersection of Canal Street and Louisiana Avenue, and that the left leg of the compass stands on the White House and the right leg stands on the Jefferson Memorial. Of course, carrying all of this a bit further, the circular drive and short streets behind the building form the head and ears of what Satanists call the Goat of Mendes or Goat's head!

Adding to speculation about some sort of Masonic/Satanic "conspiracy" influencing the construction of the District of Columbia is that supposedly an inverted five-pointed star, or pentagram, with the star pointing south, can be seen in the arrangement of the capital. It supposedly lies from the intersections of Connecticut and Vermont Avenues north to Dupont and Logan Circles, and from Rhode Island and Massachusetts Avenues going to Washington Circle to the west and Mt. Vernon Square to the east. The center of the pentagram is said to be 16th Street, where, thirteen blocks due north of the very center of the White House, the Masonic House of The Temple sits at the top of a hill. Of course, rather than all of this leading up to some sort of conspiracy, the arrangement merely demonstrates an understanding of the ancient arts of sacred geometry and astronomy, for the five-pointed star is nothing more than a representation of the star Venus, whose transit occurs once every eight years for infinity. Once again, we are met with the idea of something being built along ancient lines in order to last forever.

Interestingly, those who suspect conspiracy at the heart of the capital's construction have not recognized the significance of the park known as Meridian Hill. Historically, the name comes from a proposal in the early 1800s to establish through the mid-point of the White House an official meridian or longitudinal base point for mapmaking and other purposes. A plaque at the upper entrance to the park from 16th Street makes official note of an 1816 marker that stood on the proposed meridian. What we now know, in conjunction with an awareness of this meridian marker, is that Washington, D.C., was positioned on a 45-degree axis developed from a square determined from Desceliers's map of 1550. This axis aligns Green Oaks, Nova Scotia; Boston; Philadelphia; New York; and Washington within a reasonable proximity of modern-day coordinates, and if continued in a southwesterly direction, it bisects Roanoke, Virginia; Atlanta; Roanoke, Alabama; and New Orleans.[48]

As such, with the design of Washington, D.C., and constructions like Jefferson's Monticello, an American tradition of seemingly intimate knowledge of sacred geometry, roselines, and earth energy is formalized. This tradition has shown itself straight through the twentieth century with the work of designers such as Frank Lloyd Wright.

The United Grand Lodge in America and the Growth of the Anti-Masonic Movement

In the early decades of the nineteenth century, after a great deal of infighting between the ancient and modern factions of Freemasonry in Britain, for some reason the two groups recognized a strong sense of mutual purpose. As a result, a merger between the two was formalized when with the Articles of Union were signed on November 25, 1813, by the dukes of Sussex and Kent, the grand masters of the two lodges. Later, on December 27, 1813, the Act of Union confirmed this agreement at a joint meeting of the two lodges and the present United Grand Lodge of England came into existence. Previously, there had been distinct differences in the way each of the rival Grand Lodges in England carried out rituals. When the two Grand Lodges united in 1814, a Lodge of Reconciliation was set up to produce a standard form of ritual to be used by all. In 1816 the Grand Lodge accepted its recommendations, which amounted to expanding the simple eighteenth-century ceremonies by incorporating material from early Masonic lectures that had gradually dropped out of use. To this day Masons everywhere practice this standard form of ritual.

Freemasonry in the First Century of the New Nation

As we have seen, from even before the conception of the United States of America, Freemasonry and its followers have played a role here, perhaps consciously or unconsciously carrying on the traditions and secret knowledge brought to the New World by the Templars centuries before. Just as in the French and Indian War and the American Revolution, Masons certainly played a part in that significant conflict from 1861 to 1865 that in many ways defined the United States for all the years to come: the American Civil War.

Masons were present at the bombardment of Fort Sumter and General Lee's surrender at Appomattox, as well as most of the battles in between. Masonic history or lore holds that the opposing commanders in the first battle of the Civil War were Masons. In fact, Confederate General Beauregard, who was in charge of building the defenses at Charleston Harbor and who attacked Fort Sumter, was a Mason and a Templar Knight, which at this time was considered to be the highest level in Christian Freemasonry. Major Robert Anderson, the officer in charge at Fort Sumter who was eventually forced to surrender his command after several hours of heavy bombardment and shelling, was also a Mason, as were General Ulysses S. Grant's father and two brothers. As for Grant himself, his father often said that Ulysses intended to petition for the degrees, but was delayed by the press of duties in the Army and the presidency. In 1871, Grant in fact told a group of Knights Templar that he planned to petition to become a Mason once he returned home. The grand master for the state of Illinois had actually arranged to make him a Freemason "on sight" but Grant died before this could be accomplished. As for Robert E. Lee, Grant's adversary, it is not known for certain whether he was a Templar Knight or a Mason (two different but connected organizations), but many Southern regiments during the war fashioned themselves after the Knights Templar, including such habits as never cutting their beards and practicing celibacy.

Despite the popularity of Freemasonry, especially in the military, with the assassination of President Lincoln by John Wilkes Booth on April 14, 1865, five days after Lee's surrender to Grant, there were whispers of a Southern conspiracy involving a number of high-ranking

Masons, including Booth, that resulted once again in the necessity for secrecy on the part of the fraternity. This forced secrecy led to a number of somewhat over-imaginative Masonic members to introduce to both European and American Freemasonry the esoteric tenets of what may be called Fringe Masonry during the late Victorian era. It is known that Queen Victoria's husband, Prince Albert, supported this movement within Freemasonry.

The term Fringe Masonry is used to refer to the emergence of a variety of additional degrees within Freemasonry during this period, which happened to coincide with the time when Masonry was rapidly expanding in England. We must note, however, that though the three were coincident, there appears to be no tangible connection among the spiritualist movement, alleged mediumistic phenomena of the Victorian era, and Freemasonry. Men such as Kenneth Mackenzie and William Westcott, who were the prime promoters of Fringe Masonry, were also high-ranking traditional Masons.[49] The result was that a number of esoteric "side rites" were manufactured during the 1870s and 1880s, to the point that most of the original clues to locating the ancient meridians that waited to be rediscovered within the earlier rituals of Masonry became so garbled that today it is almost impossible to discern "that which was lost." The effect Fringe Masonry had on the larger public is still worth examining, for many believe that within the additional degrees can be found a hidden ancient knowledge, including knowledge of the roselines, that might be applied around the world.

Secret Vaults

On Oak Island, in southern Nova Scotia, a treasure hunt has played out for more than two hundred years, based largely on the discovery in 1795 of a deep and mysterious man-made shaft. Through the years, many have speculated on the existence of this Money Pit, as it has been called, yet though the history of the pit suggests a ruse of monumental proportions, the notion persists of treasure located here. Recent theories suggest that medieval Knights Templar and Prince Henry Sinclair were initially involved in the establishment of treasure—or in the appearance of treasure—on this site.

But clues to the search for Templar treasure and the Grail refugees do not, as we have seen, lie with those who sell sensational or "obvious" information, but rather become apparent to those who truly "have the eyes to see." In this chapter we have learned that Freemasonry became an established part of life in the New World and the young America. Even as it became more "mainstream," however, it retained its connection to inner knowledge and sacred geometry. Any discovery of a treasure, at Oak Island or elsewhere, depends on accessing through allegory this inner knowledge and understanding the principles of sacred geometry.

In essence, one of the primary elements of any true Masonic group is a legend or allegory relating to the original building and rebuilding of King Solomon's Temple. Associated with this is the allegory of the secret vault that lay beneath the Temple, based on Solomon's fabled depository of great secrets. Central to the teachings of the Royal Arch degree in Freemasonry is the story that among the ruins of the Temple, three sojourners discover the subterranean chamber where a long-lost secret is found.

The discovery of the secret vault by the sojourners occurred, according to Masonic tradition, on the Jews' return from their exile in Babylon. Within the York Rite version of the degree, the biblical account in Kings has been interwoven with what the Jewish historian Josephus wrote in 90 C.E. about the rebuilding of the Temple, with the crypt becoming an arched vault. In the early eighteenth century, the three sojourners were added to the story to allow a candidate to participate as a witness to the discovery on which the ceremony is based. In the Irish and Scottish versions of the ritual, the biblical reference remains true to the older story of the repair of the Temple.

Traditionally, it is told that the sojourners, who are described as the children of captivity, enter the crypt after discovering a distinctive keystone among the rubble. Following certain instructions from Zerubbabel, who is said to be of the royal house of David and of the tribe of Judah, they make a further, more important discovery relating to the word of God. These instructions include descending through the opening only when the sun, having gained its meridian altitude, illuminates the vaulted chamber. In purely speculative terms, the Royal Arch story is a simple allegory pointing the way from death to life, from darkness to light, with the crypt becoming that place of inner self where the very existence of

God is reasoned. In this manner, anything described within a Masonic context as being "cryptic" is synonymous with secrets or with what is uncovered or revealed to only the enlightened few.

What we know for certain is that the crypt legend probably dates from at least the fourth century C.E., with its many versions being derived from the writing of Philostorgius, who was born about 364. It also appears that the founders of the early Royal Arch degree garnered some of their inspiration in Samuel Lee's *Orbis Miraculum,* published in 1659.[50] According to this legend, the emperor Julian the Apostate authorized the Jews to rebuild the Temple of Jerusalem, which had been destroyed by the Roman Titus in 70 C.E. During their excavations, they discovered the crypts of Solomon's Temple. The story continues that the initial excavations were halted by a number of explosions and earthquakes that finally convinced all that it was useless to try to excavate the ruins and rebuild the old Temple.

There are variants of the legend beside those included in the English, Scottish, and Irish rites. For example, in the Book of Enoch it is said that God showed Enoch, the father of Methuselah, nine vaults in a vision and that with the help of his son he built a secret sanctuary at the bottom of the mountain of Canaan based on a design indicated by God. The nine vaults are described as being beneath one another, and in the ninth it is said that he placed a triangle of gold on which was inscribed the true name of God.

The arch itself is an architectural element that has been known and used as far back as 2000 B.C.E., but in the case of this allegory it is a long, single stone that is used to cover the space between two vertical walls. The suggestion of the arch or lintel being a sacred element of architecture has evolved from the Egyptian belief that it allowed the door to open to another dimension.

It was not until medieval times that the keystone was used in stone vaulting or arched roofing. In fact, it was the Knights Templar who were in part responsible for the introduction of the true arch, or flying buttress, during their sponsorship of the Gothic cathedrals. The medieval master masons of the time had determined that the ability of a stone arch to carry a load depends directly on the keystone, or arch stone. From an engineering perspective, it is the arch stone that disperses the weight of the superstructure through the other stones to the supporting vertical columns. This technique allowed medieval cathedrals to reach higher into the sky and thus closer to God.

What becomes clear, then, is that the ritual of the Royal Arch degree is an allegorical blend of biblical narrative, Roman and Greek history, and the medieval Knights Templar's discovery within the crypts of the Temple of Solomon. In accordance with their official history, it is known that the original Knights Templar had been granted permission to establish their headquarters in Baldwin's Palace, which stood on the former site of Solomon's Temple.

According to Hebrew scripture, when the Temple was restored after Babylon fell to the Persian empire, many of the Temple's original items were returned to Jerusalem. It is therefore assumed by many that the Ark of the Covenant was restored to the Holy of Holies, though there is no reliable record of this ever occurring. Of course, it was the Romans who destroyed the Temple for the last time. This infamous scene is shown on the carved stone known as the Royal Arch of Titus (fig. 4.12), located in Rome, but although the treasure of the Temple is shown being carted

Fig. 4.12. A relief carved on the Royal Arch of Titus depicting the destruction of the Temple of Solomon in Jerusalem by the Romans. Photograph by William F. Mann.

away by the Romans, the Ark is significantly the one artifact that is not depicted. Yet the Temple no doubt contained more than the "usual" treasure. It is probable that it housed official records pertaining to Israel's royal Davidic line. This means that if Jesus was indeed King of the Jews, then the Temple of Jerusalem might have contained proof of his heritage and other information directly relating to him—including, perhaps, evidence of his marriage.[51]

Those who devised the Oak Island Money Pit mystery over the years sought to include unmistakable evidence of Masonic involvement in the treasure scheme. No doubt many Masons would logically be intrigued by similarities in Oak Island history and the allegory they learned through their ritual. For example, the three original discoverers of the shaft on Oak Island might seem to represent the three sojourners who discover the secret vault in the Royal Arch degree. In the Masonic ritual, the candidate is lowered on a rope through a succession of trapdoors, not unlike treasure seekers who were lowered onto the many platforms found within the shaft. The tools said to be used by the three original discoverers of the pit—the pick, the crowbar, and the shovel—conveniently correspond to the implements used by the sojourners to clear a place for the foundations of the second Temple in the Masonic allegory.

Indeed, the search for the Oak Island treasure has been carried out largely by prominent and successful businessmen who were high-ranking Masons, including A. O. Creighton, Frederick Blair, William Chappell, Gilbert Hedden, and Edwin Hamilton. One of the more exceptional gentlemen to be involved in Oak Island was Reginald Vanderbilt Harris (see fig. 4.13). Aside from being the supreme grand master of the Knights Templar of Canada in 1938 and 1939, Harris was provincial grand master of the Grand Lodge of Nova Scotia from 1932 to 1935. He was also a Scottish Rite Mason, 33rd degree. Among his extensive papers bequeathed to Nova Scotia's public archives were volumes of notes on Oak Island, including the draft of a Masonic pageant that was apparently designed to accompany the rite of initiation into the 32nd degree.[52]

The allegorical ritual developed by Harris is set in 1535 at the Abbey of Glastonsbury, where the English Crown is evidently attempting to confiscate the Templars' fabulous treasures, including the Holy Grail.

Fig. 4.13. The noted Canadian Freemason Reginald Vanderbilt Harris, past supreme grand master of the Knights Templar of Canada and author of the first and most extensive book on Oak Island. Reproduced courtesy of the Sovereign Great Priory of Canada.

Secretly, a number of members spirit the Grail across the sea for safe-keeping. The allegory ends with a number of members of the order being dragged off to the Tower of London for torture and death. Intriguingly, 1535 is the same year that Jacques Cartier explored the New World under the banner of King Francis I of France, that Henry VIII of England had decided to declare himself the head of the Church of England and dissolved the English monasteries, and that the king beheaded Thomas More for his failure to submit to the Crown. It appears that R. V. Harris was trying to stress the point that the Crown had no divine right to control both church and state—and that something of immense importance coveted by the king of England secretly made its way to the New World.

It has always been speculated that both the Holy Grail and the Ark of the Covenant are among the lost treasures of the Knights Templar. Many recent authors and scholars have focused on this link, but many also believe that the Templar treasure is concealed in the man-made shaft on Oak Island. There may indeed be a physical treasure of sorts lying at the bottom of the Oak Island Money Pit, but it surely has nothing to do with the Knights Templar or the Ark of the Covenant. It is likely that whatever is hidden there can be attributed to any one of a number of pirate or military ventures of the seventeenth or eighteenth century. In truth, only by understanding sacred geometry and Freemasonry's moral allegory can the mystery of the Templar treasure finally be solved.

5
Hidden History of
a New Nation

The century and a half after the American Revolution proved to be a time of tremendous change and growth for the young United States. The country was redefined physically and psychologically as it fought two wars—one a tragic civil conflict, the other a rather more mysterious conflict between two nations with Masonic underpinnings. Through it all, Freemasonry and other secret societies preserved esoteric knowledge carried over from Europe, and as Lewis and Clark opened up the vast area west of the Mississippi, once again the secret knowledge and "treasure" of the Templars came into play. With the growth of the new nation came a geographic broadening of clues leading to what this knowledge and treasure may be.

The movement of our search for Templar treasure and Grail refugees to the American West actually begins in France, for shortly after the American Revolution, another revolution with immense potential consequences was brewing within the boundaries of that European country. One result of this conflict was a land acquisition that doubled the size of the United States of America in the early nineteenth century. Another, more secretive result was that the British Canadians and Americans entered into an undeclared race to secure definitive knowledge relating to the Templar treasure, ancient meridians, and the Grail refugees.

Changes in France

During the American Revolution, the established power in France was Louis XVI, though the real power lay with the French nobility. Sharing this control were the clergy, the army, and the public bureaucracy, whose members were drawn from an educated bourgeoisie who otherwise saw themselves as locked out of political and social advancement. These three groups joined forces in the French Revolution by, in part, embracing the philosophies of men such as Voltaire and the morals and precepts of Jacobite Freemasonry.[1] It is ironic, then, that King Louis XVI and his wife, Marie Antoinette, were held prior to their beheading in the Old Temple of Paris, the preceptory of Jacques de Molay, the last grand master of the medieval Knights Templar.[2]

It was the philosopher Taine who demonstrated how a daring Jacobin minority in France was able to enforce its will as that of "the people."* From the formation of local revolutionary committees there rose an obscure Corsican Freemason who, between 1796 and 1815, succeeded in transforming what seemed to be a string of inevitable French defeats at the hands of the British into military victories.

Napoleon Bonaparte was born in Ajaccio, Corsica, on August 15, 1769. As a boy, his genius was soon recognized and he was trained in military schools in Paris, where he studied mathematics, history, geography, and several languages. Entering the French army as an artillery officer, Napoleon was quickly promoted to brigadier general after the siege of Toulon in 1793. Following a series of military campaigns, he journeyed to Egypt in 1798, where his great Egyptian campaign ended in relative disaster.[3] On the way to Egypt, Bonaparte made a strategic detour to capture Malta and the treasure held by the Knights of Malta,

---

*Giraud, *Bibliographie de Taine* (Paris: n.p., 1902), 2–5. Taine was the French philosopher of the era that followed the Romantic age in France, which lasted from 1820 to 1850. Romanticism evolved from a reaction against the Classical school, or rather against the conventionality and lifeless rules of this school in its decadence. The Romantic school introduced the principle of individual liberty with regard to both matter and style. It was thus a brilliant epoch, peopled by men of genius and rich in beautiful work, but toward 1850 it had reached its decline, and a young generation, tired in turn of its conventions and its hollow melancholy, arose, armed with new principles and fresh ideals. Their ideal was scientific truth and their watchword was liberty. Taine was one of the most authoritative spokespeople of this era.

but after losing his flotilla to a British naval attack during the Egyptian campaign, he decided instead to attack the Ottoman Empire. Again, the French were to suffer defeat, this time at the medieval Templar foothold of Acre. It was here in August 1799 that Napoleon abandoned his troops for the first time and returned to France, where, after a coup d'état, he became counsel for life and ultimately ruler of France (fig. 5.1).

At the urging of Abbé Sieyes, one of three revolutionary directors who headed the French government at the time, Napoleon pursued Marie-Joséphine-Rose Tascher de la Pagerie de Beauharnais, the recent widow of an executed noble of Merovingian descent,[4] and married her on March 9, 1796, at the Parisian Hotel Mondragon in a civil ceremony. Sieyes had apparently been privy to the specific genealogical research of Abbé Pichon, which concluded, from the royal archives captured by the revolutionary government, that a direct descent from the Merovingian ruler Dagobert II had been maintained and included Joséphine's late husband. In time, Napoleon adopted Joséphine's son Eugène and daughter Hortense, who, as true Merovingians, added to the legitimacy of his claim to the throne of France.[5] To emphasize this connection, in 1804, when he was crowned emperor, Bonaparte decorated his coronation

Fig. 5.1. Jacques-Louis David's *Coronation of Napoleon. Reproduced courtesy of the Louvre Museum, Paris.*

robe with the golden Bees of Childeric discovered during the excavation of the tomb of Childeric I in 1653. King Childeric I was the son of Mérovée and father of Clovis, who was the most famous and influential of all Merovingian rulers.[6]

Between 1798 and 1800 Napoleon fostered plans to reestablish France in the New World following the termination of an alliance between America and France during President John Adams's administration. This quasi-war with France ended when the Franco-American Convention of 1800 concluded with the signing of the Treaty of Morfontaine. The U.S. Senate ratified the treaty shortly after Thomas Jefferson's inauguration as president, for it was Jefferson who had sympathized with the revolutionary cause in France. The treaty, designed to protect America's right of neutrality in the event of war between Britain and France, allowed for the unmolested shipping of American goods and a restricted contraband list. America was now free of hostilities with the French, and all American claims of indemnity against the French for the French seizure of American vessels was placed on hold.

President Jefferson and the Louisiana Purchase

After John Adams's tenure as president, another Founding Father, Thomas Jefferson, took office in 1801. Throughout his life, Thomas Jefferson had achieved what seemed to be the impossible. Aside from becoming the third president of the United States, he was the main author of the American Declaration of Independence, the architect and founder of the University of Virginia, the designer and owner of the sprawling estate of Monticello, and president of the American Philosophical Society. Yet even among all these laurels, it is said that some most admired him for his tolerance toward others and his preference for using reason rather than might. This quality was tested while he was in office, for during his administration sharp political conflict developed and two separate parties, the Federalists and the Democratic-Republicans, had begun to form.[7] In response, Jefferson gradually assumed leadership of the Republicans, who generally opposed a strong centralized government and championed the rights of the individual states.[8]

In some ways, of all the revolutionary visionaries in America, none was more enigmatic than Thomas Jefferson. Although his membership in Freemasonry has never been proved, his understanding of the most important tenets of Freemasonry and Rosicrucianism, an organization based on the Western Christian mysteries, was evident in all of his major endeavors. In addition, while serving as minister to France in 1785 after Benjamin Franklin, some suggest that he was introduced to the teachings of the Jesuit-trained Illuminist Dr. Adam Weishaupt. It is also suspected that during this time he became privy to the secret knowledge of the Holy Bloodline, the Templar meridians, and the earlier exploration of the New World by Prince Henry Sinclair, among others. What we know for certain regarding his connection to Freemasonry is that he utilized the harmonic architecture of the Masons in all of his designs. Curious is the fact that Monticello is situated on the axis that bisects New York, Boston, Philadelphia, and Washington, D.C., suggesting that Jefferson was indeed aware of the forces of ley lines.

One of Jefferson's most cherished architectural elements was the circle within the square. The combination of a dome or rotunda set within a square, as is found in Monticello (see fig. 5.2), or a dome set within a rectangle, as is incorporated in the Capitol building, was known to Freemasons to symbolize the union of heaven and earth. This architectural design amounted to more than merely a visual aesthetic to early Freemasons; they believed that if they created physical structures that mimicked the harmonic, golden ratio found in nature, the forces of nature would manifest through them. The Greek philosopher Hippias of Elis was the first to solve the theoretical problems of dividing an angle into three equal parts (the so-called trisection of an angle) and of squaring the circle—that is, finding a square that has the same area as a specified circle.

Along with architecture, during his lifetime Jefferson developed a vast array of other interests. In addition to being a naturalist and musician, he could converse expertly on art, science, religion, physics, astronomy, law, and literature. He also spoke several languages and could read the classics in their original Greek and Latin. Intriguingly, it is said that Jefferson disliked priests because of what he felt were their dogmatic distortions of Christ's teachings. He was branded an

Fig. 5.2. Thomas Jefferson's Monticello. Jefferson's original plans for this estate were also based on the geometric application of "squaring the circle." Photograph by William F. Mann.

atheist, among other things, and although he rarely defended himself from critical attacks, he felt compelled to write the following note to a friend:

> To the corruptions of Christianity I am indeed opposed, but not to the genuine precepts of Jesus himself. I am a Christian, but I am a Christian in the only sense in which I believe Jesus wished anyone to be, sincerely attached to his doctrine in preference to all others, ascribing to him all human excellence, and believing that he never claimed any other.[9]

Among all these achievements perhaps the most lasting for the United States was his masterminding of one of the largest land transfers in history, the Louisiana Purchase. For Americans, the presence of Spain west of the Mississippi River during the period of negotiations with the French at the beginning of the nineteenth century was not as provocative. A conflict over navigation of the Mississippi River was resolved in 1795 with a treaty in which Spain recognized the United States' right to use the river and to deposit goods in New Orleans for transfer to oceangoing vessels. The Louisiana situation did, however, reach a crisis point in October 1802, when Spain's king Charles IV signed a secret decree transferring the territory to France and the Spanish agent in New Orleans, acting on orders from the Spanish court, revoked the Americans' access to the port's warehouses. These moves consequently prompted outrage in the United States. While President Jefferson and Secretary of State James Madison worked to resolve the issue through diplomatic channels, some factions in the West and the opposition Federalist Party called for war and advocated secession by the western territories so that they might seize control of the lower Mississippi and New Orleans.

Some time before, France had secured a small presence in the Americas by establishing the sugar-rich colony of Santo Domingo, present-day Haiti. From Santo Domingo the French believed they could support the troops that they intended to post in New Orleans, but unfortunately for those in the army that were sent to Santo Domingo to suppress a rebellion by slaves and free blacks in 1802, an epidemic of yellow fever broke out. It quickly decimated the French force.[10]

France's minister of finance, François de Barbe-Marbois, who had always doubted Louisiana's worth, counseled Napoleon that the territory would be less valuable without Santo Domingo and, in the event of war, would likely be taken by the British from Canada in part because of the Acadian connection. Napoleon recognized that France could not afford to send forces to occupy the entire Mississippi Valley; thus the idea of a new empire in America was quickly abandoned, with France deciding to sell the Louisiana territory to the United States. Seizing on what Jefferson later called "a fugitive occurrence," America's agents in Paris, Monroe and Livingston, immediately entered into negotiations with French Foreign Minister Talleyrand and on April 30, 1803, reached an agreement that exceeded their authority: the purchase of the Louisiana territory, including New Orleans, for fifteen million dollars.[11] The acquisition of approximately 827,000 square miles of vast wilderness essentially doubled the size of the United States.[12] (See fig. 5.3.)

Fig. 5.3. A map of U.S. territory indicating the land acquired in the Louisiana Purchase, from History of North America (Princeton, N.J.: Princeton University Press, 1936).

Interestingly, ever since his extended stay in France, Jefferson had collected maps and books about North American geography; had read and reread the accounts of the explorations of La Salle, Joutel, Hennepin, Charlevoix, LaHontan, and, most recently, Jean Bossu; and had delved into the *Histoire de la Louisiane,* written by Le Page du Pratz. Always on the lookout for new information, he had even laid his hands on a copy of the journal of Jean-Baptiste Trudeau, a former Montrealer who eventually settled in St. Louis and who had earlier led a major expedition up the Missouri from St. Louis all the way to Mandan Indian country.[13]

In March 1803, just prior to the purchase of the Louisiana territory, under direct orders from Jefferson, a War Department cartographer named Nicholas King compiled a map of North America west of the Mississippi in order to summarize all available topographic information on the region (see fig. 5.4). Representing the federal government's first attempt to define the vast empire that was soon purchased from Napoleon, King consulted numerous published and manuscript maps, including a sketch of the Great Bend of the Missouri River taken from a survey conducted for the British North West Company by David Thompson. It was believed that this map provided the exact latitude and longitude of that important segment of the waterway, although the art of establishing longitude with a chronometer was still very new. Traveling overland in the dead of winter, Thompson spent three weeks at Mandan and Pawnee villages on the Missouri River, calculating astronomical observations. He also recorded the number of houses, tents, and warriors in the six Indian villages in the area.

At about the same time, through the urging of Jefferson, Meriwether Lewis, Jefferson's private secretary, applied himself to mastering astronomy, botany, and medicine, and the president and his aide worked out a plan that they had both been cherishing for a long while: to organize an expedition with the aim of finding a continental route to the Pacific Ocean. Before completion of the Louisiana Purchase, Jefferson recommended to Congress that Lewis be chosen to command the expedition, for both his previous service and his aptitudes and qualities, and, in his support, insisted on Lewis's "fidelity to truth so scrupulous that whatever he should report would be as certain as seen by us."

Fig. 5.4. Nicholas King's 1803 map of North America west of the Mississippi River. Reproduced courtesy of the Library of Congress.

In anticipation of the finalizing of the Louisiana Purchase, in October 1803 Thomas Jefferson was successful in steering Congress to pass a bill to sponsor an upcoming expedition to the West called the Corps of Discovery. Lewis was approved to lead the corps and in turn chose William Clark, an army captain, as his second in command. Not surprisingly, both Lewis and Clark were well-connected, high-ranking Freemasons as well.

It now appears that not only did Jefferson want to find a continental route to the Pacific, but also he fully expected Lewis to rediscover ancient roselines and perhaps even the descendants of earlier European explorers. In a letter dated June 20, 1803, Jefferson tells Lewis:

> Beginning at the mouth of the Missouri, you will take observations of latitude and longitude, at all remarkable points on the river, and especially at the mouths of rivers, at rapids, at islands, and other places and objects distinguished by such natural marks and characters, of a durable kind, as that they may with certainty be recognised hereafter. The courses of the river between these points of observation may be supplied by the compass, the log-line, and by time, corrected by the observations themselves. The variations of the needle, too, in different places, should be noticed.
>
> The interesting points of the portage between the heads of the Missouri, and of the water offering the best communication with the Pacific Ocean, should also be fixed by observation; and the course of that water to the ocean, in the same manner as that of the Missouri.
>
> Your observations are to be taken with great pains and accuracy; to be entered distinctly and intelligibly for others as well as yourself; to comprehend all the elements necessary, with the aid of the usual tales, to fix the latitude and longitude of the places at which they were taken; and are to be rendered to the war-office, for the purpose of having the calculations made concurrently by proper persons within the United States.[14]

Rather more mysteriously, Thomas Jefferson earlier advised Lewis to urge any whites he met west of the Mississippi to head back east and also ordered Lewis to be on the lookout for Welsh-speaking Indians!

The Lewis and Clark Expedition

Meriwether Lewis (see fig. 5.5) was born in Virginia in 1774, the eldest son of a family belonging to the local elite. Having been raised in the countryside, at an early age he quickly became an excellent outdoorsman and also showed a natural talent for the arts and sciences. Lewis enlisted in the regular army in 1795 and during the following years was stationed in various places, notably at Fort Pickering, which was located near modern-day Memphis, Tennessee. Here he spent some time as a commanding officer and learned the language and customs of the local Indians. William Clark (see fig. 5.5) was a little rougher around the edges. More forceful in nature than Lewis, Clark had the capacity to deal with the men who made up the corps, most of whom were not formally educated. He was also a gifted cartographer with an incredible feel for natural direction and the landscape.

Because the plan was first to go up the Missouri River to its source, Lewis assembled the selected members of the expedition near the mouth of the river in Illinois. To prepare for their spring departure, he and Clark had spent the winter of 1803–04 at nearby Camp Dubois, a small French-speaking community just outside of St. Louis. The St. Louis Frenchmen were a mixture of Louisianan/Acadians from the South, Frenchmen who had fled the French Revolution, and French Canadians from as far away as the St. Lawrence Valley.[15] This makeup suggests that the expedition was not venturing into unknown territory. Indeed, the Louisiana territory and its aboriginal inhabitants held few secrets for the expedition's contingent from St. Louis, which included a French Canadian named Georges Drouillard, who acted as interpreter on the mission. For much of the journey, the Corps of Discovery planned to follow well-established native Indian trails, which later became known as the Mormon, California, and Oregon Trails. The thirty-four men of the corps (and one Newfoundland dog) ultimately traveled eight thousand miles, measuring and mapping every step of the way.

After plowing upriver through the Great Plains, the group wintered in Fort Mandan, North Dakota, surviving only through the kindness of the Indians there—and through an amazing coincidence. The native wife of the French trapper Toussaint Charbonneau, who was hired at

Fig. 5.5. Meriwether Lewis (right) and William Clark, copies of reproductions, artists unknown. Reproduced courtesy of the Library of Congress.

Fort Mandan to act as an additional interpreter, turned out to be the long-lost sister of the leader of the Shoshone Indians. Her name was Sacagawea, and due both to her role on the expedition's journey and to the accounts of her actions by historians such as Grace Raymond Hebard and the novelist Emery Dye, she became a legendary figure. The presence of Charbonneau's Indian bride no doubt facilitated negotiations with Indians throughout the journey, for the Shoshone were horse traders who lived near the source of the Missouri at the foot of the Rocky Mountains. Of course, horses were particularly useful, if not essential, for the success of the expedition's crossing of the Great Divide.

Even with Sacagawea leading the way, however, the expedition found its most bitter disappointments ahead. The next spring they reached the great falls of the Missouri and expected to drag their goods and boats around it within a day or two. But Lewis and Clark's journals tell us that it took fifty-three days, and not until August 12, 1805, did the group finally reach the foothills location of the entrance to the Northwest Passage. When they proceeded to the top of the dividing ridge, however, all they could see was the vast Rockies spread out before them—there was no passage. In deep snow, they struggled through the mountains, taking twice as long as expected and warding off starvation by eating their horses. Finally, they were swept along down the salmon-filled Columbia River and reached the Pacific Ocean on November 18, 1805 (see fig. 5.6).

After completing their mission, Lewis and Clark retraced their steps and reached St. Louis in October 1806. At this time, Lewis entrusted Drouillard with the delivery to President Jefferson of the first letters of the expedition—including excerpts from their journals and a copy of Clark's map of the American West—to the postmaster in Cahokia, on the Mississippi River near St. Louis. Meanwhile, Lewis and Clark triumphantly led eastward through St. Louis a cavalcade that included Mandan and Osage Indian representatives. Upon their return to Washington, D.C., the two explorers were treated as national heroes, with each receiving sixteen hundred acres of the Louisiana Territory as their reward.

The following year, Jefferson appointed Lewis governor of the Louisiana Territory and Clark was made Indian agent for the West and brigadier general of the territory's militia. Yet for all their success, Meriwether Lewis tried in vain to find a publisher for his and Clark's journals, in part because his growing drinking problem had strained his relationship with President Jefferson. Ultimately, he failed to return to St. Louis that year to take up his duties as governor. Upon his arrival a year later, the city was overflowing with miners, land speculators, and eager traders who were becoming increasingly restless in anticipation of the opening up of the Louisiana Territory.

As for William Clark, on January 5, 1808, he married Julia "Judith" Hancock in Fincastle, Virginia. Perhaps significant is that Fincastle is positioned on one of the ancient meridians at 37 degrees 30 minutes north latitude, 79 degrees 57 minutes west longitude. Clark soon thereafter became a successful business partner in the newly formed Missouri Fur Company, which planned to send militia units, hunters, and boatmen up the Missouri to develop the American fur-trading industry. William Clark went on to live a full and fruitful life, first as governor of the Missouri Territory and then as superintendent of Indian affairs in St. Louis from 1822 until his death on September 1, 1838.

Lewis, by contrast, was forced to flee St. Louis in September 1809 after trying in vain to mediate between the native Indians and certain

Fig. 5.6. A map showing Lewis and Clark's route across the country

commercial interests. It is said that he wandered aimlessly until October 11, when, despondent over his position, he took his own life at Grinders Stand, an inn south of Nashville.

Some say that on that fateful night he was actually on his way to Washington to present Jefferson with some of the secrets that he had uncovered in the wilderness. What really happened on October 11, 1809, remains the subject of some speculation. His Masonic apron is still displayed in the Smithsonian Institution with what suspiciously appears to be a well-placed bullet hole. It remains surprising that Lewis was unable to find a publisher in Philadelphia for the expedition's journals. It would seem that any speculator would have loved to have the journals circulating in mass print as a ready-made advertisement for the call to adventure in the Louisiana Territory. Questions remain, too, as to Lewis's ability to establish longitude. Although he studied the art of astronomy for two years, from his journals we may infer that Lewis was at a loss much of the time when it came to observations of longitude—unless, of course, his information was somehow coded or secret.

Meridians, "White" Indians, and Mysterious Cairns

Indeed, it does appear that both Lewis and Clark had been sworn to secrecy about information that related primarily to their possible rediscovery of a series of ancient longitudinal meridians across the Louisiana Territory. We can recall the contents of the letter written by Thomas Jefferson on June 20, 1803, including his request that observations of longitude and latitude be taken at strategic locations distinguished by "other places and objects distinguished by such natural marks and characters, of a durable kind, as that they may with certainty be recognised hereafter." As the earliest stonemasons knew, only carved stones can be considered to be in any manner durable, and as Masons, both Lewis and Clark would have readily recognized the carved signs and symbols of the Craft. Further, regarding Jefferson's correspondence, what did he mean by the phrase "to comprehend all the elements necessary, with the aid of the usual tales"? To what does "the usual tales" refer?

In answer, let us examine the ancient grid beyond Chicago. At 41 degrees 15 minutes north latitude, 95 degrees 57 minutes west longitude lies the site—Council, later known as Council Bluffs, Iowa—where Lewis and Clark first met representatives of a number of the Great Plains Indian tribes. Here, atop a natural promontory at a significant bend in the river, similar to the site of Green Oaks, Nova Scotia, was an ancient gathering place known for its spiritual energy. This meridian lies between Meriden, Iowa, located to the north at 42 degrees 47 minutes north latitude, and Meriden, Kansas, found to the south at 39 degrees 11 minutes north latitude.

Applying the usual eight degrees of separation between meridians, the next meridian is found at the Missouri River–Yellowstone River confluence, located at 48 degrees 57 minutes north latitude, 103 degrees 57 minutes west longitude. The Corps of Discovery camped here and took detailed observations of latitude and longitude prior to traveling upriver.

As for Jefferson advising Lewis to be on the lookout for Welsh-speaking Indians, in 1832, George Catlin, lawyer, frontiersman, and pictorial historian, lived for several months among the Mandan Indians, near the site of present-day Bismarck, North Dakota. Significantly, he noted in his journals that the Mandans were distinctly different from all other native American tribes he had encountered, in part because most of them were "nearly white," with light blue eyes.[16] Catlin also deemed the Mandans to be "advanced farther in the arts of manufacture," than any other Indian nation, and that their lodges were equipped with "more comforts and luxuries of life." Indeed, Missouri governor William Clark himself told the frontiersman, before Catlin started up the Missouri, that he would find the half-white Mandans a strange people. Obviously the genetic strain that produced Mandans with blond hair "fine and soft as silk," blue eyes, and fair skin, was entrenched—certainly since well before the living memory of tribe members in 1832.

Catlin's affirmation within his own journals that he knew of no contact between the Mandans and Europeans prior to their encounter with Lewis and Clark in 1804 means that he himself was unaware of earlier English and French expeditions along the Missouri. Aside from records of the travels of David Thompson, it is recorded that in 1738 a French-Canadian nobleman had visited the Mandans, guided by Jean-Baptiste Trudeau. This was likely Pierre Gaultier de Varennes, sieur de Verendrye, who apparently took an expedition from his forts in present-day

Manitoba to what is now North Dakota in search of a rumored tribe of "white, blue-eyed Indians." Along the banks of the Missouri River, La Verendrye apparently found a stone cairn with a small stone tablet inscribed on both sides with unfamiliar characters. Jesuit scholars in Quebec later described the writing as Tartarian, a script similar to Norse runic writing. The tablet was shipped to France, and unfortunately there it disappeared into Jesuit archives.

La Verendrye's own notes and drawings show that he located the Mandan village in what is now MacLean County, North Dakota, between Minot and Bismarck, on December 3, 1738.[17] He described the settlement as a large and well-fortified town with 130 houses laid out in streets. Surprisingly, the fort's palisades and ramparts were not unlike European battlements and included a dry moat around the perimeter of the village. More remarkable, La Verendrye described many of the Mandans as having light skin, fair hair, and "European" features. He also described their houses as clean, "large and spacious," with separate rooms.

Thus, there existed then a group of "white" Indians who displayed European physical characteristics and employed a European strategic layout for their town. Is it a coincidence that French nobility and Jesuits were the first to discover a stone cairn along the Missouri with Norse runic carvings? Remember that the Scottish prince Henry Sinclair and his Templars would have been well aware of the significance of carved symbols and would have spoken a form of Gaelic that in later years could be mistaken for Welsh. Surely, in their travels they would have established stone cairns as surveying markers of sorts and perhaps even to act as beacons on the Great Plains if lighted with a flammable material. Amazingly, the description of these cairns is very similar to those identified in great numbers along the ancient meridian at Hatley Corners, Quebec. They are also very similar to the stone "beehive" cairns illustrated on Desceliers's map of 1550. Perhaps they even served as grave markers—maybe marking the burial site of Prince Henry Sinclair himself! If this is indeed the case, then it is quite possible that Templar treasure could have been buried with him as a kind of consecration and honor for his achievements, for here was a "giant among men" who had traveled virtually halfway around the world, reactivating a series of ancient meridians (see fig. 5.7, page 206) in pursuit of a higher level of consciousness.

Actually, just past the great falls of the Missouri lies the ancient meridian defined by a longitude of 111 degrees 57 minutes west and signifying the source of the Missouri and Yellowstone Rivers, which originate in the foothills of the Rockies at Beartooth Mountain, within the Big Belt Mountains. These mountains have significant deposits of coal, iron, gold, silver, and copper, as well as other rare and precious metals including platinum. Interestingly, one more confluence with the information we have already associated with the Templars and the Grail refugees and the significance of the New World's meridians is that the Lewis and Clark expedition was in this vicinity—somewhere between modern-day Great Falls and Helena, Montana—during the summer equinox and St. John the Baptist's feast day on June 24.

If we follow this ancient meridian to the south, it becomes evident that other early settlers felt the energy of this line. For example, the original Temple Square of the Mormons in Salt Lake City falls directly across it, as does Tempe, Arizona. Farther south still, the roseline falls across the Isla Magdalena, on the southern tip of Baja, California. Of course, the Mormons, intimately aware of their genealogy, trace their ancestors back to the Merovingian dynasty. We may wonder if it is merely coincidence that the Merovingians' primary symbol, the bee, is also the symbol for the Mormon Church and for the state of Utah. After all, it was the Mormon leader Brigham Young who declared, in an interesting choice of words, that the church would make "a rose of the desert."

This ancient roseline bisects some very significant natural features as well, such as the east end of the Grand Canyon and Oak Creek Canyon, which is located just outside of Sedona, Arizona. It also falls along the western edge of the Four Corners medicine wheel of the Navajos. In another coincidence, the state flag of Arizona is centered on a golden five-pointed star that is strikingly similar to the star of the Acadians, Stella Maris, or the Star of the Sea, the Star of the Virgin Mary.

During Lewis and Clark's time, two significant events involving the United States of America occurred that would have a profound effect on the continuation and control of this knowledge of ancient meridians in the hands of so few: The first, the War of 1812, was in part the direct result of the American purchase of the Louisiana Territory. The second,

Fig. 5.7. The map on this page, drawn in 1593 by Cornelius de Jode, is based on the same geometric equidistant projections from the north as demonstrated by the illustrative map on page 207, which applies ancient meridians across North America. The map on page 207 is an original drawing by William F. Mann.

not nearly as public but just as significant, was the formation of the United Grand Lodge of England in 1814 (see page 178). Because of a developing anti-Masonic movement over the next fifty years, this event was to play a role among the underlying causes of the American Civil War. Growing anti-Masonic feeling also may have been the reason for Jefferson and Clark remaining silent about the secrets of roselines. As

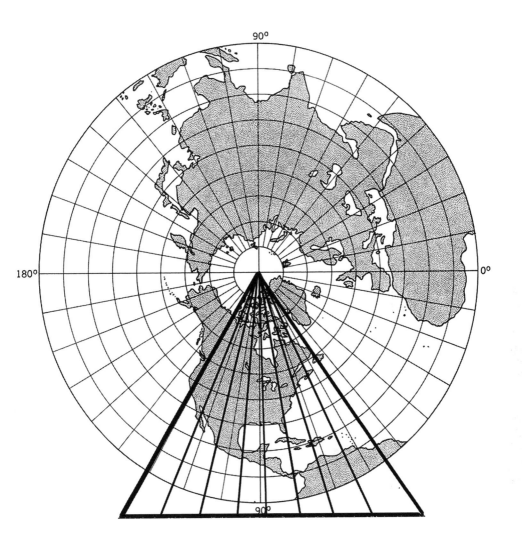

a result of these two factors, meridian secrets and any related knowledge of treasure remained the province of the whispers and rituals of fringe movements and brotherhoods, and those few remaining North American descendants of the original Grail refugees for whom many had searched during the previous four centuries—including the Mandan, those "white" Indians, who finally succumbed to disease and attrition. This meant that the Holy Bloodline would survive only through the mixture of French and Indian blood—the Métis, who inhabited the northern wilderness north of the 45th parallel.

The War of 1812 and Tecumseh

Officially, the War of 1812 occurred between the United States and Great Britain, but most of the fighting took place in the border regions between America and what was known at that time as Upper and Lower Canada. A major cause of the war was American anger over the fact that U.S. ships were being stopped and searched by the ships of the British Royal Navy and American crew members were being impressed into naval service for the British. By this time Britain was in the midst of war against France, and it had declared a naval blockade of the United States to prevent any supplies from heading to France. The British also claimed the right to seize any deserters from the Royal Navy that they found on board any foreign vessel. The Americans were also suspicious of the fast-growing shipbuilding enterprise that had blossomed under the Métis at Pentatanguishine, which is located along the ancient meridian that traverses the eastern edge of Georgian Bay on Lake Huron. The American fear was that this operation would result in an overwhelming "Grail fleet" that would rule the Great Lakes.

This interference with American shipping alone would likely not have led to war, but the American Congress at this time was dominated by a group of men known as the War Hawks, who were from mostly the western and southern states.[18] It seems that they wanted to expand into the Indian Territory of the Ohio Valley, but the Indians of the Ohio Valley traded with British merchants from Montreal to secure the guns that they needed to protect their territory from American encroachment. The Hawks intended to stop this trade by driving the British out of Canada. Like many other Americans during this era, they believed in Manifest Destiny: that it was the destiny of the United States to take over all of British North American and settle the country to the Pacific.[19]

The Americans really did not expect a great deal of opposition to any takeover of Canada, for most of the inhabitants of Upper Canada (present-day Ontario) were American in origin. Most of the people in Lower Canada (present-day Quebec), however, were of French origin. The Americans believed that both groups were eager to free themselves from British rule, but this was not the case. Instead, all the settlers there fought to protect their homeland, for they were satisfied to live under British law, which allowed them a great degree of self-government.

Consequently, the early optimism of the Americans to drive the British entirely from North America was dashed by a series of defeats at the hands of British regulars who were supported by Canadian militiamen and native warriors, among whom were the Shawnee chief Tecumseh (see fig. 5.8), others from the Ohio Valley, and Brant's Mohawk from the Grand River in Upper Canada and Caughnawaga in Lower Canada.[20]

Less than a month after the declaration of war on June 18, 1812, an American army crossed the Detroit River and invaded Upper Canada. What was initially a success for the Americans was turned into a disastrous defeat at the hands of General Isaac Brock and Tecumseh and his warriors. Fort Michilimackinac, at the entrance to Lake Michigan, was captured by the British soon thereafter and was held by them during the remainder of the war. Later the same year, the United States launched a second front on the Niagara frontier but this invasion, too, was repulsed, though Brock was killed in the battle.

For the next two years, most of the fighting took place in and around the Niagara Peninsula and on Lakes Ontario and Erie. There was also a smaller campaign in 1813–14 in Lower Canada, which spread as far south as Washington, D.C. It was during this that the British successfully marched into Washington and torched the president's mansion, after which it was repainted white, and became the White House. The war also affected the British colonies on the Atlantic, where daring sea captains from Nova Scotia and New Brunswick became licensed privateers preying on American merchant ships and keeping a portion of the profits for themselves.

The War of 1812 ended in a stalemate. Thus, the Treaty of Ghent, signed in Belgium on December 24, 1814, returned all conquered territory, leaving the situation exactly as it had been prior to the war. One major change, however, was that the residents of the British colonies of Upper and Lower Canada had gained a sense of nationhood. Together, they had fought to repel the aggressor from the south, which gave them a new pride and caused them to think of themselves as Canadians. It was the first time that they had identified themselves with the land in which they lived rather than with the countries from which they had originated. The ultimate result would be the establishment of the Confederation in 1867, the formal creation of the country of Canada.

*Fig. 5.8. The Shawnee chief Tecumseh. Print by Frederick H. Brigden, c. 1813. Repro-
duced courtesy of the National Archives of Canada.*

For our purposes, a question remains as to the underlying purpose for the aggressive stance of the Hawks in the United States leading up to the war. Is it possible that some were aware of the existence of something of immense importance that lay in part within the Ohio Valley still controlled by the Indians?

Indeed, one of the most interesting yet misunderstood aspects of the War of 1812 is the involvement of Tecumseh, the Shawnee chief who in many ways was responsible for the ultimate stalemate between the British and Americans.[21] He had envisioned the creation of a confederation of all North American tribes into one strong Indian nation and for years devoted all of his energies to this purpose, attempting to hold his people's land through diplomacy rather than bloodshed. Had he succeeded, he would have been the founder of an empire that rivaled Mexico in size. It is certainly apparent that Tecumseh supported the British in the War of 1812 in the hope that a British victory would ensure that the Indians would be able to maintain possession of their lands. Yet he was not only a great diplomat and spokesperson who ultimately gave his life for his people. It is speculated that he, along with his brother Tenskwatawa, "the Prophet," was one of the last "pure" descendants of the Grail refugees.[22]

The word Shawnee comes from the Algonquian word *shawun*, meaning "southerner." This label, however, refers to their original location in the Ohio Valley relative to other Great Lakes Algonquin rather than to an origin in the American Southeast. The Shawnee spoke an Algonquian dialect and were woodland in their culture and habits, although there is much doubt as to their ancestral home. At one time or another they had villages in South Carolina, Tennessee, Pennsylvania, Georgia, Alabama, and Ohio, an area extending across the southern reaches of the larger Algonquin nation. Although they were considered a roving people, they practiced agriculture wherever they set their villages, which were fortified through the strategic use of palisades and dry moats.

By 1656 the Iroquois of upper New York had conquered all of their rival tribes except the Susquehannock, and had started to clear the Algonquin tribes from the Ohio Valley and Lower Michigan. Most of these enemies ended up as refugees in Wisconsin, but some of the Shawnee apparently held on for a few years as Susquehannock allies, intermarrying with members of that tribe. Then in 1658 the western Iroquois attacked the Susquehannock in what was the final chapter of many years of warfare between them. Despite their lack of firearms, which the Iroquois had obtained through Dutch traders from Manhattan, not until 1675 were the Susquehannock-Shawnee defeated.

The Susquehannock and Shawnee continued as allies of the French during the French and Indian War and in 1763 fought with Pontiac against the British. They became British allies during the American Revolution, however, and led many forays against settlements throughout the colonies. Yet all of the Shawnee were enthusiastic supporters of the war. During the 1770s and 1780s, a large group left the Ohio Valley and moved across the Mississippi River into Missouri, becoming known eventually as the Absentee Shawnee. This group in turn split after 1803, with a large faction moving south to Texas.

The Ohio or Eastern Shawnee continued their resistance until the defeat of the allied Indian nations at Fallen Timbers in 1793. With the Treaty of Greenville in 1795, they were forced to cede most of their land to the American government. The result was that the Ohio Shawnee split into three groups, two of which stayed in Ohio while the third, the Anti-Greenville faction, moved west to the Wabash River in Indiana. It was during this time that Tecumseh emerged as a commanding figure among the Ohio River tribes. Except for the Shawnee who followed Tecumseh into battle, though, the nation generally adopted a neutral stance during the war. The Ohio group declared its neutrality early on and was able to remain on its lands until 1831, when members were forced to move to Kansas, Oklahoma, and Montana. The Shawnee living in Missouri were also largely neutral, but they too were eventually forced to move west to Kansas, Oklahoma, and Montana, where the bounties placed on their heads by the American government virtually eliminated them. The only remaining Shawnee today are the descendants of those who moved to Texas in 1803.

With the death of Tecumseh in October 1813, the eventual decimation of the Algonquin Nation, and the death of Thomas Jefferson on July 4, 1826, whatever remained of the ancient secret of the Holy Bloodline and the related ancient meridians would have been buried with them, deep within Native American and Métis legends and perhaps in the Masonic rituals of the United Grand Lodge of England (see chapter 4, page 178).

The Civil War

Much has been written about the Civil War, which was a monumental event that redefined both Americans and their nation. Here we will look at the causes and issues of the war between the North and the South in relation to the notion that along with the obvious factors, there existed an underlying, more secretive reason for the conflict, including the earlier secret Templar knowledge, which had been absorbed in Masonic ritual.

Of course, the American Civil War profoundly changed all of the people who were touched by it, even those who did not live in America. Within the boundaries of the United States specifically, its conclusion established the supremacy of the authority of the federal government over that of individual states, ended the institution of slavery, and stimulated the industrial growth and prosperity of the entire country. While slavery has been seen by some as the most significant cause of the war, the issues of an individual state's right to govern itself and the South's feeling that it was not fairly represented in Congress as a result of prewar legislations appear to have been at the heart of the South's attempt to secede from the Union.[23]

The Missouri Compromise was the first effort by Congress to defuse the sectional and political rivalries triggered by Missouri's request late in 1819 for admission to the Union as a state in which slavery would be permitted. At the time, the United States contained twenty-two states, evenly divided between slave and free. The admission of Missouri as a slave state would upset that balance and set a precedent for the expansion of slavery into other states. The compromise worked out by the Senate and the House provided for Missouri being admitted as a slave state and Maine, which was part of Massachusetts at that time, as a free state—on the condition that except for Missouri, slavery would be excluded from the Louisiana Purchase lands north of latitude 36 degrees 30 minutes, the southern boundary of Missouri.

It seems significant that the entire length of the Missouri River falls north of this designation, which suggests that the river was deemed to be of immense importance, even if it meant allowing slavery to continue. It was Henry Clay, of Kentucky, speaker of the House, who fought to secure passage of the compromise. In fact, his support was so ardent that he is generally regarded as its author.[24] Interestingly, as spokesman of western expansionist interests and leader of the War Hawks, it was Clay who first stirred up enthusiasm for war with Great Britain and helped bring on the War of 1812. Then, in 1814 he resigned from Congress to aid in the peace negotiations leading to the Treaty of Ghent, earning him the title "the Great Compromiser."

Many Southerners criticized the Missouri Compromise because it established the principle that Congress could make laws regarding slavery. Northerners, on the other hand, criticized the compromise for allowing slavery to continue. Nevertheless, the act helped hold the United States together for more than thirty years. In 1854, however, it was repealed by the Kansas-Nebraska Act, which established local choice regarding slavery in those states despite the fact that both were north of the compromise line. In the Dred Scott case, three years later, the Supreme Court declared the Missouri Compromise unconstitutional on the grounds that the Fifth Amendment prohibited Congress from depriving individuals of private property without due process of law.

Adding fuel to the smoldering fire between North and South regarding slavery and abolition were the actions of John Brown, who led a massacre of proslavery settlers in Kansas and organized a raid on the federal arsenal in Harpers Ferry, Virginia, in 1859. It was his intention to foment a slave uprising and to create a black republic. To Southerners, John Brown was a ruthless symbol of all that they feared from abolitionists, but while Republican leaders denounced Brown's use of violence, he conducted himself with dignity during his trial for treason and as such became a martyr to many in the North when he was found guilty and hanged on December 2, 1859.

With the election of Lincoln as president in 1860, South Carolina's secession from the Union became a foregone conclusion.[25] It was this mix of secession and fomenting abolitionism that ultimately ignited the Civil War. South Carolina had long been waiting for an event to occur that would unite the South against antislavery forces. Once the outcome of the election was certain, a special South Carolina convention declared that "the Union now subsisting between South Carolina and other states under the name of the United States of America is hereby dissolved." By February 1, 1861, six more Southern states had seceded, and on February 7 the seven states adopted a provisional constitution for the Confederate States of America.

Less than a month later, on March 4, 1861, Abraham Lincoln was sworn in as president of the United States. In his inaugural address he refused to recognize the secession, considering it "legally void." His speech closed with a plea for restoration of the Union, but the South turned away and on April 12, Confederate guns fired upon federal troops stationed at Fort Sumter in Charleston, South Carolina. The fort dominated the harbor, which was previously identified as being located on the 79 degrees 57 minutes west longitudinal meridian defined through Desceliers's map of 1550. Could this have been a symbolic as well as a strategic volley to those "on-the-square"? Again, it is curious that another strategic point on the grid pattern of ancient meridians would become both a physical and a symbolic focal point of actions between the practitioners of York Rite Masonry (the North) and Scottish Rite Masonry (the South).

After four long years of war, the Union siege of the Confederate capital of Richmond, Virginia, signaled the end of the conflict. Under the command of General Grant, the Union Army marched into the city and Confederate forces under General Lee moved west. One week later, on April 9, 1865, Lee surrendered his Army of Northern Virginia at the Appomattox courthouse. Joseph E. Johnston, who was in charge of the Army of Tennessee in North Carolina, surrendered his troops to General Sherman shortly thereafter. Confederate naval units did not surrender immediately and some continued to fight on the high seas until as late as November 1865.

One result of the Civil War was the awakening of a sleeping industrial giant in America, for it was realized that within the newly defined expanse of the United States there lay enough natural resources to create the strongest nation on earth. Significantly, a good portion of these natural resources lay along the ancient roselines that span the country. Also, if the ultimate purpose of those in control of the United States was to influence the future state of the world by becoming its New Jerusalem (though this is only conjecture at this point), then locating religious artifacts representing great divinity, even including members of the Holy Bloodline, would have been essential to America's claim of spiritual superiority. It is historical fact that both Bonnie Prince Charlie and, subsequently, George Washington were offered the kingship of the United States, but both of them turned down the position. We'll never know why, but we might speculate that somewhere within the Americas there remain descendants of the Holy Bloodline who have a more rightful claim to the kingship of the New Jerusalem. As we'll now see, clues to the continuing existence of ancient Templar knowledge slowly disseminated from Europe and abroad.

Rennes-le-Château, St. Anthony and St. Paul, and Templar Clues in the West

In June 1885, only about twenty years after the conclusion of the Civil War in America, the village of Rennes-le-Château in southern France received a new parish priest, Abbé Berenger Saunière.* His tenure, as we will see, is significant in that in a roundabout way it brings us more information about the Holy Bloodline and ancient roselines and the connections between these and the American Midwest that grew as a result of the actions of Thomas Jefferson and Lewis and Clark and the changes wrought by the Civil War.

In 1891, Abbé Saunière started a modest restoration of the village church of Mary Magdalene that had been consecrated in 1059. During the renovations, the abbé supposedly discovered that one of the two Visigoth columns that supported the altar stone was hollow and that inside there were four parchments preserved in sealed wooden containers (see fig. 5.9, page 218). Two of the parchments were genealogies dating from 1244, the year the Cather stronghold of Montségur surrendered to northern French forces, and 1644. The other two, which appear to be encoded Latin texts, had apparently been composed by an earlier priest of Rennes-le-Château, Abbé Antoine Bigou, in the 1780s. Both have subsequently been deciphered and the following interpretation has appeared in many books devoted to Rennes-le-Château:

---

*Baigent, Leigh, and Lincoln, *Holy Blood, Holy Grail*, 24–32. A great deal of the material used in this book concerning the life of Berenger Saunière and the mystery of Rennes-le-Château was originally derived from Gérard de Sède's *L'Or de Rennes*, but the bulk of the story has come from *Holy Blood, Holy Grail*.

BERGERE PAS DE TENTATION QUE POUSSIN TENIERS
GARDENT
    LA CLEF PAX DCLXXXI PAR LA CROIX ET CE CHEVAL
DE DIEU
    J'ACHEVE CE DAEMON DE GARDIEN A MIDI POMMES
BLUES

(Shepherdess, no temptation, that Poussin, Teniers, hold the key;
peace 681, by the cross and this horse of God, I complete [or
destroy] this daemon of the guardian at noon. Blue apples.)*

Another interpretation from the second parchment reads:

A DAGOBERT II ROI ET A SION EST CE TRESOR ET IL EST
LA MORT.

(To Dagobert II, king, and to sion belongs this treasure and he is
there dead.)[26]

The story goes that following his discovery, Saunière was sent to Paris
by his superior, the bishop of Carcassone, with instructions to seek out
Abbé Bieil, director general of the Seminary of St. Sulpice (which, we
have learned in chapter 1, was built on the ancient Paris roseline). Having
duly presented himself to Bieil, Saunière spent three weeks in Paris in the
company of Bieil's nephew Émile Hoffet, who was a known occultist. It
was during this time that he was introduced to Emma Calvé, an operatic
diva and high priestess of the Parisian esoteric subculture, with whom he
would have a long affair. During his stay in Paris, the priest also spent
time in the Louvre, where he purchased reproductions of three paintings:
a portrait, by an unidentified artist, of Pope Celestin V; a work by David
Teniers the Younger that has subsequently been identified as *St. Anthony
and St. Paul;* and finally and most interesting to our study here, Nicolas
Poussin's second version of *Et in Arcadia Ego—Les Bergers d'Arcadia.*

---

*Although this deciphering has appeared in many books devoted to the mystery of
Rennes-le-Château, including *L'Or de Rennes*, *Holy Blood, Holy Grail* was the first to
present in English a summary of the French research into the mystery. Therefore, Baigent,
Leigh, and Lincoln receive acknowledgment for the decoding on page 26 of their book.

JESVSCVRGOANTCCSEXdTPESPaSCShacyENJTTbeThqaNIaMVRaT
FVEKdoTIaZa*VVSMoKIyVVS qVEMMSVSCTYTaVITIYESVSFedCERVNT
.laVIEM*TTCaENaPMTbTETOMaRThahMINISTRRabaTlhaSaRVSO
VERoVNXVSEKaTTE*dTSCoVMlENTdTlVSCVJMMaRTaleRGoaCbCEP
TTlKTbKaMYNNGENTTJNaRdTPFTSTTCTqPRETTOVSTETVNEXTTPE
dPESTERVaETEXTEJRSTTCayPTIRTSNSVISPEPdESERTPTETdoMbESTM
PLFTTaESTEEXVNGETNTTOddEREdTXalTERGoVRNVMEXdGTSCTPVhl
TSETVTXTVdaXSCaRJoRTTSqVIYEKaTCVhMTRadTTTVRVSqTVaREhoCCVN
bEN VIVMNONXVENVTTGRECENPdTSdENaaRVSETddaTVMESGTE
GENTES? dIXINVFEMhoECNoNqVSTadEEGaENTSPERRTINEbEaT
adCVTMSEdqVhINFVRElKTETlOVCVIoShCabENSECaqVaEMVTTTEba
NMTVRPOTKabETEdTXTTEJRGOIEShVSSTNEPTLlaMVNTTXdIERMS
EPVIGTVKaEMSEdESERVNETILlqVdPaVPSERESENhTMSEMPGERhа
bEMTTSNobLTISCVMFMEaVTETMNONSESMPERhaVbEllSCJOGNO
VIlIEKOTZVRbaMVqlTaEXTMVdaCTSTqVTaTlOlTCESTXETVENE
aRVNTNONNPROTEPRTESVmETaNTVMMSEdVTLVZaRVMPVTdER
ЕhАTqVEMKSVSCTaOVTTaMORRTVTSCPOGTTaVKERVNTahVTEMP
RVTNCTPEJSSaCEHCdoTVMVMTETlaZCaRVMTNaTERFTCTKRENTq
lVTaMYlVTTPROPqTERTlhXVMabThGNTCXVGTaaETSNETCRCd
dEbaNTTNTESVM

NO ↓ IS

JESV. MEdEla. VVLNERVM ✦ SPES.VNa. PoENITENTIVM.
PER. MaGdalaNa. laCHYMaS ✦ PECCaTa. NoSTRa. dILVaS.

Fig. 5.9. One of the Rennes-le-Château parchments supposedly found by Abbé Saunière. From Gérard de Sède, *Le Tresor Maudit (The Accursed Treasure).*

Upon his return to Rennes-le-Château, Saunière, who seemed to have acquired a great deal of money and a newly defiant attitude toward the Church, undertook a series of rather mysterious projects: In the church-yard he erased the headstone inscription on the sepulchre of Marie de

Blanchefort (fig. 5.10), the marquise d'Hautpoul (though this inscription had already been copied). He also authorized the building of a replica of a medieval tower, the Magdalene Tower, which was designed to house his ever-growing library. Intriguingly, it was built across an ancient roseline, which again hints at knowledge of ancient meridians being somehow associated with the Magdalene. He also constructed a rather grand country house, the Villa Bethania, though he never occupied it. Finally, he oversaw the restoration of the church itself, incorporating a number of oddities, including strange sculpture and the backwards placement of the Stations of the Cross.

If Poussin's painting indeed holds a clue to the rediscovery of a series of ancient meridians and the potential location of a spiritual or physical treasure in the New World (see chapter 3, page 121), then Teniers's painting *St. Anthony and St. Paul* (see fig. 5.11) could be examined in the same light.

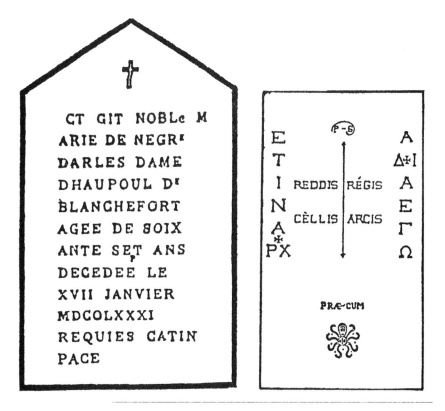

Fig. 5.10. A copy of the inscription on the headstone and horizontal slab at the grave of Marie de Blanchefort. From Eugene Stubelin, Pierres G. de Languedoc.

What is immediately striking in relation to the story of Rennes-le-Château and that of Green Oaks and Oak Island, Nova Scotia, is that Anthony was the patron saint of the medieval Knights Templar. St. Anthony the Hermit was born in a village south of Memphis in Upper Egypt in 271 C.E. Following the death of his parents, as tradition has it, he heard those words that Christ uttered to the rich young man who asked how he could enter heaven: "Go, sell what thou hast, and give it to the poor, and thou shalt have treasure in Heaven."[27]

Soon thereafter Anthony became a model of humility and charity, selling his estate and giving the profits to the poor. It is told that his only food was bread with a little salt, and he drank nothing but water. He ate sometimes only once in three or four days and never before sunset. When he rested, he lay on a rush mat or the bare ground. The story goes that before his death, St. Anthony visited his monks, for he was then the head of a desert monastery, and told them he would not die among them. His orders were that he be buried in the earth beside his mountain cell by two of his disciples, Macarius and Amathas. Hastening back to his solitude on Mount Kolzin near the Red Sea, he soon died,

Fig. 5.11. David Teniers the Younger's painting St. Anthony and St. Paul. Note how the painting is bisected by the cross and observe the relative application of light and dark. Reproduced courtesy of the Ashmolean Museum, Oxford.

whereupon his disciples followed his orders and buried his body secretly in that place.

The life of St. Anthony could easily have inspired the Knights Templar in their quest for the Grail. The Knights would surely have related to Anthony's discarding of all earthly treasures and comforts in his search for wisdom and closeness to God. Other stories tell of St. Anthony's ongoing struggle with the many temptations of the flesh, to which the Templars must have also related. The logic follows that Prince Henry Sinclair and those Templars who accompanied him across the wilderness of the New World took solace in the knowledge that the spirit of St. Anthony was evident through their own actions. Clearly, Prince Henry and his fellow Knights, working to complete their designated tasks in the wilderness of the New World, would have found peace in the knowledge that like them, their patron saint had forsaken all individual earthly possessions and desires in order to pursue his calling. Coincidently, St. Anthony is the patron saint to whom a prayer is said to recover a lost or stolen article—perhaps, in this case, the Templar treasure—relics or genealogies or something much more precious: the lost wisdom of the ancients.

It seems that Teniers's painting reveals the underlying concept of a series of ancient roselines established across the landscape, with the central meridian being the crucifix that splits the painting into two equal parts. In the "eastern" half of the painting there is light, representative of civilization, while in the "western" half of the painting, we find St. Anthony in the dark wilderness, debating whether to follow the hidden knowledge that lies in his small library of books or the formal teachings of the Church, represented by St. Paul himself. Here is the true meaning of the temptation of St. Anthony.

If we symbolically relate this painting to the landscape and geography of the New World, we may first notice that adjacent to the city of St. Paul/Minneapolis, Minnesota, lies the village of St. Anthony, which originally encompassed the area at 45 degrees 15 minutes north latitude. Interestingly, *St. Anthony and St. Paul* was painted sometime just before Teniers's death in 1694, a date that coincides with the history of the state of Minnesota: Following the visits of several French explorers, fur traders, and missionaries, including Joliet and Marquette, the region was claimed for Louis XIV—who had shown an immense personal interest in Poussin's 1640–42 painting *Et in Arcadio Ego*—by Daniel Greysolon, sieur Duluth, in 1679. In another light, Teniers's painting could be symbolically viewed as the next clue to or continuation of the area west of that found underlying Poussin's painting, which was based on Champlain's explorations between 1604 and 1632.

When La Salle explored the Great Lakes region all the way to Illinois, a Franciscan Recollet by the name of Louis Hennepin accompanied him. In January 1680 the party was forced to split up, with La Salle sailing to Ontario for supplies while Hennepin and the rest of the group explored the St. Croix River and Upper Mississippi. The Sioux apparently captured Hennepin and his crew in April of that year. It was during this time that they reached what is now St. Anthony Falls, which Hennepin supposedly named for his favorite saint. The story goes that in July of the same year, Hennepin was rescued by a French voyager and returned in 1682 to France, where he wrote and published the story of his exploration.

Of course, one way of traveling westward from the Great Lakes would have been to enter the St. Croix River at Duluth at the western tip of Lake Superior, sail south to the Mississippi, then continue on to St. Louis, where the Missouri meets the Mississippi. In this manner, the painting by David Teniers the Younger is a conceptual map leading the intrepid explorer into St. Anthony's wilderness beyond the falls. The learned initiate would have recognized the clues in Teniers's painting, which, when connected to the corresponding journals of the early French explorers and St. Anthony's associations to the stories of the Knights Templar, would have led him to the New World hinterland. Significantly, by 1888 iron ore became the dominant trade of the Great Lakes, with the state of Minnesota providing a good deal of the iron ore used in steelmaking in the United States. If you look carefully at the left edge of David Teniers's painting, within the shadows, there appears what may be the saint's lowly hovel or perhaps an entrance to an underground mine or tomb of sorts. It is known that the heads of every royal dynasty in Europe sought out Teniers's work and that one of his more famous paintings is entitled *The Alchemist* (see fig. 5.12). Here, then, is another clue as to what was unquestionably the real treasure of the Templars: the vast natural resources within the New World that provided the medieval Templars with their military edge.

Fig. 5.12. David Teniers the Younger's The Alchemist. *Note how the alchemist depicted in this painting resembles St. Anthony as depicted in the painting St. Anthony and St. Paul. Reproduced courtesy of the Pallazzo Pitti, Galeria Palatina, Florence, Italy.*

What was attributed, throughout Europe, to alchemical magic was actually being supplied by a secret network of mining and maritime activity, which relied on mapping the New World using a system that evolved from an ancient knowledge controlled by those of the "inner circle." Simply put, the major portion of raw materials required to produce weaponry superior to that of all European factions lay along the roselines of the New World. As sworn guardians of the Holy Bloodline, the Templars positioned the Grail refugee settlements along these ancient meridians in a symbolic gesture of support for and recognition of the Bloodline's direct lineage to the Kingdom of Heaven.

6

A New Jerusalem

Local tradition in Guelph, Ontario, Canada, has it that in 1863 the short-lived emperor Maximilian von Hapsburg of Mexico, with the support of the Scottish Rite Freemasons, began a colossal stone church on what is still known in Guelph as the Catholic Hilltop. It is said that foundations for a structure six times the size of the present-day Church of Our Lady (see fig. 6.1) were set into the hilltop in anticipation of Guelph becoming the headquarters of a Holy Kingdom in the New World—a New Jerusalem.[1]

Guelph, the Royal City

The site for the city of Guelph was selected by a popular Scottish novelist named John Galt, who had been appointed in 1827 as the Canadian superintendent of a British development firm known as the Canada Company. It is said that he chose the name Guelph for the new town in honor of the British royal family, as it had apparently never been used as a place-name before. The name Guelph comes from Welfen, the family name of the House of Hanover, which ruled Great Britain at the time. Thus, Guelph is still known today as the Royal City.

Local history has it that John Galt chose the most prestigious and prominent site within the town's boundaries for the Catholic Church to be constructed in honor of his friend Alexander MacDonnell, who was Upper Canada's first Catholic bishop. It was Bishop MacDonnell who

Fig. 6.1. The Church of Our Lady, built on part of the foundation of the colossal stone cathedral planned for Guelph's Catholic Hilltop in 1863. Photograph by William F. Mann.

had helped him form the Canada Company by providing both crucial advice and capital at a time when Galt's negotiations with the British government had stalled. Galt's plan was quite imaginative: Guelph was meant to resemble a European city, complete with squares, broad main streets, and narrow side streets, resulting in a variety of block sizes and shapes. Galt had designed the town following a Baroque plan with a series of streets radiating from a focal point at the Grand River. What ultimately developed on Catholic Hill was an ecclesiastical campus, a complex of five stone buildings that today acts as a terminating vista. The complex forms dominate the city and local zoning ordinances continue to prohibit blocking of the view from any vantage point.

Interestingly, Galt was not himself a Catholic. In fact, he came from a Scottish Presbyterian background. It is not even known whether or not he was a Scottish Rite Freemason. What we do know is that his extraordinary gift to the Roman Catholics led to his dismissal from the Canada Company. Galt's initial grant had also included a huge area surrounding Catholic Hill, but this land gift was drastically reduced after his departure. Apparently, the formidable archdeacon Strachan of York, now Toronto, was not amused by Galt's gift of a smaller hill to the Anglicans. In 1827, Upper Canada was strictly an Anglican preserve and Roman Catholics were still denied basic civil liberties there. In fact, the British Parliament did not pass the Catholic Emancipation Act until 1829.

Though he might not have been a Mason himself, John Galt certainly came from the right part of the world for Scottish Rite Freemasonry. Charles Radclyffe's estates were not far from Irvine, the Scottish seaport where Galt was born. Yet only one mention of Galt occurs in John Ross Robertson's *History of Freemasonry in Canada*.[2] In 1829, when he returned to London to defend himself, albeit unsuccessfully, against charges of extravagance and insubordination for his grant of lands to the Catholic Church, Galt carried a letter from a Simon McGillivray, the grand master for Upper Canada, who had been sent from Britain in 1822. As a high-ranking Scottish Rite Freemason in the nineteenth century, McGillivray likely would have been a deeply religious Christian who believed in the mysteries of Christ. McGillivray was also one of many Scottish Rite Freemasons who were directors of the Canada Company.

What exactly were John Galt's motives in his gift of land and a church to the Catholics in Guelph? What if there remained descendants of the Holy Bloodline within the Golden Horseshoe region of Lake Ontario, individuals who had secretly been transferred for their own safety to the more northerly countryside surrounding Guelph during the fighting in the War of 1812? If a number of the directors of the Canada Company were high-ranking Scottish Rite Freemasons, they might well have had an inkling as to the location and protective energy of the Templar meridians in the area. It will come as no surprise to learn that Guelph is situated relatively close to the ancient roseline positioned at 79 degrees 57 minutes west longitude. Perhaps, then, the city is spiritually dedicated not to the House of Hanover, but to an altogether different royal family instead.

If the Hapsburgs were in fact involved in the development of Guelph as a rose settlement, then perhaps the reason for their involvement lies within the pages of *Holy Blood, Holy Grail*.[3] The first emperor of Austria, Francis I, who at the time held the title of Holy Roman Emperor, was an ardent Scottish Rite Freemason and supporter of the royal Stuarts. He was also a contemporary and friend of Charles Radclyffe, and his estates in Lorraine were said to have provided sanctuary to exiled royal Stuarts from Scotland. During the period that he was Holy Roman Emperor (between 1804 and 1806), Francis's court in Vienna was known as the Masonic capital of Europe. During this time he became the greatest promoter of Scottish Rite Freemasonry and was personally responsible for the spread of the order throughout Europe.

As we have learned in chapter 4, Scottish Rite Freemasonry claimed to have descended directly from the medieval Knights Templar and promised initiation into greater and more profound mysteries—supposedly preserved and handed down in Scotland and passed on to French royalty, including Bonnie Prince Charlie—than did other varieties of Freemasonry. Thus, as the authors of *Holy Blood, Holy Grail* claim, Scottish Rite Freemasons continued well into the nineteenth century their dream of reviving the Holy Roman Empire. According to this vision, a new holy empire was to be ruled jointly by the Hapsburgs and a radically reformed Roman Catholic Church, supported by the Scottish Rite Freemasons. The new empire would be genuinely holy and secular, embracing all Christians who, like those in ancient Rome, followed the true mysteries of Jesus. Their dream was finally to be realized in Guelph, Ontario.

Maximilian's von Hapsburg's right-hand man in Guelph was Father John Holzer, a Jesuit priest. Like many other Catholic priests in Upper Canada, Holzer attempted to create a separate society for Roman Catholics during his stay in the New World. An Austrian like Maximilian, Holzer had been sent directly to Upper Canada by the Society of Jesuits in 1848. He turned out to be relentless in his zeal, building schools, a hospital, an orphanage, a convent, and a rectory in Guelph during the 1850s and early 1860s. Indeed, he succeeded in all that he set out to accomplish except for the building of the huge Hapsburg church on Guelph's Catholic Hilltop.

Unfortunately, the spiritual and physical foundation of Maximilian's "visionary" church was abandoned following Holzer's death and in 1876 the smaller Church of Our Lady was begun on a section of the same foundation. This is the church that dominates the Guelph skyline to this day, along with its associated convent school for the Loretto Sisters and the St. Ignatius College for boys. The Jesuit presence remained in the city, and in 1913 a Jesuit retreat, St. Stanislaus Novitiate, was founded there for Anglophone novices in Guelph. It was later named Loyola College.

Coincidentally, within the University of Guelph's Scottish and Scottish-Canadian collection in the archives of the McLaughlin Library there are housed seven ancient Rosslyn charters, among them three with seals. Not surprisingly, the collection has been described by many Scottish historians as one of the finest in the world and undoubtedly the best in North America. The collection itself combines a wealth of material including regional history that presents an intriguing dilemma: It almost appears that someone has left many clues to the connection between an early Sinclair descent and the subsequent settlement of a number of Sinclairs in and around the royal city of Guelph.

The earliest charter in this collection is dated March 20, 1491, and deals with the transfer of the barony of Pentland from Oliver Sinclair, the son of Earl William, the builder of Rosslyn. The letter is from Oliver to his son George, who married Agnes, daughter of Robert, Lord Chrichton of Sanquar. George died without an heir and the estate passed to his brother William, who died in 1554. The next charter, dated November 8, 1513, transfers the barony from George to William. William, who was knighted by James V, married Alison Hume and was succeeded by his son William, who died after 1602.

The next charter chronologically is dated August 25, 1542, and is from James V to his son William and confirms him in the barony of Pentland. This charter includes the great seal of James V, who reigned from 1512 to 1542. It was this same William of Rosslyn who married Elizabeth, daughter of Sir Walter Kerr of Cessford, and they had two sons, Edward and William, and three daughters. The last four charters in the collection are from William to his sons Edward and William and are dated 1542, 1554, and two from 1574. The first of these has a small red seal with a legend in Gaelic, which is indecipherable. The third charter, dated 1574, bears the seal of Sir William Sinclair and is signed "W. Santclair of Roislin, Knecht."[4]

According to the official genealogy of the early Sinclairs provided by Father Hay, it was Edward Sinclair who married Christian, daughter of George Douglas of Parkhead, but he died without heirs and was succeeded by his brother William, who married Jean, daughter of Edmonston. It is known that this William built the vaults and great archway of Rosslyn Castle (see fig. 6.2) as well as one of the arches of the drawbridge—all, it is believed, to protect the Rosslyn treasure.

Officially, it is said that this collection of Sinclair charters was purchased for two reasons: First, it provides examples of seals of the time and period, and second, the charters relate to other items already in the collection. In this respect, the oldest item in the whole Guelph collection is a letter written by Henry Sinclair, the second Sinclair, earl of Orkney, son of Prince Henry Sinclair and father of earl William Sinclair, designer of Rosslyn Chapel. Though in Scots, it is still quite understandable. In the letter, to Lord Sinclair, baron of Rosslyn, Henry appoints David Menzies as tutor testamentary to his son William Sinclair. Again, in this city, the physical and spiritual foundation of a New Jerusalem, someone went to a great deal of trouble and expense to ensure that this dynastic connection to the physical and spiritual foundation of a New Jerusalem would be available for those with the eyes

Fig. 6.2. A depiction of Rosslyn Castle (from an eighteenth-century lithograph)

to see and understand. This action seems to confirm that the early New World guardians of the Holy Bloodline had understood all too well that ultimately Acadia would be lost as a Grail refuge and that other arrangements would be required for the safekeeping of the remaining descendants of the Holy Family.

Acadia: A New World Avalon

As we have already seen, it is thought that it was in Acadia—now Nova Scotia—that the Templars first sought to find a New World refuge for the Grail, the Holy Bloodline connecting the House of David to the Merovingian dynasty through the descendants of Jesus and Mary Magdalene, and refuge it was until the British exiled the Acadians in 1755.

On December 6, 2003, however, a bilingual proclamation was signed by Adrienne Clarkson, the governor general of Canada, and the official Canadian representative of Queen Elizabeth II, acknowledging the wrongs done to Acadians who were deported from Nova Scotia 250 years ago for refusing to plead allegiance to the British Crown. The document acknowledges that on July 28, 1755, military representatives of "the Crown made the decision to deport the Acadian people," without the express consent of the reigning monarch.[5] The proclamation announced that beginning in 2005, July 28 would become "A Day of Commemoration" of the Acadian expulsion, otherwise known as le Grand Dérangement, the Great Upheaval.

Today, in Nova Scotia alone there are over forty thousand people who claim Acadian descent. They are found in several regions of the province, although many of them are concentrated in the area of Clare, Digby County, the first settlement established by returned Acadian exiles. Clare lies on the south shore of Baie Sainte-Marie, a deep inlet in the northwestern part of Nova Scotia, separated from the Bay of Fundy by a spit of land called Digby Neck. In English terms it is still known as the French Shore, but to the Acadians it has always been la Ville française. There are certainly larger concentrations of Acadians elsewhere in Canada, especially in the Maritime provinces of New Brunswick, Prince Edward Island, and Cape Breton, but the isolation of the French Shore and the homogeneity of its population have preserved a distinct Acadian character in Clare.

All together, some three quarters of Clare's ten thousand residents are Acadian. Although they have had an Acadian member of the legislature since 1836, they are just beginning to win francophone rights. Only since 1981 have they been able to educate their children in French. The independent Université Sainte Anne has grown from a small Jesuit college to become Nova Scotia's only francophone university, and its affiliate, the Centre Acadien, is diligently preserving historical and contemporary Acadian culture.

The Festival Acadien de Clare is the oldest Acadian celebration in the Maritimes and throughout the summer the play *Evangeline* is performed in Acadian French. In fact, the Acadian linguistic revival in the last quarter-century has made Clare a unique bastion of the ancestral dialect. Acadian conversations conducted in Clare include linguistic idiosyncrasies that can be traced to the French spoken some three hundred years ago in the Poitou region of western France, from which the first Acadians set sail. What makes this all the more remarkable is that the original dialect has been lost forever in France.

The general area around the French Shore is known as the "Land of *Evangeline*" (fig. 6.3), in recognition of Henry Wadsworth Longfellow's masterpiece of 1847, *Evangeline: A Tale of Acadie*. Though Longfellow himself had never visited Nova Scotia, his epic poem was tremendously popular, meshing a fictional love story with the tragic tale of the expulsion of the Acadians from their homeland between 1755 and 1763. He apparently based the poem on an account found in Thomas Chandler Haliburton's *History of Nova Scotia*.[6] According to Acadian tradition, Evangeline's real name was Emmeline and she was the daughter of the Acadian Benedict Bellefontaine.[7] It is said that the heroes of the poem—Gabriel Lajeunesse, the son of Basil the blacksmith, and René LeBlanc—are not fictitious but rather were also real-life Acadians at the time of the expulsion.

In the poem two lovers, Evangeline and Gabriel, who first meet on the windswept meadows of Grand Pre, are separated during the expul-

Fig. 6.3. The "Land of Evangeline" in Acadia. Photograph by William F. Mann.

sion. Following several arduous journeys, they are finally reunited, but by then the aged Gabriel lies dying. For Acadians, the poem has come to symbolize the historic struggle of the Acadian people. For others, the poem may harken back even further to the suppressed story of Jesus and Mary Magdalene.

The area including the national historic site of Grand Pre has become a focal point for all things Acadian (see fig. 6.4), and in recognition of its importance, the Canadian government has added Grand Pre to its list of possible UNESCO World Heritage Sites. A scenic path called the Evangeline Trail runs from the Bay of Fundy's tidal surges near Grand Pre to Nova Scotia's rocky southernmost tip near Yarmouth, commemorating many of the region's important sites, such as St. Charles's Church, where the Acadian men were assembled at the command of the British governor, Charles Lawrence, and his Halifax Council, and were told that they were to be deported.

After the bitter expulsion (see fig 6.5), when ten thousand Acadian men and women were rounded up and evicted on separate ships, the British government in Nova Scotia gave the Acadian farms to English-speaking Protestant colonists who were mostly of Scottish and Irish descent. But to the Acadians, Acadie was still home, and after the Treaty of Paris of 1763 finally settled the French-English war, the Acadians returned, only to be tolerated by the British provided they swore allegiance to the Crown and settled in the colony's most distant parts.[8]

Before the expulsion, the Acadians were successful farmers, but when they resettled in Clare, where the soil was poor and the landscape heavily forested, they were forced to become lumberjacks and woodworkers. They also turned to fishing the rich Bay of Fundy and the Grand Banks. Unfortunately, in recent years the fishing industry has died off and modern-day Acadians lean increasingly on tourism, finding economic as well as cultural sustenance in their Acadian roots.

The first Acadians had names such as Belliveau, Comeau, Doucet, Dugas, Gallant, LeBlanc, Robichaud, Saulnier, and Mellanson, whose family origins provide a hint that many Acadians, specifically the Mellansons, were in all probability descendants of the Holy Family. In 1657 two French brothers, Pierre and Charles Mellanson, arrived with

Fig. 6.4. The church and statue of Evangeline at Grand Pre. Photograph by William F. Mann.

Fig. 6.5. A print depicting the expulsion of Acadians from Nova Scotia, artist and date unknown. Reproduced courtesy of the National Archives of Canada.

their parents in Port Royal, Acadia, rather mysteriously aboard an English ship, the *Satisfaction,* which also carried Sir Thomas Temple, the newly appointed English governor of Acadia.[9] The story goes that Pierre and Charles Mellanson were Protestants who became Roman Catholic prior to marrying French girls. Yet their arrival in the colony was supposedly three years after Nova Scotia had come under English control. Surely they would not have converted in a Protestant-controlled colony. Many scholars have tried to explain the puzzling origins of the Mellanson family. It was at one time generally believed that the Mellansons were of Scottish origin. But a priest named Father Clarence d'Entremont has established that the Mellansons are of French descent.[10] Evidently, the father, Pierre La Verdure, was a French Huguenot who went to England, where he married an Englishwoman named Prescila Mellanson. Their sons, Pierre and Charles, established what is still known as the Mellanson Settlement in the former Port Royal section of Nova Scotia.

The older son, Pierre, who is identified in early records as a stone-mason, married the esteemed Marie-Marguerite Muis d'Entremont, the daughter of the lord of Pomcoup, Philippe Muis d'Entremont. Charles married Marie Dugas, the daughter of the armorer Abraham Dugas and Marguerite Doucet of Port Royal. Charles Mellanson was also called La Ramée or Sieur de La Ramée and Pierre Mellanson was also known as La Verdure or Sieur de La Verdure.[11]

The Mellanson Settlement (see fig. 6.6) was located on the north shore of the Dauphin (now Annapolis) River, approximately four miles downriver from the town of Port Royal (later Annapolis Royal). Under the British, the settlement was part of a wider area sometimes known as Oak Point or Pointe-aux-Chesnes. Like the other Acadian settlements scattered along the river, it was an agricultural community where family members and neighbors worked cooperatively in the distinctive "dike land" agriculture unique to colonial North America and practiced to reclaim low-lying salt marshes. Because it was situated on the approach to the fort at Port Royal/Annapolis Royal, engineers recorded the Mellanson Settlement on several eighteenth-century maps, providing an unusually detailed record of a pre-deportation Acadian settlement.[12]

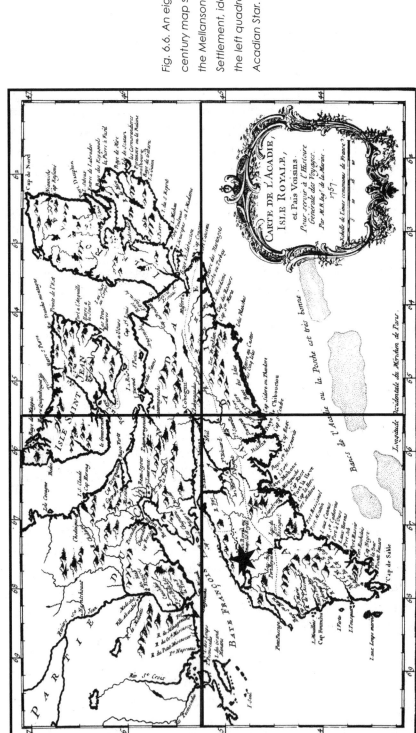

Fig. 6.6. An eighteenth-century map showing the Mellanson Settlement, identified in the left quadrant by the Acadian Star.

Fig. 6.7. The dancing fox and the apple appearing on the Mellanson coat of arms

The Mellanson coat of arms (fig. 6.7) seems to hold some symbolic keys to the family's true origin. The shield is split horizontally in two; on the right side there is a deep purple-red fox dancing on its hind legs across a green promontory, while on the left there is a green apple.

Perhaps these symbols have something to do with the notion that the female lineage of the Mellansons, represented by the deep purple-red vixen, or female fox, was of Merovingian descent, for the root word *mel* means "of a darkish color," thus representing the depths of the sea. (We can recall that the Merovingians were supposedly descended from a union between a princess and a sea king.) One suggestion is that the root of *mel* lies in the the purple murex dye the Phoenicians used to color their woven cloth, an important trade item. It is said that embroidered linen dyed with Phoenician purple was used in the Holy of Holies. In Greek, the derivative of *mel* is *melas,* meaning "black," or *mullos,* referring to a marine fish or mollusk. From these connections, we are left with the idea that the name Mellanson is somehow connected to the sea. There is also the notion that the lineage is connected to emerald green, the color of the promontory upon which the vixen dances, which naturally represents the fertility of the goddess.

As for the apple, it is known, of course, as the forbidden fruit from its connection to the Tree of the Knowledge of Good and Evil in the Garden of Eden and the temptation of Eve. In scientific terms, the apple is the fruit *(pomme)* of the genus *Malus* belonging to the family Roseaceae. As such, anyone found lying under an apple tree is said to be "under the rose," dreaming of a forbidden secret. One Greek myth that portrays the apple as the ultimate prize is the story of the judgment of Paris, a contest among the three most beautiful goddesses of Olympus—Aphrodite, Hera, and Athena—for a golden apple that was addressed to "the fairest."[13]

The story begins at the wedding of Peleus and Thetis, to which all of the gods are invited except for Eris, the goddess of discord. When she nevertheless appears at the festivities, she is turned away, and in her wrath she casts the golden apple among the assembled goddesses. Because all three goddesses lay claim to the apple, Zeus is asked to mediate and thus commands Hermes to lead the three to Prince Paris of Troy, who is to decide the issue. Appearing before Paris, the three goddesses each present gifts of her favor: Athena offers him many heroic victories, Hera offers him great wealth, and Aphrodite offers him Helen, the most beautiful woman alive, as his wife. Unfortunately, Helen is married to Menelaus, king of Sparta. From this offer ensues the Trojan War, led by the wrathful goddesses Hera and Athena, when Sparta demands their queen be returned. The ultimate result is the fall of the great empire of Troy and perhaps a lasting perception that all queens are exceptionally beautiful but inherently guileful and wickedly manipulative.

A later example of these attributes is found in the portrayal of King Arthur's stepsister, Morgan Le Fay. In his book *Celtic Folklore,* John Rhys writes that he believes Morgan Le Fay was originally a mermaid of the same breed as the Breton *morgens*.[14] As such, her name may have changed from Modron to Morgan in Brittany, where there was a belief in a certain type of water fairy called a Morgans or Mari-Morgans.[15]

Coming full circle, Avalon, the mystical heaven of sorts in the tales of King Arthur, is depicted as a magical island that is hidden behind deep, impenetrable mists that part only for those who believe the island truly exists. Ironically, until the mists part, there is no way to navigate to the island. When Arthur is mortally wounded at Camlann, Morgan

Fig. 6.8. The Death of Arthur, c. 1859, by James Archer. In this work, Morgan Le Fay prepares to bear Arthur across the water to Avalon. Reproduced courtesy of the Mansell Collection, London.

Le Fay takes him to Avalon to be healed and to await a call to return to Britain (fig. 6.8).

Avalon could be said to be a place in the spirit realm, the Otherworld, where peace reigns and where even the enmity between Morgan and Arthur no longer holds. In Avalon there also lies Nimue, the damsel of the lake, who becomes the keeper of Excalibur. In fact, Avalon is said to be the place where Excalibur was forged. It is said that in Avalon no thief or enemy lurks and only unbroken peace and harmony exist.

To many, the land of Acadia/Nova Scotia is synonymous with the wondrous land of Avalon. It is a land of raw power and mysterious happenings. Enveloped much of the time by swirling mists that result from the mixing of the warm Gulf Stream and colder Atlantic current, Nova Scotia's shorelines are hauntingly beautiful and melancholy. It doesn't take much imagination to picture an Irish curragh emerging from the mists, bearing the wounded body of King Arthur. He is then received by the native people, who offer their home and all that they have to the weary travelers, without question or judgment. In this Acadian heartland, because of its temperate climate, groves upon groves of apples flourish even to this day, so that Nova Scotia is still known by many as the "apple isle."

Perhaps this is the origin of the concept of Morgan spiriting away the soul of Arthur across the sea to Avalon—to the real Arcadia now known as Nova Scotia.

The Fox-Ojibwa

Reflective of the myths of time gone by, some have recently claimed that the Templars brought the Ark of the Covenant with them across the Atlantic to the New World. Once here, it is said that they entrusted the First Nations to be its ultimate guardian.[16] The land to which they escaped, inhabited by the Algonquin Nations, is characterized by karst topography, which results from softer sandstone eroding from limestone to produce many caves and crevices. Like the fox in his lair that is safe from the hound, the New World Templars and members of the Holy Bloodline, aided by the First Nations, would find in these caves temporary refuge from the ever-probing agents of the Church and others who sought to discover their whereabouts.

Many historians have failed to realize that at one time the Fox-Ojibwa Nation was the largest and most powerful of the Algonquin–Great Lakes tribes. Since then, members have been known by a variety of names, including Ojibwa, Chippewa, Bungee, Mississauga, and Salt-eaux, and their true size and population throughout North America tend to have been underestimated. In fact, during the seventeenth century they were perhaps the single most powerful nation east of the Mississippi and quite possibly the most powerful in North America. Because their true territory was well north of the main flow of settlement, however, their victories over both other native and colonial enemies have never been duly noted. It was the Ojibwa, for instance, who finally defeated the powerful Iroquois and forced the Sioux to leave Minnesota.[17] The Ojibwa's power grew largely from their overwhelming superiority and cunning in military strategy, which led to yet another name for their nation: the Fox.

We know that the sudden and mysterious arrival of the Ojibwa at Sault Ste. Marie sometime around 1500, following a great migration from the east, displaced several of the resident tribes. As a result, the Menominee were pushed south into an alliance with the Winnebago, and the Cheyenne and Arapaho began a series of movements that eventually took them to the upper plains of Colorado and Montana. Continued Ojibwa expansion west along the shores of Lake Superior also brought them into conflict with the Dakota and Assiniboine of the Great Plains. While some whites came later for the minerals and timber, this harsh territory in the northern United States and in Canada even today remains largely unpopulated. In addition, most of the Ojibwa territory had poor soil and a short growing season, which did not attract extensive settlement. Because of this relative isolation, eventually, the Ojibwa Nation extended from Ontario in the east to Montana in the west.

The date of the first meeting between the French and the Ojibwa is uncertain because the French at first did not distinguish among the Huron, the Ottawa, and the Ojibwa, who were all part of the larger Algonquin Nation. Champlain is reported to have met some Ojibwa at the Huron villages along Georgian Bay in 1615, and three years later, while exploring Lake Huron, Champlain's right-hand man, Étienne Brulé, traveled far enough to the north that he most likely met Ojibwa. But it was not until 1623, when he reached the falls of St. Mary's River—Sault Ste. Marie—that we can be sure of a meeting between the Ojibwa and the French.[18]

Because of this limited exposure, the Ojibwa have been able to retain much of their traditional culture and language. Certainly, most North Americans have heard of Longfellow's poem *Hiawatha*. Unfortunately, the poet mixed up his tribes—the name Hiawatha was borrowed from the Iroquois, but the stories are entirely Ojibwa. In fact, a good deal of native North American legend and folklore that exists today can be credited to the Ojibwa, who are said to be the direct descendants of the original natives who crossed the Bering Strait into the Americas during the last ice age. Similar to most Algonquin tribes, the Ojibwa passed down their history orally, from memory, though in some rare instances, they used birchbark scrolls and a kind of pictographic writing that was similar to Mi'kmaq hieroglyphics.

Between 1400 and 1650, most Ojibwa practiced a classic Woodland culture, but because various groups within the tribe lived in markedly diverse areas topographically and geographically, there were major differences in culture within the nation. Like all Native Americans, the Ojibwa adjusted to their circumstances. For example, after reaching the Northern Plains, the Bungee or Plains Ojibwa adopted the buffalo culture and became very different from the eastern Ojibwa in their art, ceremony, and dress.[19] Toward the southern part of their range, in Michigan, Illinois, Wisconsin, and Ontario, Ojibwa villages were larger and more permanent due to the cultivation of corn, squash, and beans, the "three sisters." Eventually, however, as the main force of the Ojibwa moved north, the nation's southern tribes were eventually absorbed by the Wendot, Petun, Neutral, and Huron.[20]

Historically, it is said that the Métis Nation of Canada evolved in the northwest in the eighteenth and nineteenth centuries, but only now are the Métis people themselves questioning the extent of their ancestry in Canada. Said to be born of a mixture of French and Scottish fur traders and Cree, Ojibwa, Saulteaux, and Assiniboine women, the Métis in the northwest have developed as a separate people, distinct from other Indians and Europeans.

We may well wonder if a particular clan within the Ojibwa Nation could be the descendants of the Templars and those Mi'kmaq tribes that intermarried with them and moved inland from the eastern seaboard during the fifteenth century. Perhaps the formation and eventual disappearance of the Massassauga tribe was the result of this earlier interaction between Sinclair and his Templars and the Algonquin Nation. It certainly now seems as though this is one secret that the First Nations have never revealed. Even Brulé, who would spend most of his time among the native Indians and ultimately incur the wrath of Champlain for certain indiscretions, would not discover the ultimate secret that a portion of the Holy Bloodline intermarried with the First Nations.

There are several Ojibwa legends attesting to the notion that more is known about the story of the Templars in the New World than has been told. One of the most prominent is that of the three sisters: The legend holds that ancient mariners found three islands lying in the waters of Thunder Bay. These have consistently offered shelter from the storms that forever lash Lake Superior. According to Ojibwa legend, the "Three Sisters" have a very strange origin indeed:

It is said that of the four daughters of a great Ojibwa chieftain, the youngest was "the fairest of them all," constantly relating her conversations with the spirits of the forest to her family. Endeared to her father by her sweet nature and otherworld sensibility, the girl was ridiculed by the three elder sisters.

One day, the young maiden heard the great and kindly voice of Nanna Bijou, the Great Spirit, say that he had chosen her to be the bride of his son, North Star. That evening she related the story and told of the God's instructions of when and where she was to meet the Great Spirit's son. The sisters laughed mockingly and accused her of losing her mind. The chief, angered by their cruel treatment of his youngest daughter, beat the daughters with a strip of deer hide. Full of hate because of their punishment, the sisters planned the younger girl's death.

Recalling the place and time of the meeting, they followed their sister into the woods. It is said that North Star, being a spirit, could not be seen by the elder sisters. Thus, as the young sister embraced North Star, the three sisters shot their arrows into her heart. But instead of falling, their sister was borne gently upwards to the sky by the spirit. Alas, the arrows also pierced North Star's heart. Frightened at what they saw, the sisters ran wildly through the woods. The Great Spirit, furious at their deed, turned them into stone and hurled them into the waters of Thunder Bay.[21]

This Ojibwa legend clearly shares a number of elements with Greek and Celtic mythology: for instance, the archetypes of the wicked triple goddess and the supreme spirit turning her to stone because of her deeds. Elements of the tragic separation and ultimate death of the two lovers also relate to Longfellow's narrative poem *Evangeline,* which has its roots in the Greek and Roman tragedies of Selene and Endymion, Artemis and Orion, and Diana and Aktaeon. But how could one of the oldest native legends possess these archetypes unless there was direct European influence prior to the accepted historical contact between the French and the Ojibwa?

According to other oral traditions of the Ojibwa, the Daybreak People—the Abenaki—vowed to stay in the east even though "the prophet of the First Fire" told the native people to move or be destroyed.[22] Within Mi'kmaq legend, it is the man-god Glooscap who takes on the persona of the prophet of the First Fire. It is also said that the *midi,* the shamans, remembered the prophet of the First Fire speaking of a turtle-shaped island that would be one of seven stopping places during the Ojibwa migration. Intriguingly, there are two islands in the area of Ojibwa migration that fit this description: Montreal Island and Milton Outlier, a small glacial feature from the last ice age, located along the meridian of 79 degrees 57 minutes west longitude and positioned just north of the town of Oakville on the northwestern shore of Lake Ontario.

One interpretation of an Ojibwa birchbark scroll has identified all seven major stopping places of the great migration: Montreal Island; Niagara Falls; the inland turtle-shaped "island" that can be only Milton Outlier; Manitoulin Island; Sault Ste. Marie; Spirit Island, close to the mouth of the St. Croix River; and Madeline Island, in the Apostle Islands of Lake Superior.[23] It is said that the *megis* (turtle) shell rose up out of the water or sand at each locale and the Ojibwa knew to stop when they found a turtle-shaped island and "the food that grows on water," meaning wild rice. On a more practical level, islands of this nature would be chosen as stopping places because they offered a defensive refuge of sorts.

Milton Outlier (see fig. 6.9) is one of the more prominent features found along the Niagara Escarpment, now designated as a UNESCO World Biosphere Reserve. The escarpment itself is the result of prehistoric geological upheaval and glacial erosion. Four hundred and forty-five million years ago, in an age known to geologists as the Ordovician Era, there was a sea in the Michigan basin. At that time, North America was tropical and land plants and animals did not yet exist. The Michi-

Fig. 6.9. Milton Outlier. Photograph by William F. Mann.

gan Sea, however, was full of life, including shellfish and corals. The dolomitic limestone face that resulted from this population originates at Niagara Falls and winds north to Georgian Bay and Manitoulin Island in Lake Huron. Extending the full length of this magnificent natural feature is an ancient Indian trail now known as the Bruce Trail.

Knowing the extent of the escarpment and the barrier that it presented, the Ojibwa could have traveled inland in their migrations, first by canoe until they reached the great falls, and then overland along the Bruce Trail either on foot during the summer or by sled dog during the winter, until they reached Georgian Bay. There they could again follow the coastline of the Great Lakes by canoe until they reached their final destination. In doing so, the Ojibwa were following one of a number of ancient routes that perhaps, as we shall see, had been established by ancient Celts as they made their way to the copper mines of Lake Superior, on the shores of Kitche Gumeeng.[24]

Madeline Island, in the Apostle Islands of Lake Superior, is significant because the Ojibwa believe that their ancestors migrated there from the east coast of North America and that it was their final stopping place after many years of migration resulting from the prophet of the First

Fire's dream that they must either move or be destroyed. Interestingly, this island, which is among a group of islands named after the Apostles, suggests that Mary Magdalene was indeed the most favored follower of Jesus. Its connection to the Ojibwa migration calls to mind the arduous journey the Magdalene undertook along with her uncle, Joseph of Arimathea, across the Mediterranean to the southern shore of France and Ste. Maries de la Mer.

The researcher Peter Champoux has hit upon an intriguing natural geometry that relates amazingly well to the migration pattern of the Ojibwa: In *Gaia Matrix* he demonstrates how the geopositions of major Indian settlement areas now known as Niagara Falls, Chicago, Duluth, and Sault Ste. Marie establish a pentagonal geometry that encloses most of the Great Lakes.[25] The central point of what he calls the Great Lakes Pentagon (see fig. 6.10) is where the lakes converge in Sault Ste. Marie, which was a well-known gathering place for Native Americans. What this suggests is that through the proper application of sacred geometry and meridian knowledge, which was veiled in oral tradition or moral allegory, the Celts and Vikings possessed uncannily accurate maps of the Great Lakes region, if not of the entire North American continent. As a result of this treasured knowledge and resulting maps, both secret roseline settlements and their related underground mines could be revealed to the true initiate—among whom were the Templars, who used this knowledge to establish meridian settlements as refuges and sites where precious ore could be accessed and the practice of smelting and steelmaking could occur in secret.

Meridians, Ancient Observatories, and Pre-Christian New World Trade

In *America* B.C.: *Ancient Settlers in the New World*, one of the more important pieces of evidence that author Barry Fell highlights as linguistic proof of pre-Christian travel to the North America and resulting trade between the Old and New World—perhaps, as we have hinted, through the Celts and Vikings—are the texts inscribed in the rocks at Peterborough, Ontario, Canada.[26] It is here that there is evidence of a voyage or voyages of a Bronze Age Scandinavian king, Woden-lithi, to

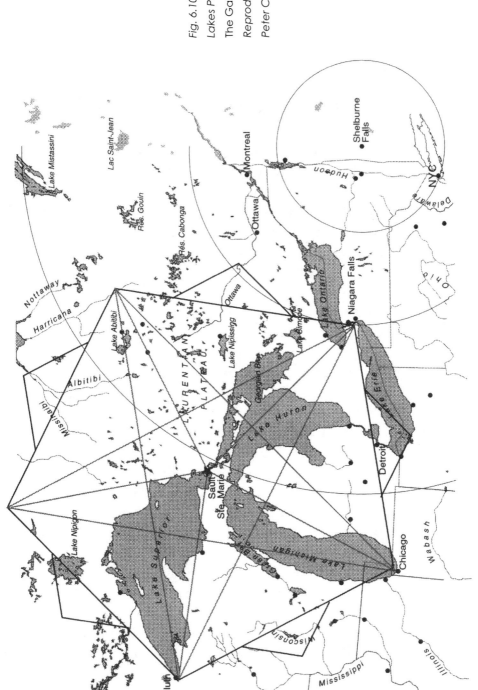

Fig. 6.10. The Great Lakes Pentagon, from The Gaia Matrix. Reproduced courtesy of Peter Champoux.

North America around 1700 B.C.E. According to Fell, Woden-lithi's main purpose for visiting America was to barter textiles with the Native Americans in return for metallic copper ingots.[27] These texts are written in an ancient script and yet use alphabets that have survived to the present in remote parts of the world. If interpreted correctly, the evidence points to the certainty that pre-Christian traders had been visiting or settling in the Americas for thousands of years.

According to Fell's interpretation, some seventeen centuries before the time of Christ, King Woden-lithi and his men sailed across the Atlantic and entered the St. Lawrence River. The text on the rocks says that their homeland was Norway and that the king was from the capital at Ringerike, which is located west of the head of Oslo Fjord.[28] Somehow, he and his party traversed the Lachine Rapids and reached the north shore of Lake Ontario, near what is now Toronto and the ancient meridian positioned at 79 degrees 57 minutes west longitude. From here they attempted to go beyond Niagara Falls but found it impossible and instead made their way up the inland water route now known as the Trent-Severn Waterway. At a place today called Petroglyphs Park, just outside of Peterborough, the Norse established a colony that became a religious and commercial center. It seems that Woden-lithi remained in Canada for five months, from April to September, trading his cargo of woven material for copper ingots from the Lake Superior mines, with the local natives acting as middlemen for the northern Indian tribes.

Within the inscription that was left behind are records of the Norse journeys, their religious beliefs, a standard of measurement for cloth and cordage, as well as astronomical observations for determining the Norse calendar year. These observations confirm that the Norse New Year began in March and provide for the exact determination of the dates of the winter and summer solstices. The numerous rock carvings depict the central sun god and moon goddess and certain astronomical axes that cut across the site, all of which confirms an amazing knowledge of the constellations and understanding of the motions of the sun through the signs of the zodiac.[29]

Another of the better-known New World astronomical sites is Mystery Hill, called America's Stonehenge, in North Salem, New Hampshire. Apart from the numerous stone chambers on the site, there is also a stone circle made up of five principal standing stones. It has been determined that one of these lies due north of the center observation point. The other four stones have been shown to mark the sunrise and sunset points on the horizon for the midsummer and midwinter solstices. The major astronomical significance of Mystery Hill seems to have been associated with the summer and winter solstices, and regulation of the calendar by the vernal and autumnal equinoxes.

Interestingly, these ancient observatories tie in to Acadia as it existed before the deportation of its citizens in 1755. When the marquis de Chabert first arrived in Acadia from France in 1746, he charted a number of harbors in the region, but in doing so he noted numerous discrepancies that could not be officially explained. When he returned to France in 1747, he explained that "all the marine maps were defective for almost all the coasts of this part of North America," surmising that the discrepancies were due to the lack of accurate astronomical observations and establishment of a prime longitudinal meridian.[30] Thus in 1750, under direct instructions from the king of France, Chabert returned to Cape Breton and Acadia and constructed the first "official" observatory in Canadian territory, at Fort Louisbourg.

Unfortunately, nothing remains of this structure. We know that it existed because Chabert produced maps and a report, *Voyage fait par ordre du Roi en 1750 et 1751 dans l'Amerique septentrionale,*[31] from astronomical observations gathered there. It is intriguing that given Louisbourg's foggy climate, the site was hardly appropriate for an observatory. Chabert explains his choice, however:

> I had principally to fix with exactitude the longitude of Louisbourg, both in order to facilitate the landing of vessels coming into that port and in order that in the drawing of maps one could start from this point in locating all others on the coasts of this part of North America on their true meridians, which task required an exact determination of this point . . . [32]

He went on to use the observatory as a survey station, with his objective being to include observations on the tides and "diverse operations of practical geometry," as well to conduct detailed stellar and lunar observations.[33] Perhaps Chabert's work extended from his desire to map the eastern coastline using a series of true meridians. Unfortunately, the real truth concerning Chabert's mission was lost, along with the French desire to establish a New Jerusalem in New France, when Fort Louisbourg was surrendered to the British in July 1758.

7

Everlasting Elements

In *The Woman with the Alabaster Jar*, Margaret Starbird makes the point that the deepest and most hidden meaning of the early medieval alchemists and their symbols was not chemical—it was theological, philosophical, and psychological.[1] It was at this time that the natural person was seen as "lead" and the transformed divine spiritual being was seen as "gold."[2] This transformation was deemed to be guided by the Holy Spirit, and the process by which the transformation occurred was either a near-death experience or giving birth or, more commonly, certain esoteric initiations.

In far more ancient times, an understanding and knowledge of metals and their properties was considered the ultimate secret or divine right of a royal house. From the earliest times, this wisdom was synonymous with wealth and power. The battle for control of the secret process of turning base alloys into steel for weapons, as well as the process of refining gold and other valued metals, was constant and fierce. The scriptures tell us that Moses received instructions on how to construct the Ark of the Covenant (see fig. 7.1) from God himself, and that he passed on this knowledge to King David.* Throughout his life, David prepared for the construction of the Holy Temple by setting aside the necessary physical

---

*According to the *Catholic Encyclopedia*, per the sacred narrative recorded in Exodus 25:10–22: God Himself had given to Moses the description of the Ark of the Covenant, as well as that of the tabernacle. God's command was fulfilled to the letter by Beseleel, one of the "skilful men" appointed by Moses "to devise and to work in gold, and silver, and brass, and in engraving stones and in carpenters' work" (Exodus 37:1–9).

materials, commanding the Levites and others in their duties, and giving the plan for the Temple to Solomon. Thus, according to tradition, the Messiah, who will build the third Temple, will come from the Davidic dynasty. Here lies the simple reason that so many individuals over time

Fig. 7.1. A representation of the Ark of the Covenant. In this Masonic context, the Ark is displayed under the Masonic Royal Arch.

have tried to make claim to a Davidic lineage—that is, whoever controls the temple controls direct contact with God.

Another famous example of one who possessed this "divine" wisdom is King Solomon. Shortly after he is anointed king at the age of twelve, God appears to Solomon in a dream in which he invites the king to make a request for himself. Solomon answers: "I am but a small child . . . Give therefore your servant an understanding heart to judge your people." His request pleases God, who tells him: "Because you have not requested riches and honor but only that which would benefit all the people, I will give you not only an understanding heart like none other before or after you . . . but also riches and honor like no other king in your days" (1 Kings 3:7–13).

King Solomon went on to rule as king for forty years, and during this time Israel prospered, with the building of the first Temple, designed to house the Ark, as its crowning achievement. The Bible tells us that kings from all over the world came to hear Solomon's wisdom, which included not only that of the Torah, but also secular knowledge of the sciences.

Because Prince Henry would have been immersed in the symbolism associated with the rebuilding of the Temple from his position within Freemasonry and his association with the Templars, some of the keys to unlocking the true secrets of the Knights Templar are to be found within what are known as *The Little Keys of Solomon*. Ancient tradition suggests that those who possess these secret writings possess the understanding and knowledge of where the New Temple of Jerusalem may be found. *The Little Keys of Solomon* are known to relate, on one level, to the esoteric principles that could be found within the ancient mysteries. According to ancient writings, the keys include the proper application of astronomy, dualism, numerology, androgyny, and the hidden fifth element—etymology—all found within a long-lost ancient Hebrew manuscript known as *The Key of Solomon*.

On another level, *The Little Keys of Solomon* may be seen as the descendants of King Solomon and the House of David, including Jesus and his purported offspring. If the Templars truly considered themselves to be adepts and possessors of ancient wisdom, then they would have considered Jesus to be the living body and continuance of that wisdom. Furthermore, if the Templars possessed written proof of Jesus' understanding and knowledge of the ancient mysteries far beyond the four gospels, then Jesus himself would be viewed as a key to unlocking the ancient mysteries.

In *The New Atlantis,* Francis Bacon's magnum opus, the philosopher speaks of an "Island Solomon house . . . whereby concealed treasures which now seem utterly lost to mankind shall be confined to so universal a piety."[3] In this learned romance, Bacon supposes that a vessel lands on an unknown island called Bensalem, over which a certain king Solomon reigned in days of yore. It has been established that the vessels of the Phoenician king Hiram of Tyre and King Solomon were at sea for forty-two days before reaching the gold mines of Ophir. Thus, North America appears not only to be a good candidate for the location of King Solomon's mines and the land of Ophir, but also, in all probability, to be the private source of gold for both the Templars and the Stuarts.

The New Atlantis was published in 1627, shortly after the founding of the English colonies in the Americas. Bacon expressed his views on the new colonies several times, including a speech to Parliament claiming that the New Kingdom on Earth (Virginia) was as it is in the Kingdom of Heaven. In a clear reference to King Solomon's Temple in a New Jerusalem, Bacon describes the founding of the colonies in Virginia in 1606 as a spiritual as well as a political act.

While chancellor of England under the reign of King James I, Bacon immersed himself in a mystical, hermetic philosophy and practiced alchemy. Once he wrote that alchemists were like the sons of the man who told them he had left gold buried in the vineyard. After vigorous digging, they found no gold, but they had turned up the soil and mold around the roots of the vines and so produced a plentiful vintage. Thus, said Bacon, the quest for gold brought to light many useful inventions and advanced society in innumerable ways.

In *Wisdom of the Ancients,* Francis Bacon also warned against "the commodity of wit and discourse that is able to apply things well, yet so as was never meant by the first authors."[4] In other words, he posits that many people look to provide meaning where no meaning has ever existed and many people believe that a treasure lies hidden where no treasure has ever existed. Nevertheless, Bacon himself, as a self-described "latter-day symbolist of pagan mysteries," deduced from the myths an extraordinary abundance of "concealed instruction and allegory," for "parable has ever been a kind of ark, in which the most precious portions of the sciences were deposited."

Yet Bacon's largest and most enduring claim to fame is the theory suggesting that he wrote Shakespeare and that his original manuscripts lie in a vault beneath Oak Island, deposited there by the earliest privateers, who supported Bacon's hatred of the Spanish. This theory comes from those who say that William Shakespeare couldn't have written the works to which he is credited; whereas, Francis Bacon possessed all the qualities that Shakespeare lacked. It is an interesting theory, to say the least, but to associate it with Oak Island must in some way be a clue to Bacon's at least partial understanding of the bigger puzzle.

Aside from Francis Bacon's literary and political manipulations, there is overwhelming evidence that he was part of a secret society, perhaps the Priory of Sion or the Rosicrucians or another more obscure order. He may well have resurrected the dormant underground remains of the medieval Knights Templars or the Priory of Sion to satisfy a longing for the divine knowledge that he believed was his. We do know that Bacon was obsessed with codes and ciphers and that he initiated the use of watermarks on paper.* When we consider that a majority of the watermarks used in Bacon's time and after related to the unicorn, the Merovingian bear, the snake or worm (shamir), the Grail, and the Pillars of the Temple, Bacon's role suddenly seems to loom larger in the overall puzzle of the Templars in the New World. Could it be that his spiritual New Atlantis was in fact Prince Henry Sinclair's New Jerusalem?

Margaret Starbird considers the symbolism of the watermarks to be political as well as doctrinal, and that the heresy to which many of them allude is related to that of the Holy Grail: During the twelfth century, the Cathars believed that Jesus was an earthly vessel of the spirit of God and that his teachings about the ancient mysteries would lead them to personal enlightenment and transformation. Many of the watermarks (see fig. 7.2) were indeed heretical as far as the Church was concerned, indicating a belief in a married Jesus who was the royal heir of David.

---

*For a far more extensive and illustrative look at the subject of these curious watermarks, please refer to Fanthorpe and Fanthorpe, *The Secrets of Rennes-le-Château*, 92–96, and Frank Higenbottam, *Codes and Ciphers* (London: English Universities Press, 1973).

Fig. 7.2. Some common unicorn watermarks. Reproduced from Margaret Starbird,
The Woman with the Alabaster Jar *(Rochester, Vt.: Bear and Company, 1993).*

One of the most distinctive of all the watermarks was the unicorn. According to Harold Bayley's book *The Lost Language of Symbolism,* the unicorn represented Christ, the archetypal bridegroom, one of the favored motifs in medieval Europe.* There are also a great number of watermarks that depict the lion, which is understood to symbolize the lion of the tribe of Judah. Thus the coat of arms of the British royal family and of Canada, which depict the lion, suggest descendency from the House of David. In other cases, watermarks reflected the three-pronged iris lily, the *fleur-de-lis,* which was the symbol used to identify the Merovingian bloodline. Bayley has even found several watermarks that combine the three-pronged iris lily and the lion, thus making a veiled reference to the royal bloodline of both Israel and France—the line of the princes of Judah, the very same princes who are prevalent throughout the basic rituals of Freemasonry! Thus, in our search for the New

---

*All references made to unicorn watermarks have originated from Harold Bayley, *The Lost Language of Symbolism* (New York: Barnes and Noble, 1968), although Margaret Starbird, in *The Woman with the Alabaster Jar,* was the first to relate the medieval themes of the Sacred Marriage and the Lost Bride to the modern concept of the Grail Family.

Jerusalem, we once again return to this society that was so prevalent in the founding of America.

A Return to Rosslyn Chapel

As evidenced by the carvings of Rosslyn Chapel, Prince Henry Sinclair was likely immersed in the earliest tenants of Freemasonry. Therefore, it is reasonable to assume that he would have secreted any treasure relating to knowledge of both the roselines and an ancient Davidic bloodline in both the historical and the symbolic aspects of the Royal Arch degrees, which speak of the discovery of the ancient vaults or crypts below Solomon's Temple. It makes sense, then, that any concrete Templar "treasure" would have been stored within natural crypts or vaults positioned along ancient meridians at key energy and observation points where future temples could be established. The real treasure, of course, was the very knowledge of meridians, or roselines, that guided Sinclair. Making this theory seem all the more logical is that these rose points would have been known to and revered by Native Americans and thus, being considered sacred, would have been perpetually guarded and yet left undisturbed.

Within Freemasonry's Royal Arch degree there is a lesser-known series of "side" degrees that are part of Cryptic Masonry. Those who practice Freemasonry believe it is a distinct privilege to be conferred in the Council of Cryptic Masons, for there are no more beautiful or meaningful degrees in all Freemasonry. Given these accolades, the degrees of Ancient Cryptic Masonry are centered on the story of the initial preservation, loss, and recovery of the Word. Symbolically, the Word is said to represent man's search for life's purpose and the nature of God, all the while teaching him humility and reverence.

As is the case for many of the Masonic degrees, the true origins of the degrees of Cryptic Masonry are shrouded in mystery. It is generally accepted that they first appeared in North America under the auspices of Phillip P. Eckel, who lived in Philadelphia in the years immediately after the American War of Independence. Nothing much is known of Eckel's activities regarding these degrees or their source. It is believed that he was associated with the influx of Germanic immigrants to the United

States, specifically to Pennsylvania, and that he was a close associate of Benjamin Franklin. This suggests that Eckel brought the degrees with him from one of the Continental Rites in Europe that were so popular in the early to mid-1700s.

Parts of Cryptic Masonry are said to resemble degrees that were attached to what was known as the Rite of Misraim; other parts seem to be nearer in form to the Rite of Memphis, which evolved out of what is called High Egyptian Masonry.

Another side degree presented with Cryptic Masonry is that of the Royal Ark Mariner. This degree is described as one of the oldest, if not the oldest, rite in all of Masonry. Surprisingly, it stands entirely alone and totally unrelated to any other degrees. The ceremony of elevation into the Royal Ark Mariners is a truly initiatory rite. It is based on the triumvirate of wisdom, strength, and beauty, as are other degrees in the Craft, but in this instance, the degree refers particularly to the wisdom of Noah in constructing the Ark (see fig. 7.3), his strength of character, and the beauty of his workmanship. But there are other significant messages in the degree, and even for the experienced Mason there is a powerful reminder of our reliance on a spiritual as well as a material enlightenment.

Rather logically, considering its relation to Noah, the symbol of this degree is the rainbow, harkening to God's convenant with the survivors of the Flood once they found dry land—"I will never again curse the ground for man's sake and I will never again destroy every living thing by flood as I have done this time. While the earth remains, seedtime and harvest, cold and heat, winter and summer and day and night shall not cease"—and his blessing of Noah and his sons ("Be fruitful and multiply and fill the earth").

The idea of making a covenant or pact with God is certainly a concept that has withstood the test of time. The problem is that if you don't succeed in following through on your promise, you stand to incur the wrath of God. Of course, the worst thing that could happen to you is death, but more likely you would be subjected to periods of melancholy or depression. In many cases, this is what befell those medieval alchemists who forfeited all worldly comforts, including the love of their family, for the unattainable philosopher's stone. There is a wonderful woodblock print called *Melancholia* (see fig. 7.4, page 260)

Fig. 7.3. An illumination of Noah and the Ark, a facsimile of an original book page attributed to an unknown artist in the southern Netherlands, c. 1450

Fig. 7.4. Albrecht Durer's Melancholia, 1514. Reproduced courtesy of the Metropolitan Museum of Art, New York.

that was created by the artist Albrecht Durer in 1514, which expresses the sense of confusion and despair encountered by the struggling alchemist. Surrounded by the hermetic symbols of the royal art and tools of the craft, even the winged hermaphrodite, representing a balance of male and female genius, cannot solve the puzzle. The trouble is that the alchemist has chosen to stay within the confines of the laboratory and not experience the spiritual enlightenment of following the rainbow across the sea. More than likely, this is one level of symbolism that can be found within David Teniers the Younger's *The Alchemist* (fig. 5.12, page 223). As noted previously, Teniers found it appropriate to depict St. Anthony and the alchemist as the same person. The irony here is that the practicing alchemist has failed to realize the true origin of alchemy, which can be found only within the ancient science and knowledge of the earth's properties, not through some "divine" intervention in the confines of a laboratory. Perhaps this is the simple realization followed by the Mellanson family across the ocean into a wilderness that represented to many the ancient Arcadia.

Green Oaks, Nova Scotia

As we have learned, at Green Oaks, in Arcadia, a topographical feature known as Anthony's Nose is located on a mountainside adjacent to the Shubenacadie River, which runs a deep, muddy red due to the tidal surge coming from Minas Basin and the Bay of Fundy. Certainly St. Anthony the Hermit is not buried at Green Oaks, but because the saint was revered by the Knights Templar for his austere and disciplined way of life, Prince Henry Sinclair and his followers surely considered the landscape to be symbolic of St. Anthony's earlier struggle in the wilderness of the Old World.

This is one principle that Prince Henry and the refugees no doubt followed as they traveled across the New World: They likely saw reflected in New World locations specific landmarks of the Old World. We can assume, then, that in looking to establish a New Jerusalem, they sought many of the same features of Old Jerusalem (see fig. 7.5).

The recently incorporated exploration firm Templar Gold Explorations Ltd. has analyzed the springwater that flows from the Green Oaks site and, intriguingly, has found its contents to contain the following elements in varying levels: aluminum, antimony, arsenic, barium, beryllium, boron, cadmium, chromium, cobalt, copper, iron, iridium, lead, manganese, molybdenum, nickel, niobium, rubidium, selenium,

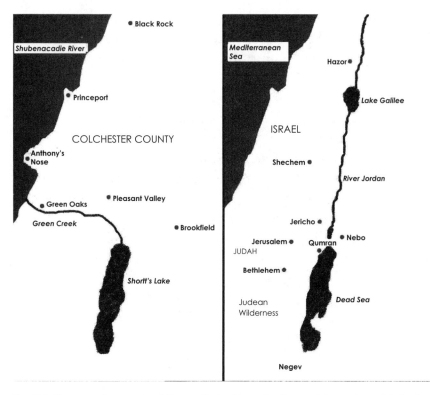

Fig. 7.5. Comparative maps of Green Oaks, Nova Scotia, and Jerusalem. Original drawing by William F. Mann.

silver, strontium, and thallium, titanium, uranium, vanadium, and zinc. Among the elements in this list are the metals required to produce a high-strength, low-alloy steel. Large deposits of limestone and coal are also readily available in the area, as are commercial-sized deposits of both gold and platinum.

As related in Laurence Gardner's most recent book, *Lost Secrets of the Sacred Ark,* considerable scientific attention has recently been directed toward unique forms of elemental matter.[5] Derived from gold and platinum and other transition elements, this matter has been labeled as monatomic—that is, achieving a single atomic state. This matter was first discovered by the American David Hudson in the 1980s, when he applied for several patents for what he described as Orbitally Rearranged Monatomic Elements (ORMEs). New understandings in physics suggest, however, that these substances are diatomic or small atomic cluster condensates and they are now generally referred to as ORMUS or M-state elements.

According to Laurence Gardner, M-state elements possess some unique properties. Experiments relating to thermo-gravimetric analysis have revealed that at certain high temperatures, the material weight of M-state elements will substantially reduce, even to the degree that they will levitate. It was also discovered that in specific circumstances they have the ability to become superconductive and to resonate in parallel dimensions, which means that they are natural superconductors of sorts with a null magnetic field, repelling both north and south magnetic poles while having the ability to levitate and store any amount of light and energy within themselves. For all their properties, these materials might seem to be the pure essence of God.

Certainly the presence of such M-state substances at Green Oaks, aside from their spiritual connections, only confirms that a combination of a number of natural factors and materials in the area ensured that the inhabitants of the thriving agricultural and mining community in Arcadia lived a full and healthy life.

A New World Arcadia

In Greek mythology, Arcadia was a sanctuary on the Acropolis and the home of Pan, who helped the Athenians win an important victory over the Persians and received the sanctuary in exchange for his aid. It was also a district in the central region of the Peloponnesian peninsula of Greece. In later literature a fanciful version of Arcadia was the setting for poetic evocations of pastoral life. While the actual terrain of the Greek Arcadia is harsh and mountainous, the idealized landscape of the literary Arcadia is gentle and fertile and is home to uncorrupted shepherds and pagan deities. The qualities of this imaginary Arcadia must have readily come to the mind of the refugees who first made Arcadia/Acadia their home. Here was a sanctuary for the outlawed Knights Templar and the Holy Bloodline, where its inhabitants could lead simple lives in close harmony with both nature and the land's native inhabitants.

Yet, as the marquis de Chabert had realized some 350 years later, in order to navigate farther inland, the travelers would need to establish a prime meridian. Luckily, the Templars already possessed knowledge of the ancient meridians, which had been developed over centuries of astronomical observations by those initiates who had come before them. Evidence of ancient stone-circle observatories still exist at Green Oaks and further evidence has recently been discovered at an area known as Bear Cove, a small inlet on the eastern shore of St. Margaret's Bay, Nova Scotia. There a stone platform has been exposed that was the ancient surveyor's starting point paralleling the northern latitude of Oak Island, located just to the west in Mahone Bay (fig. 7.6). Knowing the exact latitude and longitude of this platform likely allowed the true initiate, through a continuous application of the Pythagorean theorem, to map the entire New World and to follow the subsequently determined rose-lines across what they considered to be their New Jerusalem.

Fig. 7.6. The stone platform at Bear Cove on St. Margaret's Bay, Nova Scotia. The two upright stones, or pillars, are aligned in a true east–west direction, providing a unique surveying platform. Photograph by William F. Mann.

Memorial Pillars

From the earliest times, it was customary to record historical events or exhibit gratitude for divine intervention with the erection of pillars. The ancient Phoenician writer Sanchuniathon, a contemporary of Solomon, tells us that Hypsourianos and Ousous, who lived before the Flood, dedicated two pillars to the elements fire and air. In addition, Josephus has recorded that in the antediluvian era, Seth, the third son of Adam and Eve, erected pillars:

> For that their inventions might not be lost before they were sufficiently known, upon Adam's prediction, that the world was to be destroyed at one time by the force of fire, and at another time by the violence of water, they made two pillars, the one of brick, the other of stone; they inscribed their discoveries on them both, that in case the pillar of brick should be destroyed by the flood, the pillar of stone might remain, and exhibit those discoveries to mankind, and would also inform them that there was another pillar of brick erected by them.[6]

Hence, two pillars, Jachin and Boaz (see fig. 7.7), which Hiram cast in bronze per Solomon's instructions, were placed in the eastern front of Solomon's Temple as a memorial to the children of Israel. Jachin represented male strength and Boaz represented female beauty. Together, the pillars recall the Pillars of Hercules, which served as the central feature of the Phoenician temples of Baal Melkart, supreme lord of the Phoenicians and their patron of ancient mariners and navigators. These pillars commemorated the strait that led into the Atlantic, which was viewed as Paradise or the Otherworld.

Keeping in mind this tradition of memorializing, it makes sense that the seafaring Prince Henry looked to establish his new temple in a New Jerusalem in just such a symbolic manner to honor both the Supreme Being and the ancient navigator. If we assume that he and his entourage moved inland to avoid detection, then the two natural pillars—Rattlesnake Point, the southeastern pinnacle of the Milton Outlier (fig. 7.8, page 267), and Mt. Nemo—that form part of the Niagara Escarpment, both positioned on the ancient meridian of 79 degrees 57 minutes west

UP THE RIGHT PILLAR
CALLED ITS NAME

HE SET UP THE LEFT
AND

Fig. 7.7. Jachin and Boaz, the two pillars of Solomon's Temple

longitude in the small town of Milton, Ontario, take on considerable significance. Remarkably, one of these pillars is made of clay and the other is made of stone, reflective of the two pillars that survived the Flood, according to Masonic tradition.

In the topography of this area, Rattlesnake Point is the shining brow that catches the rays of the morning sun. Here is Taliesin, one symbol of the Celtic godhead. In the Celtic language, a "pinnacle" is referred to as a *nosshead*, with *noss* meaning the head of the horse, the "godhead." Interestingly, Nosshead, Scotland, in the far north, in Caithness, is the ancient seat for Clan Sinclair. It is where the Sinclair and Girnigoe Castles are located, close to the Nosshead itself. Since ancient times, fires were lit atop the promontory (the "shining brow") to act as beacons to sailors, and a lighthouse was built on the same spot more than a hundred years ago. In 1998 the Clan Sinclair archivist Ian Sinclair established a study center in the former Nosshead Lighthouse Estate with the goal of providing a resource for historians

Fig. 7.8. Rattlesnake Point, in Ontario. Photograph by William F. Mann.

and genealogists. The location of Niven Sinclair's library within the center incorporates a number of exceptional and invaluable historical texts, ranging from the genealogical records of the Sinclairs to a copy of the Domesday Book.

Another interesting aspect of the location of these pillars, the Milton Outlier, comes from studies conducted at the nearby University of Guelph: Apparently, some cedars growing on the "brow" of the Outlier are more than two thousand years old. These ancient eastern white cedars, stunted and twisted because of the harsh climate along the cliff face, are sustained by minute *cryptoendoliths*—organisms that grow inside the limestone rock. These gnarled cedars recall the Glooscap legend of the seventh man who wanted to live forever: Glooscap clasped him by the loins, lifted him up, and set him down again with a twist, transforming him into a gnarled old cedar tree.

The cedars on Rattlesnake Point also relate to Rosslyn Chapel's famous Apprentice Pillar, richly carved in both pagan and Masonic symbolism that reflects ancient teaching and beliefs. Legend has it that the architect of the pillar, an apprentice mason, was murdered by his master in a fit of jealous rage after the master returned from a pilgrim-age to the Holy Land and witnessed the beauty of the finished carving. Interestingly, in Masonic tradition it is believed that the martyr Hiram, architect of Solomon's Temple and creator of the pillars Jachin and Boaz, refused to surrender the secret of the *shamir,* a worm or ser-pent of wisdom whose touch split and shaped stone. Therefore, eight worms or shamirs are grouped in a rough octagon around the base of the Apprentice Pillar (see fig. 7.9). According to Andrew Sinclair, author of *The Sword and the Grail,* these serpents also represent the number of points on the Maltese cross of the Knights of the Order of the Temple of Solomon.*

As for the spiral vines depicted on the Apprentice Pillar (fig. 1.5, page 20), to our eye they might be seen to represent the double helix of a DNA strand; to the eyes of those living at the time of the chapel's design, the intertwining of ancient royal bloodlines from the earliest times. They also recall the intertwined snakes of the caduceus, the ancient Greek symbol of the healer.

Bringing this symbolism full circle, Jesus, who was known as a healer, was symbolized not only by the unicorn, but also by the cedar tree. In Ezekiel 17:22–25, a prophecy referring to Jesus' death and resurrection is directly associated with this evergreen:

> And the Sovereign Lord says: I will take a tender shoot from the top of a tall cedar, and I will plant it on the top of Israel's highest mountain. It will become a noble cedar sending forth its branches and producing seed. Birds of every sort will nest in it, finding shelter beneath its branches. And all the trees will know that it is I, the Lord, who cuts down the tall tree and helps the short tree to grow tall. It is I who makes the green tree wither and gives new life to the dead tree. I, the Lord, have spoken! I will do what I have said.

---

*Sinclair, *The Sword and the Grail,* 2–3. Within *The Sword and the Grail,* Andrew Sinclair offers one of the best descriptions of the chapel and other workings at Rosslyn and how sacred geometry and symbolism were applied during their late medieval construction.

Fig. 7.9. The serpents at the base of Rosslyn Chapel's Apprentice Pillar. Photograph by William F. Mann.

The cedar and the unicorn are clearly related symbols. Indeed, the twisted white cedars on Rattlesnake Point (fig. 7.10) actually resemble the single horn of the unicorn. In addition, Native Americans deemed the white cedar to possess both healing and wisdom powers, while the medieval Church recognized the unicorn as a symbol of Christ in part because the unicorn was believed to have special powers of healing: For instance, the touch of a unicorn's magical horn was said to purify poisonous waters, and a cure for snakebite was a powder said to be ground from the mythical animal's horn. In medieval art, the unicorn is portrayed dipping his horn into a stream or a fountain, as if offering purification or being anointed.

Carrying these associations further, in the Middle Ages the anointing of the "horn" or "head" of the bridegroom/king of Israel was part of the ritual known as *hieros gamos*.[7] This rather erotic imagery included the bridegroom/king in the form of the unicorn, with lifted head or "horn," seeking the lap of the bride/goddess (the deer under the apple tree in the garden) for the consummation of the sacred marriage. Such imagery can

Fig. 7.10. An ancient cedar on Milton Outlier. Photograph by William F. Mann.

be seen in the famed Unicorn Tapestries displayed at the Cloisters of the Metropolitan Museum of Art in New York City[8] (see fig. 7.11)—and can be seen on the Desceliers's map of 1550, where the unicorn is standing beneath the apple tree waiting for his deer bride.

Carrying this symbolism to the New World, in Acadia there is an old song called "Vole, mon Coeur, vole!" which tells of three daughters

Fig. 7.11. An image of a unicorn from the famous Unicorn Tapestries at the Cloisters in New York City

of the prince who wait under an apple tree for their beloved princes. Researched by Marius Barbeau, it has been translated by R. Keith Hicks:

Our old orchard has a tree,
Joy in my heart, oh joy!
An old orchard has a tree,
And it bears apples red. And it bears apples red, red, red, red,
And it bears apples red.

Green and fresh, the leaves are green,
Joy in my heart, oh joy!
Green and fresh, the leaves are green,
And in its red fruit is sweet,
And in its red fruit is sweet, sweet, sweet,
And in its red fruit is sweet.

Daughters of the prince are three,
Joy in my heart, oh joy!
Daughters of the prince are three,
And sleeping 'neath the boughs,
Are sleeping 'neath the boughs, boughs, boughs,
Are sleeping 'neath the boughs.

The youngest maid awakens,
Joy in my heart, oh joy!
Youngest maid awakens,
"Sister, awake! 'Tis dawn!
Sister, awake! 'Tis dawn, dawn, dawn!
Sister, awake! 'Tis dawn!"

Naught I see but moonbeams,
Joy in my heart, oh joy!
That shines on our true loves,
That shines on our true loves, loves, loves,
That shines on our true loves.

Our three knights in battle
Joy in my heart, oh joy!
Our three knights in battle,
They fight for us all three,
They fight for us all three, three, three,
They fight for us all three.

And when they have conquered,
Joy in my heart, oh joy!
And when they have conquered,
We'll be their joyful brides,
We'll be their joyful brides, brides, brides,
We'll be their joyful brides.

But if they're defeated
Sad be my heart, oh sad!
We all will still be true,
We all will still be true, true, true,
We all will still be true.

This song refers us back again to the Desceliers's map of 1545, which depicts three sisters and a group of Europeans gathered around or greeting Jacques Cartier, suggesting a royal wedding that has taken place in the wilderness of Canada. Interestingly, at the western edge of the map's illustration there is an area that corresponds approximately to the Milton Outlier, and here there is a band of natives in non-European clothing who sport beards and carry lances and are shown among a grove of apple trees.

Consecrating a New Temple

If we were looking to establish a new Temple of Jerusalem at the summit of the New World, what might be the purest symbol of God's essence that could be used to consecrate the site? Assuming for a moment that the Knights Templar had discovered the relics that could lead to the ultimate downfall of the Church—the bones of Jesus—would it not have been appropriate to consecrate the chosen site with these? Naturally, this would have shaken the established Church to its very foundations, for the Christian faith is based on the assumption that Christ died on the cross and on the third day ascended into heaven—that there was no body left in the tomb after he had risen. If in fact Jesus' burial place in Jerusalem had been discovered by the Knights Templar, and his remains were brought to southern France on their return from the Holy Land, this would explain the absolute ruthlessness with which the Church and its agents, the Jesuits, followed the Templars to the ends of the earth.

There are related claims that Jesus survived the crucifixion and traveled in person to the Languedoc or that his embalmed body was brought to that area of southern France by family and friends, including Mary Magdalene herself. If any of this is true, it would in no way lessen the manner in which Jesus should be perceived and honored. Even Charles Towne, who describes himself as a Protestant Christian, says that there is no reason to expect that the Bible is correct in every way. When asked about his beliefs, he responded, "I have enormous respect and adoration for Christ and what he did," but added that he did not know whether Christ was actually the son of God.[9] Neither should such assertions about Christ after the crucifixion lessen the good that he represents or the mysteries that surround him.

Many, of course, will dismiss such possibilities as either nonsense or downright heresy, but the fact is that during medieval times, many within the Catholic Church itself believed the Holy Bloodline to be true. If the true nature of the Templar treasure was a mysterious fifth gospel or royal genealogies, these could always be dismissed as forgeries, even if they proved through carbon dating to match the time of Christ. But with today's advances in DNA testing, any DNA of Christ obtained through his relics—his bones, for example—could be matched to the DNA of known living members of the Davidic lineage. This explains the recent excitement relating to the finding of the ossuary of James, the brother of Jesus, even though it was eventually determined to be a fake. If the Merovingian claim of a direct connection to the House of David is true, it would explain the underlying reason for a great number of geopolitical manipulations that have occurred over the past two thousand years.

One conclusion from all of this is that, in keeping with legend, the Templars were indeed in possession of the bones of an important ancient person and they used their knowledge of ancient meridians to spirit away these relics to the New World—a New Jerusalem. There, they hid them within the hollow pillar of the new Temple—Rattlesnake Point—just north of Oakville, Ontario, Canada. From this we might assume that the bones of Mary Magdalene are buried within the adjacent second pillar of the Temple, Mt. Nemo. And under the shadow of these two stone sentries, descendants of the Knights Templar and Holy Bloodline made their way to a new Paradise and Garden of Eden.

Other associations can be drawn from this area of Ontario: Mount Nebo is an elevated ridge in what is now western Jordan that provides a panoramic view over ancient Palestine and the valley of the Jordan River. On a clear day the West Bank city of Jericho is also visible from the summit. According to the final chapter of Deuteronomy, Mount Nebo is where Moses was given a view of the Promised Land before dying at the age of 120.

When viewed from the air, the Milton Outlier is shaped like a ship or an ark of sorts. Rising high above the valley that surrounds it, the pinnacle is a perfect location for both an open-air temple that reaches to the heavens and an astronomical observatory. Overlooking Lake Ontario, some twelve miles to the south, a lone sentry positioned on the promontory would have a commanding view of the area and would have been the first to notice any ships on the southern horizon and thus warn the Ojibwa/Huron village at nearby Crawford Lake (see fig. 7.12). Curiously, the valley that must be crossed to reach the village is called Nassagaweya Canyon. In the Algonquian language, the word *nassagaweya* means "crossed sticks." Could this be a reference to those who wore the red cross on their white tunic and inhabited the Outlier and the adjacent valley? Masonic tradition does maintain that the earliest lodges could be found in the deepest valleys or on the highest hills.

One more significant association to this part of Ontario can be found, once again, in the work of Nicolas Poussin. The very last picture that Poussin painted is *Winter* (see fig. 7.13), which was completed as part of a series known as *Seasons,* created between 1660 and 1664 for the duc du Richelieu. According to Alain Merot, an expert on Poussin, the four *Seasons* paintings are "historical" scenes in which four landscapes are fused into a single image embracing humankind, nature, and

Fig. 7.12. A reconstructed Ojibwa/Huron Indian village at Crawford Lake. Photograph by William F. Mann.

Fig. 7.13. Nicolas Poussin's Winter. Reproduced courtesy of the Louvre, Paris.

the march of life.[10] *Winter* is said to depict the Flood, which represents the Last Judgment, and Noah's Ark, the saving of the faithful.

The painting shows a massive floodplain beyond a great falls, access to which is framed by two natural limestone pillars. On one pillar we see a bronze serpent slithering its way to the pinnacle, and near the other, on the higher ground surrounding it, is a family in a canoelike boat, seeking safety from the water. At the top of this pillar is a cedar tree and just beyond it we can make out what appears to be an Indian village. In the far distance is Noah's Ark, which seems to be heading toward the western sun, which lies beyond a majestic hilltop. In the foreground, a survivor clings to the head of a horse; another appears to float on top of a wooden slab.

When we compare the landscape in this painting to the specific location and features identified around Milton, Ontario, the similarities are beyond question. How might Poussin have learned about this place in the New World? Might Richelieu himself have exposed to Poussin further details of the extent of the Western world as revealed by the explorer Champlain? Within Poussin's painting, the natural limestone pillars of Rattlesnake Point are symbolized by the snake on one and the Holy Family near the other. In this comparison the great falls symbolize Niagara Falls, with the survivor and the horse representing the "Golden Horseshoe" area of the western end of Lake Ontario, while the native village is the Crawford Lake Indian village. The massive floodplain is representative of the ancient Michigan Sea, which formed during the Ordovician Era. We can see in all of this symbolism a connection to an understanding and knowledge developed prior to the Flood, which is here symbolized by Noah's Ark. The conclusion we may draw from this painting is that this ancient wisdom and the Holy Bloodline survived the Flood, and that something related to the wisdom or the Bloodline can be found in the two pillars of the new temple.

The Wisdom of Solomon in a New Elysium

When the ancient Egyptians worshipped Thoth and his hidden works as "the personification of the mind of God," they were in fact recognizing wisdom. In actuality, early Freemasons regarded Thoth, not St. Anthony, as their original patron. According to old Masonic tradition,

Thoth played a major part in preserving the earliest knowledge of Free-masonry and transmitting it after the Flood. This so-called Thoth connection sets this knowledge within the ancient and enduring context of a royal wisdom tradition stretching back to those times in ancient Egypt when pharaohs were considered to be both gods and men—both the incarnation and the living embodiment of the gods.

In Greek mythology, the spirits of the exalted dead were carried on the wings of a horse to the Elysian Plains, depicted as beautiful meadows or fields, or islands of the blessed, which were located in the far west near the shores of an immense ocean. The Elysian Plains were a place where certain heroes of the fourth race, ruled by Rhadamanthus, never experienced death and were said to dwell in perfect happiness. In later myth, the Olympic Titans were also seen as living there, after being reconciled with Zeus under the rule of Kronos. It was held by Pindar that all who had three times passed blamelessly through life lived there in bliss. Later, Elysium would come to be located in the Underworld as the abode of those whom the judges of the dead found worthy.* It thus came to be seen as a paradise of the heroes found either in the Underworld or in the far west. It was here that the likes of Achilles and Hercules were said to live on in pleasant surroundings and in the company of other man-gods, forever continuing their heroic pursuits, taking part in the hunt, or savoring a banquet.

Through his own heroic deeds, Prince Henry Sinclair has achieved something of the same status as the Egyptian pharaohs or the Greek man-gods, for it was he who fulfilled the prophecies of the Bible and established a new temple within a New Jerusalem. It was his secreting of sacred treasure along the ancient meridians in the fourteenth century that in some ways figured largely in the New World events of the next six hundred years. In addition, as the appointed guardian of the Holy Grail, he was perpetuating a spiritual quest that later inspired men such as Benjamin Franklin, George Washington, Thomas Jefferson, Lewis and Clark, and even Frank Lloyd Wright to their heroic achievements and remarkable feats of human endeavor.

---

*In Virgil's *Aeneid,* Aeneas and the Sibyl seek out the Elysian Fields, where Aeneas meets the spirit of Anchises, his father, who reveals to him the workings of the universe and the purifications through which men can be admitted to Elysium.

As such, according to Masonic tradition, the conclusion can be drawn that at a secret "rose" location between Great Falls and Helena, Montana, at the base of the foothills of the great western Rockies, there lies the hero of this story—Prince Henry Sinclair—and within lies a book of sorts whose value far outweighs even that represented by the relics of the Holy Family or the Ark of the Covenant. This book, *The Key of Solomon*, grants to its possessor all of the ancient wisdom that can be deduced through the parable of Noah's Ark, including complete knowledge of the seven liberal arts and sciences, from the very essence of God to chemistry, physics, biology, and mathematics. It also provides knowledge of the ancient meridians and an understanding of all things magical, including alchemy, divination, and the secret of the shamir. Where else might the keys to such wisdom be interred but at the base of the symbol of enlightenment, the goddess Helena?

Clues to this ultimate knowledge can be found within a number of sources ranging from the ancient Egyptian, Greek, and Roman myths to the scriptures. Ancient Jewish tradition teaches that God dictated to Moses the first five books of the Bible—the Torah—letter by letter, and that human events, past, present, and future, are encoded in the Hebrew scriptures following an encryption system that can be described and unlocked with the proper key. Bible code theories have certainly existed for thousands of years, but in 1990 Dr. Robert Aumann, professor of mathematics at the Hebrew University of Jerusalem, was the first to analyze the question digitally. The results of his four-year study on the computer analysis of hidden codes found in the first five books of the Hebrew scriptures were published in 1994 in the journal *Statistical Science*. In the article, Dr. Aumann writes that there is "very strong scientific evidence that under intense scientific experimentation the bible code phenomenon is shown to exist and is provable as a true phenomenon."[11] Since then, a number of books relating to the secret codes of the scriptures have been published, ranging from Barbara Thiering's *Jesus and the Riddle of the Dead Sea Scrolls* to Michael Drosnin's *The Bible Code*.

Sir Isaac Newton was supposedly obsessed with the notion that a secret wisdom lay concealed within the pages of the Bible. He believed that a radically different method of interpretation could lead to the true meaning of the Holy Grail. Newton, once a grand master of the Priory of Sion, also believed the Egyptians concealed under the veil of religious rites and hieroglyphic symbols mysteries that were beyond the capacity of common man to fathom. Among these was the knowledge that the earth orbited the sun and that the sun remained at rest.

Of all the work associated with the spiritual pursuit and understanding of this ancient wisdom, the theories of C. G. Jung rise to the top. Jung's work in the field of psychoanalytical studies was very different from that of his contemporaries, for he recognized inner spiritual truth as being present within the psyche of every individual.[12]

From a historical point of view, it is Jung's personal quest for the original experience of the creative spirit in the unconscious psyche that brings him so close to the spiritual movements that began to appear in the West in the twelfth and thirteenth centuries. These movements included alchemy, which sought to follow the prompting of the inner soul and to discover a more direct, inner experience of the divine without the help of an intermediary such as a priest.

The Grail romances also have a spiritual affinity with these movements. For example, one of the romances tells that whenever Joseph of Arimathea listens to the counsel of the Grail, he hears the voice of the Holy Spirit speaking to him in his heart. The Grail is seen as a direct and distinct conduit to the voice of God and therefore to God himself. Consequently, Perceval's Grail quest can be interpreted as the seeking of knowledge that can be achieved only through an inner, individual experience of the Holy Spirit. If we associate the Holy Spirit with its earliest form, Mother Earth, we soon realize that in essence Perceval is looking to become one with nature. For the mystical adept of the Middle Ages, the Grail was a symbol of our inner soul or spirit. Accordingly, the great secret that Jung believed to be hidden within the stories of the Grail is the mystery of the transformation of God in the soul of man.

At the same time, with the growth of alchemy and its understanding of transformation came the start of the concept of *lumen naturae,* "the light of nature," which was considered to be a kind of intuitive knowledge of all that is good and rich enkindled by the Holy Spirit in the heart of humans. For the alchemist, the lumen naturae was a source of knowledge or attainment of wisdom equal to the highest spiritual revelation. As such, it fit with alchemy's constant search for an experience of the divine. The most important symbol for this divinity was the philosopher's stone, the *lapis,* which also became a symbol of eternity and the inner wisdom of man. Hence, the alchemist considered the philosopher's stone to have all the attributes of the Trinity, and thus to be nothing less than the exact image of God.

Freemasonry and the spiritual psychology that has been derived from its symbolic structure have also been likened to this quest to identify the Divinity that exists in all men. Masonic tradition sees the complete human being as having four levels: flesh, a psyche or soul, a spirit, and a direct contact with the Divine Source. It proposes that the human psyche itself contains four levels that reflect this larger four-level structure. Specifically, it is represented by the Temple of Solomon, which is described as a three-story temple within which we can be conscious of a fourth, higher "rose" level—the omnipresence of the Divinity.

Finding Hidden Treasure

For centuries, humankind has speculated on the existence of an ancient wisdom and and has imagined its brotherhood of knightly guardians. Seen as more precious than the physical relics of the Holy Family or a Templar treasure is the treasure of the Divine Word, the real key of Solomon.

Legend holds that Solomon was able to construct the Temple only by summoning Asmodeus, a fallen angel who became king of the demons, and controlling him with his magical ring. Asmodeus, as guardian of the Underworld, possessed the knowledge of the shamir, which allowed the true initiate to split and carve stone without tools and which, according to Asmodeus, was given by God to the Angel of the Sea. But the angel trusted no one with the shamir except the moorhen, which had taken an oath to guard it carefully.

The story goes that the moorhen took the shamir with her to mountains that were uninhabited by humans, then, with the shamir, split the mountains and injected the crevices with seeds, which grew and covered the rocks. Ironically, it was this action that allowed humans to inhabit the mountains.

Now Solomon, who coveted the shamir, commanded Asmodeus to find the nest of the moorhen and to lay a piece of glass over it. When the moorhen returned to her nest and found that she could not reach her young, she fetched the shamir and placed it on the glass. Asmodeus shouted then and terrified the bird so that she dropped the shamir and flew away. Once in possession again of the coveted shamir, he bore it to Solomon. In the meantime, the moorhen was so distressed at having broken her oath to the Angel of the Sea that she committed suicide.

In time, though the temple was completed, Solomon refused to allow Asmodeus to return to the Underworld. The king told Asmodeus that he did not understand wherein the greatness of the demons lay if a demon guardian could be kept in bonds by a mere mortal. Canny Asmodeus replied that if Solomon would remove his chains and lend him the magic ring, he could prove his own greatness, and to this Solomon agreed. The demon thereby stood before the king; then, with one wing touching heaven and the other reaching to the earth, he snatched up Solomon and flung him far from Jerusalem. Asmodeus then disguised himself as Solomon and assumed the throne of the king.

For three long years Solomon journeyed in faraway lands, begging for his daily bread among strangers and atoning for his sins. At the end of the third year, God took mercy upon him and caused Naamah, the daughter of the Ammonite king, to fall in love with him. In his anger over his daughter's choice, the Ammonite king had the lovers taken to a barren desert in the hope that they would die of starvation. Solomon and Naamah wandered until they finally came to a city near the sea. When Naamah began preparing a fish that they had bought in the market for their meal, she found in its belly the magic ring that belonged to her husband—the same ring that he had given to Asmodeus and which, after having been thrown into the sea by the demon, had been swallowed by a fish. Solomon put the ring on his finger and was transported back to Jerusalem. There, King Solomon exposed Asmodeus and drove him back to the Underworld. He then ascended the throne once again and was granted the gift of judgment.

Of course, there are many hidden messages in this legend, but the underlying moral for our purposes is that the guardians of the Underworld, or Otherworld, whether they are angels or demons, and the "magic" that they guard should never be disturbed or possessed. What are the exact coordinates of the Templar caches in the New World? With an awareness of the ancient meridian knowledge that Prince Henry Sinclair and his fellow Templars employed to hide their treasure, whatever it was, we might discover these exact places—but we might think twice before doing so. On the other hand, perhaps the quest for the Templars' ancient wisdom is meant to be neverending, challenging seekers to ascend to ever higher levels of personal knowledge.

The fact remains that Prince Henry Sinclair and his fellow travelers dedicated their lives to the protection of their secrets, and many throughout the history of the New World have, in some way, dedicated theirs in the interest of discovering these secrets. As Proverbs 9:1 tells us, "[W]isdom, and wisdom alone, built her house"; and according to Proverbs 25:2, "[I]t is the glory of God to conceal a thing: but the honour of kings is to search out a matter." In the end, the seeker of wisdom is immeasurably richer, for he follows in the footsteps of the ancient kings. But for those who seek to find the treasure of Prince Henry and the Templars, the lesson of Solomon must prevail: Let those who have the understanding use it with wisdom.[13]

Epilogue
ALL THAT WAS LOST

In this book, historical background consisting of a number of seemingly unrelated Old and New World figures, events, and places have been threaded together to reveal not only clues in a centuries-old treasure hunt, but also a probable answer to the question of what the Holy Grail truly represents.

It is intriguing in itself to consider the coincidences and potential rationale contributing to our understanding of why Canada and the United States developed as separate nations, but when these circumstances are combined with the ancient mysteries of Egypt and the secrets of Freemasonry, we can begin to see the depth of forces at work in the creation of these nations of the New World.

It seems that throughout the centuries, every major event that has fashioned the character of the New World has been influenced by the quest for what has come to be known as the Templar treasure. The founding of New France and the American colonies, the French and Indian War, the American War of Independence, the American Civil War, the Louisiana Purchase, and the Lewis and Clark expedition all have in common the veil of secrecy that first descended when Prince Henry Sinclair and his Knights Templar came to these lands so many centuries ago with the primary goal of protecting the Holy Bloodline.

Since the time of the earliest New World explorers and settlers, basic Masonic/Templar principles—including sacred geometry and moral allegory and Grail/Goddess veneration—have played an intricate part in the everyday lives of the people who journeyed here as well as of the worldly kings and politicians who played out their strategy, military and otherwise, upon these shores.

As we have seen in these pages, the Holy Grail may be a genealogical record of the Grail Family, a firsthand account written by either Jesus or Mary Magdalene herself, or associated relics—perhaps even the bones of Jesus. Or it may be something as all-encompassing as the wisdom of the ancients, including knowledge of the meridians that have been used for centuries to determine longitude and latitude, and the "alchemical" knowledge of how to make steel. What is important is not the nature of the Holy Grail—that is, what it is actually discovered to be; what is important is that the reader takes away from this book the desire to continue his or her own quest, which includes both a marveling at and continued questioning of life's mysteries and the official recorded history of the New World.

As we have seen, for each question that has been answered, there remains a host of others: What really happened to Prince Henry Sinclair and his Templar followers immediately after they established their first "rose" settlement in a New Arcadia? Did the Templars disperse and intermarry with the natives throughout the larger Algonquin Nation to establish strategic trading alliances that continued to have an impact on the Old World? What became of these first families, including their offspring of mixed cultures? Does the history of these culturally mixed families give the Métis an unprecedented claim to North America? Could such a claim—which may include a claim to the Merovingian bloodline—eventually be played out in world courts and in the halls of Europe's royalty?

Did the Templars possess an alchemical knowledge of metallurgy that is only today being rediscovered? Some scholars have even suggested that the Templars possessed the knowledge to turn lead into gold and to manipulate the basic properties of elements, thereby defying gravity and allowing humans to fly. Or could it be that the medieval Templars had uncovered nothing more than a treatise on the basic arts and sciences regularly practiced today by engineers, surgeons, biochemists, surveyors, and others?

And what of the role of Freemasonry in the birth and growth of the nations of the New World? Is the French/Scottish Freemasonry that was originally introduced to the New World over six hundred years ago the same as the Freemasonry existing today? We may conclude that it is not, given that during the seventeenth and eighteenth centuries, the Church was able to infiltrate the rituals of Freemasonry and sanitize them of all pre-Christian notions and mystery. Unfortunately, what has been lost by the Church's elimination of the ancient is any connection between the Christian mysteries and the early mysteries tied to the earth's forces—the mysteries practiced by the aboriginal natives before they were influenced by Europeans. Part of these mysteries is the knowledge of the ancient meridians, earth's energy lines, which allowed such initiates as Prince Henry Sinclair to fulfill their own covenants.

As we have learned, one of the more exceptional gentlemen to be involved in the Oak Island treasure mystery was Reginald Vanderbilt Harris, a well-respected lawyer who wrote the first comprehensive book on the island and the Money Pit. Aside from being the supreme grand master of the Knights Templar of Canada in 1938 and 1939, Harris was provincial grand master of the Grand Lodge of Nova Scotia from 1932 to 1935. He also bore several titles within Capitular Masonry, the Order of the High Priesthood, the Royal Ark Mariners, Constantinian Masonry, and the York Rite College, and was a 33rd-degree Scottish Rite Mason.

It bears repeating that among Harris's extensive papers were volumes of notes on Oak Island, including the draft of an allegorical ritual within a Masonic pageant that was apparently designed to accompany the rite of initiation into the 32nd degree. The allegory is set in 1535 at Glastonbury Abbey, where the English Crown is evidently attempting to confiscate the Order's fabulous treasures, including the Holy Grail. But members of a secret order spirit away the Grail across the sea for safekeeping. The allegory ends with a number of suspected members of the Order being dragged off to the Tower of London for torture and death.

Beyond the obvious connections between this allegory and one of the subjects of this book—the location of Grail settlements in the New World—it is intriguing to note that 1535 is the same year that Jacques Cartier explored the New World under the banner of King Francis I of France. It was also the year that Henry VIII of England decided to declare himself the head of the Church of England and dissolved the English monasteries because he coveted their money. The year 1535 was also the year that the king ordered Thomas More beheaded for his failure to submit. With all of these confluences, it seems that R. V. Harris was trying to suggest that the crown had no divine right to control both church and state—and that something of immense importance that the king of England coveted had secretly made its way to the New World under the banner of Scottish Rite Masonry.

Allegory aside, Prince Henry Sinclair, we have learned, was instrumental in the transmission to the New World of something undeniably significant to the European Church and monarchs. He was a man of medieval Europe, a man of reason and chivalry born in a world of the Black Death and the Crusades and a rising Church. The true purpose of this man and his fellow Knights Templar, who safeguarded the Holy Bloodline, was nothing less than to establish a New Jerusalem, to rebuild the city and its Temple, to make a place where all people could live in harmony and be free to recognize God in any chosen form. This would also explain why the Templars acted as guardians to the Grail refugees, the descendants of the Holy Bloodline: What more profound symbol of a direct connection to God could exist than an unbroken lineage to the Kingdom of Heaven?

This, of course, leads to perhaps the greatest question of all: How will the Roman Church react when a purported descendant of the Holy Bloodline steps forward to claim his or her rightful position in the House of David and Peter? Some of the history recounted in these pages illustrates how long the Church has desired to eliminate the possibility of this event. Will it openly accept the inevitable, or will it battle the claims with the tenacity it has displayed during the past two thousand years? Only time will answer these questions.

Many people may say that the Holy Grail ultimately represents Truth. But it has been demonstrated throughout history that humankind can recognize Truth only through parable or allegory, for in any other guise, it will destroy us. In many ways, this is what the Bible, native Indian myth, Arthurian legend, and even Masonic ritual and practices tell us. Of course, any individual has the ability to reason what the Truth may be. Yet, because of its power, the Truth of earth's ultimate secret can be presented only through the archetypes and symbols so often found in art and literature, the language of luminaries such as René d'Anjou, Leonardo da Vinci, and Nicolas Poussin.

These were men who recognized the Truth. They were men of reason and substance who discovered the means to produce light where previously there was only dark. The Truth they presented would be revealed only to the adept, the initiated who knew how to see. The true mystery can be revealed only to those who have been initiated through a series of rituals or who have been on a quest through the wilderness—those who have followed rites that have been practiced since the earliest times.

From looking anew at history—its events and people, great and seemingly inconsequential—it has become obvious that what today may be accepted as the gospel truth may in fact be based on earlier myth or legend, which, in turn, if followed far enough back into ancient times, has a truthful origin.

One of the keys, therefore, to determining Truth is to accept that the tenets of Christianity precede by ages the birth of Christ. They stretch back to a time before the Great Flood. As we have seen here, we cannot rely on our history to supply the Truth, for most historical events have resulted not from divine intervention, but rather from the manipulations of those who desire control.

The Truth lies behind and beyond our history, if we have the eyes to see.

⊓⊙TES

Chapter 1: Treasured Secrets

1. William Jefferson Clinton, *My Life* (New York: Knopf, 2004), 44–45.
2. Michael Baigent, Richard Leigh, and Henry Lincoln, *Holy Blood, Holy Grail* (New York: Delacorte, 2004), 77.
3. Ibid., 69.
4. Ibid., 76.
5. Norman Cantor and Harold Rabinowitz, eds., *The Encyclopedia of the Middle Ages* (New York: Viking, 1999), 436.
6. Ibid., 437.
7. Dan Burstein, ed., *Secrets of the Code* (New York, Perseus, 2004), 360.
8. Ibid., 357.
9. Ibid.
10. Cantor, *The Encyclopedia of the Middle Ages,* 87.
11. Ibid., 82.
12. Bernard of Clairvaux, *On the Song of Songs,* Kilian Walsh, trans. (Spencer, Mass.: Cistercian Publications, 1976), 24.
13. Ibid., 12.
14. Louis Charpentier, *The Mysteries of Chartres Cathedral* (New York: Avon, 1980), 147.
15. Michael Walsh, *Butler's Lives of the Saints: Concise Edition,* rev. ed. (San Francisco: HarperSanFrancisco, 1991), 56.
16. Baigent, Leigh, and Lincoln. *Holy Blood, Holy Grail,* 209–44.
17. Frederick J. Pohl, *Prince Henry Sinclair: His Expedition to the New World in 1398* (London: Davis-Poynter, 1974), 10.

18. Ibid., 54.
19. Michael Baigent and Richard Leigh, *The Temple and the Lodge* (New York: Arcade, 1991), 160–67.
20. Pohl, *Prince Henry Sinclair,* 16–25.
21. Ibid., 47–57.
22. Ibid., 178–79.
23. Ibid., 129.
24. Robert Charroux, *Treasures of the World* (Middlebury, Vt.: P. S. Eriksson, 1962), 60–70.
25. Barry Fell, *America b.c.*, rev. ed. (New York: Pocket Books, 1989), 93–111.
26. Tim Wallace-Murphy and Marilyn Hopkins, *Templars in America* (York Beach, Maine: Weiser, 2004), 64.
27. Michael Anderson Bradley, *Holy Grail Across the Atlantic* (Toronto: Hounslow Press, 1998), 246–47.
28. William F. Mann, *The Knights Templar in the New World* (Rochester, Vt.: Destiny Books, 2004), 108–17.
29. William Hutchinson, *The Spirit of Masonry* (New York: Whitefish, Mont.: Kessinger, 2004), 79–80.
30. Christopher Knight and Robert Lomas, *Uriel's Machine* (Rockport, Mass.: Fair Winds Press, 2001), 207–12.
31. E. C. Krupp, ed., *In Search of Ancient Astronomies* (Columbus, Ohio: McGraw-Hill, 1979), 67–68.
32. Charles H. Hapgood, *Maps of the Ancient Sea Kings: Evidence of Advanced Civilization in the Ice Age* (Kempton, Ill.: Adventures Unlimited Press, 1997), 1–2.
33. Ibid., 49.
34. Ibid.,
35. Ibid., 16–17.
36. Ibid., 32–33.
37. Ibid., 50–54.
38. Crichton E. M. Miller, *The Golden Thread of Time* (Rugby, Warwickshire, England: Pendulum, 2001), 76–86.
39. Pohl, *Prince Henry Sinclair,* 155–67.
40. Bradley, *Holy Grail across the Atlantic,* 144–46.
41. Silas Tertius Rand, *Legends of the Micmacs* (New York: Johnson Reprint Corp., 1971), quoted in Pohl, *Prince Henry Sinclair,* 165–66.
42. Fell, *America b.c.,* 93–111.
43. Colin Platt, *The Atlas of Medieval Man* (New York: St. Martin's, 1994), 164.
44. Baigent, Leigh, and Lincoln, *Holy Blood, Holy Grail,* 138–44.

45. Christopher Allmand, *The Hundred Years' War: England and France at War c. 1300–c. 1450* (Cambridge: Cambridge University Press, 1988), 75–83.

46. Baigent, Leigh, and Lincoln, *Holy Blood, Holy Grail,* 139.

47. Ibid., 446–47.

48. Ibid., 168, 173–75.

49. Richard Andrews and Paul Schellenberger, *The Tomb of God: The Body of Jesus and the Solution to a 2,000-Year-Old Mystery* (Boston: Little, Brown and Co., 1996), 140.

50. Ibid., 336.

Chapter 2: The Lost Templar Colonies

1. Mann, *The Knights Templar in the New World,* 4.

2. Gavin Menzies, *1421: The Year China Discovered America* (New York: HarperPerennial, 2004), 4–6.

3. Michael Anderson Bradley, *Grail Knights of North America: On the Trail of the Grail* (Toronto: Hounslow Press, 1998), 262–63.

4. Ibid., 349–53.

5. Joseph Muzzy Trefethen, *Geology for Engineers* (Princeton, N.J.: Van Nostrand Co., 1959), 28.

6. Ian Wilson, *The Columbus Myth* (Toronto: Simon and Schuster, 1991), 141–150.

7. Raymond H. Ramsay, *No Longer on the Map* (New York: Ballantine, 1973), 173.

8. Ibid., 175–76.

9. Ibid., 121–32.

10. Mann, *The Knights Templar in the New World,* 49–59.

11. Wallace-Murphy and Hopkins, *Templars in America,* 157–67.

12. Suzanne Carlson, "Loose Threads in a Tapestry of Stone: The Architecture of the Newport Tower," in *NEARA Journal* 35, no. 1 (summer 2001).

13. Stephen C. McCluskey, *Astronomies and Cultures in Early Medieval Europe* (Cambridge: Cambridge University Press, 2000), 26–28.

14. William S. Penhallow, "Astronomical Alignments in the Newport Tower," in *NEARA Journal* (March 21, 2004).

15. Steven Sora, *The Lost Colony of the Templars* (Rochester, Vt.: Destiny Books, 2004), 214–23.

16. Ibid., 163–64.

17. Samuel Eliot Morison, *The Great Explorers* (New York: Oxford University Press, 1978), 62–64.

18. Sora, *The Lost Colony of the Templars,* 164.

19. From "The Written Record of the Voyage of 1524 of Giovanni da Verrazano" as recorded in a letter from Verrazano to King Francis I of France, July 8, 1524, in Lawrence C. Wroth, trans. and ed., *The Voyages of Giovanni Verrazano, 1524–1528* (New Haven, Conn.: Yale University Press, 1970), 133–43.

20. Thomas Bertram Costain, *The White and the Gold* (Garden City, N.Y.: Doubleday, 1954), 16–18.

21. Ibid., 21–22.

22. Ibid., 32–33.

23. Rasmus B. Anderson, ed., *The Norse Discovery of America* (University Press of the Pacific, 2002), 142.

24. Costain, *The White and the Gold,* 32.

25. Ibid., 38–41.

26. Geoffrey Ashe, *Avalonian Quest* (London: Methuen, 1982), 13–20.

27. Bradley, *Grail Knights of North America,* 293–306.

28. Peter Willis, *Dom Paul Bellot: Architect and Monk* (Newcastle-upon-Tyne, England: Elysium Press, 1996), 134.

29. Hans Wolff, ed., *America: Early Maps of the World* (Munich: Prestel, 1992), 58–59.

30. Ibid., 60.

31. Bradley, *Grail Knights of North America,* 383–87.

32. Tim Wallace-Murphy, Marilyn Hopkins, and Graham Simmans, *Rex Deus: La Véritable Secret de la dynastie de Jésus* (Paris: Éditions du Rocher, 2001), 235.

Chapter 3: Recorded Beginnings

1. Costain, *The White and the Gold,* 51.

2. Ibid., 157–58.

3. Ibid., 62–66.

4. Samuel de Champlain, *The Works of Samuel de Champlain,* vol. 1, edited by Henry P. Biggar (Toronto: University of Toronto Press, 1971.), xv.

5. Bradley, *Holy Grail Across the Atlantic,* 251–53.

6. Costain, *The White and the Gold,* 31–32.

7. Ibid., 50–60.

8. Champlain, *Works,* vol. 1, 232–54.

9. Bradley, *Holy Grail Across the Atlantic,* 224–25.

10. Ibid., 199–258.

11. John J. Robinson, *Born in Blood* (New York: M. Evans and Co., 1989), 13–15.

12. Costain, *The White and the Gold*, 60–61.

13. John Smith, *A Map of Virginia* (Oxford: Joseph Barnes, 1612), 3.

14. Costain, *The White and the Gold*, 105–10.

15. Mark Finnan, *The First Nova Scotian* (Halifax: Formac, 1997), 107–16.

16. Francine Bernier, *The Templars' Legacy in Montreal* (Kempton, Ill.: Adventures Unlimited Press, 2003), 108–10.

17. Finnan, *The First Nova Scotian*, 95–96.

18. Alphonse Deveau and Sally Ross, *Acadians of Nova Scotia: Past and Present* (Halifax: Nimbus, 1992), 18.

19. Bernier, *The Templars' Legacy in Montreal*, 74–78.

20. Ibid., 150.

21. Ibid., 243.

22. Ibid., 118–21.

23. Costain, *The White and the Gold*, 114–15.

24. Ibid., 124–30.

25. Bernier, *The Templars' Legacy in Montreal*, 149–52.

26. Bradley, *Holy Grail Across the Atlantic*, 275–78.

27. Baigent, Leigh, and Lincoln, *Holy Blood, Holy Grail*, 39.

28. Mann, *The Knights Templar in the New World*, 24–26.

29. Baigent, Leigh, and Lincoln, *Holy Blood, Holy Grail*, 185–86.

30. Henry Lincoln, *The Holy Place* (New York: Arcade, 2004), 62–63.

31. Mann, *The Knights Templar in the New World*, 93–96.

32. Wallace-Murphy and Hopkins, *Templars in America*, 200.

33. Bernier, *The Templars' Legacy in Montreal*, 56–65.

34. Ibid., 74–75.

35. Ibid., 39–40.

36. Costain, *The White and the Gold*, 106–108.

37. Bernier, *The Templars' Legacy in Montreal*, 23–24.

38. Costain, *The White and the Gold*, 98–101.

39. Deveau and Ross, *Acadians of Nova Scotia*, 25–27.

40. Costain, *The White and the Gold*, 169–72.

41. Ibid., 435.

42. Ibid., 356–59.

43. Richard E. Bohlander, ed., *World Explorers and Discoverers* (New York: Macmillan, 1992), 135–42.

44. Ibid., 143–44.

45. Costain, *The White and the Gold*, 360.

Chapter 4: New World Foundations

1. Baigent and Leigh, *The Temple and the Lodge,* 227–28.
2. Ibid., 211–13.
3. Robert Lomas, *The Invisible College: The Royal Society, Freemsaonry, and the Birth of Modern Science* (London: Headline, 2002), 6–7.
4. Baigent and Leigh, *The Temple and the Lodge,* 224–25.
5. Ibid., 229–35.
6. Ibid., 236–39.
7. Laurence Gardner, *Bloodline of the Holy Grail* (Rockport, Mass.: Fair Winds Press, 2002), 329–34.
8. Baigent and Leigh, *The Temple and the Lodge,* 266–67.
9. Gardner, *Bloodline of the Holy Grail,* 339.
10. Baigent and Leigh, *The Temple and the Lodge,* 148–49.
11. Ibid., 150–51.
12. Ibid., 192.
13. Albert Mackey, *Encyclopedia of Freemasonry* (Whitefish, Mont.: Kessinger Publishing, 1991), 235.
14. Baigent and Leigh, *The Temple and the Lodge,* 264–68.
15. Ibid., 269.
16. Sinclair, *The Sword and the Grail,* 49, 166.
17. Mackey, *Encyclopedia of Freemasonry,* 251.
18. Lomas, *The Invisible College,* 125.
19. David Wood, *Genesis* (Kent, UK: Baton Press, 1985), 243.
20. Lomas, *The Invisible College,* 155–64.
21. Ibid., 78.
22. Baigent and Leigh, *The Temple and the Lodge,* 277–78.
23. Lesley Choyce, *Nova Scotia: Shaped by the Sea* (Toronto: Penguin Books Canada, 1997), 69.
24. Baigent and Leigh, *The Temple and the Lodge,* 250–52.
25. Kenneth MacKenzie, *The Royal Masonic Cyclopedia* (Whitefish, Mont.: Kessinger, 2002), 635–37.
26. Baigent and Leigh, *The Temple and the Lodge,* 279–86.
27. Reginald Vanderbilt Harris, "Templarism in Canada," pamphlet no. 17, Canadian Masonic Research Association, 1964.
28. Baigent and Leigh, *The Temple and the Lodge,* 281.
29. Choyce, *Nova Scotia: Shaped by the Sea,* 107–11.
30. Dean W. Jobb, *The Acadians: A People's Story of Exile and Triumph* (Mississauga, Ontario: Wiley and Sons, 2005), 47–53.

31. Deveau and Ross, *Acadians of Nova Scotia*, 26.

32. Baigent and Leigh, *The Temple and the Lodge*, 307–308.

33. Ibid., 284.

34. Ibid., 337.

35. Ibid., 313.

36. Ibid., 338.

37. Ibid., 324–25.

38. Sora, *Secret Societies of America's Elite*, 139–40.

39. Ibid., 160–67.

40. Baigent and Leigh, *The Temple and the Lodge*, 325–33.

41. Mackey, *Encyclopedia of Freemasonry*, 325.

42. Ibid., 326.

43. Sora, *Secret Societies of America's Elite*, 170–71.

44. Baigent and Leigh, *The Temple and the Lodge*, 350.

45. Ibid., figure 36.

46. Spiro Kostof and Greg Castillo, *A History of Architecture* (New York: Oxford University Press, 1995), 625.

47. Ibid., 626.

48. Mann, *The Knights Templar in the New World*, 72.

49. MacKenzie, *The Royal Masonic Cyclopedia*, 1–7.

50. Ibid., 45.

51. Baigent, Leigh, and Lincoln, *Holy Blood, Holy Grail*, 362–66.

52. William S. Crooker, *Oak Island Gold* (Halifax: Nimbus, 1993, 84–85.

Chapter 5: The Hidden History of a New Nation

1. Baigent and Leigh, *The Temple and the Lodge*, 286, 313.

2. Ibid., 133.

3. David G. Chandler, *The Campaigns of Napoleon* (New York: Scribner, 1973), 286–332.

4. Ibid., 42–47.

5. Bradley, *Holy Grail Across the Atlantic*, 306.

6. Ibid., 310–11.

7. Jon Kukla, *A Wilderness So Immense: The Louisiana Purchase and the Destiny of America* (New York: Knopf, 2003), 44–50.

8. Ibid., 78–90.

9. O. I. A. Roche, ed., *The Jeffersonian Bible* (New York: Clarkson Potter, 1964), 14, 348.

10. Chandler, *The Campaigns of Napoleon,* 621–33.

11. Thomas Fleming, *The Louisiana Purchase* (Hoboken, N.J.: Wiley, 2003), 5–9.

12. Ibid., 11–12.

13. Ibid., 12–21.

14. Donald Jackson, ed., *Letters of the Lewis and Clark Expedition with Related Documents* (Champaign: University of Illinois Press, 1979), 89.

15. John Logan Allen, *Passage Through the Garden: Lewis and Clark and the Image of the American Northwest* (Champaign: University of Illinois Press, 1974), 16–18.

16. George Catlin, *Letters and Notes on the Manners, Customs, and Condition of North American Indians,* letters 10–16 (New York, Dover, 1973).

17. Pierre Gaultier de Varennes de la Verendrye, *Journals and Letters of Pierre Gaultier de Varennes de la Verendrye and His Sons* (New York: Greenwood Press, 1968).

18. Reginald Horsman, *The Causes of the War of 1812* (New York: Octagon Books, 1972), 13–17.

19. Ibid., 33–34.

20. John Sugden, *Tecumseh: A Life* (New York: Henry Holt, 1998), 17.

21. Ibid., 124–48.

22. Ibid., 233–35.

23. Patricia L. Faust, ed., *Historical Times Illustrated Encyclopedia of the Civil War* (New York: HarperCollins, 1991), 37.

24. Ibid., 40.

25. Ibid., 57.

26. Baigent, Leigh, and Lincoln, *Holy Blood, Holy Grail,* 2.

27. Michael Walsh, *Butler's Lives of the Saints,* 15–16.

Chapter 6: *A New Jerusalem*

1. James C. Boyajian, *Portuguese Trade in Asia under the Habsburgs, 1580–1640* (Baltimore: Johns Hopkins University Press, 1992), 436.

2. J. Ross Robertson, *History of Freemasonry in Canada* (Whitefish, Mont.: Kessinger, 2003), 95.

3. Baigent, Leigh, and Lincoln, *Holy Blood, Holy Grail,* 434.

4. William Sinclair Charter, 1574, University of Guelph Scottish Collection, Guelph, Ontario.

5. Deveau and Ross, *Acadians of Nova Scotia, Past and Present,* 62–63.

6. Thomas Chandler Haliburton, *History of Nova Scotia* (Belleville, Ontario: Mika, 1973), 46, 88.

7. Ibid., 36–38.

8. Deveau and Ross, *Acadians of Nova Scotia, Past and Present,* 64.

9. Margaret C. Melanson, *The Melanson Story* (self-published, 2003) 1–5.

10. Ibid., 6–7.

11. Ibid., 7–8.

12. Ibid., 9–10.

13. Robert Graves, *The White Goddess: A Historical Grammar of Poetic Myth* (New York: Farrar, Straus, and Giroux, 1966), 214, 230, 284.

14. John Rhys, *Celtic Folklore* (New York: Gordon, 1974), 14.

15. Ibid., 15.

16. William S. Crooker, *Oak Island Gold,* 187–92.

17. Carl Waldman, *Encyclopedia of Native American Tribes,* rev. ed. (New York: Facts on File, 1999), 57.

18. Ibid., 58.

19. Ibid., 99–101.

20. Ibid., 163.

21. Olive Patricia Dickason, *Canada's First Nations: A History of Founding Peoples from Earliest Times* (Oxford: Oxford University Press, 2001), 20–21.

22. Ibid., 90–98.

23. Peter McFarlane and Wayne Haimila, *Ancient Land, Ancient Sky* (Toronto: Alfred A. Knopf, 1999), 152–59.

24. Ibid., 163.

25. Peter Champoux and William Stuart Buehler, *Gaia Matrix* (Franklin Media, 1999), 117.

26. Fell, *America B.C.,* 239–40.

27. Ibid., 1–22.

28. Ibid., 256–57.

29. Ibid., 260–68.

30. Joseph Bernard, Marquis de Chabert, *Voyage Roi,* 1st ed. (Paris: De L'Imprimerie Royale, 1753), introduction.

31. Ibid., 1.

32. Ibid., 2.

33. Ibid., 3.

Chapter 7: *Everlasting Elements*

1. Margaret Starbird, *The Woman with the Alabaster Jar* (Rochester, Vt.: Bear and Company, 1993), 101.
2. Ibid., 102.
3. Francis Bacon, *The New Atlantis*, in Sidney Warhaft, ed., *Francis Bacon: A Selection of His Works* (Toronto: Macmillan, 1965), 448.
4. Francis Bacon, *The Wisdom of the Ancients*, in Sidney Warhaft, ed., *Francis Bacon: A Selection of His Works*, 274–77.
5. Laurence Gardner, *Lost Secrets of the Sacred Ark* (London: Thorsens, 2003), 108–23.
6. Josephus Flavius, *Antiquities of the Jews* (New York: Thomas Nelson, 1999), 1.2.3.
7. Starbird, *The Woman with the Alabaster Jar*, 36–38, 137.
8. Ibid., 138–39.
9. Dennis Overbye, "Laser Co-Inventor Wins Religion Prize," *Toronto Star*, Thursday, March 10, 2005.
10. Alain Merot, *Nicolas Poussin* (New York: Abbeville Press, 1990), 248–49.
11. Witztum, Rips, and Rosenberg, "Equidistant Letter Sequences in the Book of Genesis," *Statistical Science*, August 1994.
12. Pedro Kujawski and P. de Salles, "In Service to the Psyche: The Grail Legend in C. G. Jung's Individuation Process," in John Matthews, ed., *The Household of the Grail* (London: Aquarian Press, 1990), 185–97.
13. From Pierre Saint-Maxment Feugère and Gaston de Koker, *Le Serpent Rouge* (SRES Verites Anciennes, 1981).

BIBLIOGRAPHY

Adams, Dickinson, ed. *The Papers of Thomas Jefferson: Jefferson's Extracts from the Gospels.* Princeton, N.J.: Princeton University Press, 1983.

Addison, Charles G. *The History of the Knights Templar.* Kempton, Ill.: Adventures Unlimited Press, 1997. First published in London, 1842.

Aitchison, Leslie. *A History of Metals.* 2 vols. New York: John Wiley and Sons, 1960.

Allen, John Logan. *Passage Through the Garden: Lewis and Clark and the Image of the American Northwest.* Champaign: University of Illinois Press, 1974.

Allmand, Christopher. *The Hundred Years' War: England and France at War c. 1300–1450.* Cambridge: Cambridge University Press, 1988.

Alofsin, Anthony. *Frank Lloyd Wright—The Lost Years, 1910–1922: A Study of Influence.* Chicago: University of Chicago Press, 1993.

Ambrose, Stephen E. *Lewis and Clark: Voyage of Discovery.* Washington, D.C.: National Geographic Society, 1998.

Andersen, Hans Christian. *The Complete Fairy Tales and Stories.* Translated by E. C. Haugaard. New York: Anchor Press/Doubleday, 1974.

Anderson, Rasmus B., ed. *The Norse Discovery of America.* University Press of the Pacific, 2002.

Andrews, Richard, and Paul Schellenberger. *The Tomb of God: The Body of Jesus and the Solution to a 2,000-Year-Old Mystery.* Boston: Little, Brown and Co., 1996.

Ashe, Geoffrey. *Avalonian Quest.* London: Methuen, 1982.

———. *King Arthur's Avalon.* London: Collins, 1966.

———. *Kings and Queens of Early Britain.* London: Methuen, 1982.

————. *Land to the West*. London: Methuen, 1986.

————. *Mythology of the British Isles*. London: Methuen, 1990.

Ashe, Geoffrey, ed. *The Quest for America*. New York: Praeger Publishers, 1971.

————. *The Quest for Arthur's Britain*. London: Granada Publishing Limited, 1968.

Authwaite, Leonard. *Unrolling the Map*. New York: Reynal and Hitchcock, 1935.

Baigent, Michael, and Richard Leigh. *The Dead Sea Scrolls Deception*. London: Corgi Books, 1991.

————. *The Elixir and the Stone*. London: Viking, 1997.

————. *The Temple and the Lodge*. New York: Arcade, 1991.

Baigent, Michael, Richard Leigh, and Henry Lincoln. *Holy Blood, Holy Grail*. New York: Delacorte, 2004.

————. *The Messianic Legacy*. London: Jonathan Cape, 1986.

Baker, Daniel B., ed. *Explorers and Discoverers of the World*. Washington, D.C.: Gale Research, Inc., 1993.

Ball, Martin J., and James Fife, eds. *The Celtic Languages*. London: Routledge, 2002.

Barbour, Philip. *The Three Worlds of Captain John Smith*. Boston: Houghton Mifflin Company, 1964.

Bayley, Harold. *The Lost Language of Symbolism*. New York: Barnes and Noble, 1968.

Begg, Ean C. M. *The Cult of the Black Virgin*. London: Arkana, 1985.

Bennett, John G. Gurdjieff. *The Making of a New World*. London: Turnstone Books, 1973.

Bergin, Joseph. *Cardinal Richelieu: Power and the Pursuit of Wealth*. New Haven, Conn.: Yale University Press, 1985.

Bernard of Clairvaux. *On the Song of Songs*. Translated by Kilian Walsh. Spencer, Mass.: Cistercian Publications, 1983.

Bernier, Francine. *The Templars' Legacy in Montreal: The New Jerusalem*. Kempton, Ill.: Adventures Unlimited Press, 2003.

Billon, Frederick L. *Annals of St. Louis—The French and Spanish Period*. St. Louis: Nixon-Jones Printing Co., 1886.

Bird, Will R. *Off-Trail in Nova Scotia*. Toronto: The Ryerson Press, 1956.

Birks, Walter, and R. A. Gilbert. *The Treasure of Montségur*. London: Thorsons Publishing Group, 1987.

Blake, Peter. *The Master Builders: Le Corbusier, Mies van der Rohe, Frank Lloyd Wright*. New York: Alfred A. Knopf, 1960.

Bohlander, Richard E., ed. *World Explorers and Discoverers.* New York: Macmillan Publishing Company, 1992.

Bolon, Carol R., Robert S. Nelson, and Linda Seidel. *The Nature of Frank Lloyd Wright.* Chicago: University of Chicago Press, 1988.

Bord, Janet, and Colin Bord. *Mysterious Britain.* London: Granada Publishing Limited, 1974.

Boudet, H. *La Vraie Langue celtique et le cromleck de Rennes-les-Bains.* Nice: Belisane, 1984. Facsimile of 1886 original.

Bowen, Catherine Drinker. *Francis Bacon: The Temper of a Man.* Boston: Little, Brown and Company, 1963.

Bowra, C. M. *From Virgil to Milton.* New York: St. Martin's Press, 1962.

Boyajian, James C. *Portuguese Trade in Asia under the Habsburgs, 1580–1640.* Baltimore: John Hopkins University Press, 1992.

Bradley, Michael. *Holy Grail Across the Atlantic.* Toronto: Hounslow Press, 1998.

———. *The Columbus Conspiracy.* Toronto: Hounslow Press, 1991.

———. *Grail Knights of North America: On the Trail of the Grail.* Toronto: Hounslow Press, 1998.

Brooks, H. Allen. *The Prairie School—Frank Lloyd Wright and His Midwest Contemporaries.* Toronto: University of Toronto Press, 1972.

Brown, Dan. *Angels and Demons.* New York: Atria, 2000.

———. *The Da Vinci Code.* New York: Doubleday, 2003.

Brydon, R. *A History of the Guilds, the Masons, and the Rosy Cross.* Roslin, Midlothian: Rosslyn Chapel Trust, Rosslyn Chapel, 1994.

Budge, E. A. Wallis. *The Egyptian Book of the Dead.* New York: Dover Publications, 1967.

———. *An Egyptian Hieroglyphic Dictionary,* vols. 1 and 2. New York: Dover Publications, 1978.

———. *The Gods of the Egyptians,* vols. 1 and 2. New York: Dover Publications, 1969.

———. *Osiris and the Egyptian Resurrection,* vols. 1 and 2. New York: Dover Publications, 1973.

Burstein, Dan, ed. *Secrets of the Code: The Unauthorized Guide to the Mysteries behind* The Da Vinci Code. New York: CDS Books, 2004.

Butler, Alan. *The Goddess, the Grail and the Lodge.* Winchester, UK: O Books, 2004.

Butler, Alan, and Stephen Dafoe. *The Templar Continuum.* Belleville, Ontario: Templar Books, 1999.

Camille, Michael. *Gothic Art: Glorious Visions.* New York: Harry N. Abrams, 1996.

Campbell, Joseph. *Myths to Live By.* New York: Arkana, 1971.

Canada Department of Mines and Resources. *Geology and Economic Minerals of Canada.* Ottawa: 1947.

Canada Department of Tourism and Culture. *Nova Scotia Travel Guide.* Halifax: 1993.

Carlson, Suzanne. "Loose Threads in a Tapestry of Stone: The Architecture of the Newport Tower." *NEARA Journal* 35, no. 1 (summer 2001).

Cary, Max, and E. H. Warmington. *The Ancient Explorers.* London: Methuen and Company, 1929.

Catlin, George. *Letters and Notes on the Manners, Customs, and Conditions of North American Indians.* 2 vols. New York: Dover Publications, 1973.

Cavendish, Richard, ed. *Encyclopedia of the Unexplained.* London: Arkana, 1989.

Chabert, Joseph Bernard, Marquis de. *Voyage Roi.* Paris: De L'Imprimerie Royale, 1753.

Chadwick, Nora. *The Celts.* Harmondsworth, UK: Penguin, 1971.

Champlain, Samuel de. *The Works of Samuel de Champlain.* 6 vols. Edited by H. P. Biggar. Toronto: University of Toronto Press, 1971.

Chandler, David G. *The Campaigns of Napoleon.* New York: Scribner, 1973.

Chaplin, Dorothea. *Mythological Bonds between East and West.* Copenhagen: Einar Munksgaard, 1938.

Charpentier, Louis. *The Mysteries of Chartres Cathedral.* New York: Avon, 1980.

Charroux, Robert. *Treasures of the World.* Middlebury, Vt.: P. S. Erikkson, 1962.

Chatelaine, Maurice. *Our Ancestors Came from Outer Space.* London: Pan Books, 1980.

Choyce, Leslie. *Nova Scotia: Shaped by the Sea.* Toronto: Penguin Books Canada, 1997.

Churton, Tobias. *The Golden Builders: Alchemists, Rosicrucians and the First Free Masons.* Lichfield, UK: Signal Publishing, 2002.

Clark, Andrew Hill. *Acadia: The Geography of Early Nova Scotia to 1760.* Madison: University of Wisconsin Press, 1968.

Clark, Kenneth. *Leonardo da Vinci.* London: Penguin Books, 1959.

Clarke, George Frederick. *Expulsion of the Acadians: The True Story.* Fredericton, New Brunswick: Brunswick Press, 1980.

Clayton, Peter A. *Chronicle of the Pharaohs.* London: Thames and Hudson, 1994.

Clinton, William Jefferson. *My Life*. New York: Alfred A. Knopf. 2004.

Coldstream, Nicola. *Medieval Architecture*. Oxford: Oxford University Press, 2002.

Collins, Andrew. *Gateway to Atlantis: The Search for the Source of a Lost Civilization*. London: Headline Book Publishing, 2000.

Coppens, Philip. *The Stone Puzzle of Rosslyn Chapel*. The Netherlands: Frontiers Publishing and Adventures Unlimited Press, 2004.

Costain, Thomas B. *The White and the Gold: The French Regime in Canada*. New York: Doubleday, 1954.

Creighton, Helen. *Bluenose Ghosts*. Toronto: McGraw-Hill Ryerson, 1957.

———. *Bluenose Magic*. Toronto: McGraw-Hill Ryerson, 1968.

———. *Folklore of Lunenburg County, Nova Scotia*. Toronto: McGraw-Hill Ryerson, 1976.

Crooker, William S. *Oak Island Gold*. Halifax: Nimbus Publishing, 1993.

———. *The Oak Island Quest*. Windsor, Nova Scotia: Lancelot Press, 1978.

Dabney, Virginius. *Virginia: The New Dominion*. Garden City, N.Y.: Doubleday, 1971.

Daraul, Arkon. *Secret Societies, Yesterday and Today*. London: Frederick Muller Limited, 1961.

Davidson, Robert F. *The Old Testament*. London: Hodder and Stoughton, 1964.

Delaney, F. *The Celts*. London: Grafton Books, 1989.

Delpar, Helen, ed. *The Discoverers: An Encyclopedia of Explorers and Exploration*. New York: McGraw-Hill, 1980.

Deveau, Alphonse, and Sally Ross. *The Acadians of Nova Scotia: Past and Present*. Halifax: Nimbus Publishing, 1992.

Devoto, Bernard, ed. *The Journals of Lewis and Clark*. Mariner Books, 1997.

Diefendorf, Barbara B. *Beneath the Cross: Catholics and Huguenots in Sixteenth-Century Paris*. Oxford: Oxford University Press, 1991.

Dingledine, Raymond C., Lena Barksdale, and Marion Belt Nesbitt. *Virginia's History*. New York: Scribner's, 1956.

Dobbs, Betty J. T. *The Foundations of Newton's Alchemy*. Cambridge: Cambridge University Press, 1975.

Dodge, Stephen C. *Christopher Columbus and the First Voyages to the New World*. New York: Chelsea House, 1991.

Dor-Ner, Zvi, and William Scheller. *Columbus and the Age of Discovery*. New York: William Morrow, 1991.

Doyle, Sir Arthur Conan. *Sherlock Holmes: The Complete Novels and Stories*, vols. 1 and 2. New York: Bantam Books, 1986.

Drosnin, Michael. *The Bible Code.* New York: Simon and Schuster, 1997.

Duncan, Dayton, and Ken Burns. *Lewis and Clark: The Journey of the Corps of Discovery.* New York: Alfred A. Knopf, 1997.

Duriez, C. *The C. S. Lewis Handbook.* Essex, UK: Monarch, 1990.

Eco, Umberto. *Foucault's Pendulum.* London: Picador, 1990.

———. *The Name of the Rose.* London: Picador, 1984.

Erdeswick, S. *A Survey of Staffordshire.* London: J. B. Nichols, 1984.

Eschenbach, Wolfram von. *Parzival.* Translated by Helen M. Mustard and Charles E. Passage. New York: Vintage, 1961.

Elting, John R. *Amateurs, to Arms! A Military History of the War of 1812.* Chapel Hill, N.C.: Algonquin, 1991.

Etlin, Richard A. *Frank Lloyd Wright and Le Corbusier: The Romantic Legacy.* Manchester: Manchester University Press, 1994.

Evans, James. *The History and Practice of Ancient Astronomy.* Oxford: Oxford University Press, 1998.

Everett, Felicity, and Struan Reed. *The USBORNE Book of Explorers, from Columbus to Armstrong.* London: USBORNE Publishing, 1991.

Fabricius, Johannes. *Alchemy.* Northamptonshire, UK: The Aquarian Press, 1976.

Fairbairn, James. *Crests of the Families of Great Britain and Ireland.* Revised by Laurence Butters. Rutland, Vt: Charles E. Tuttle, 1968.

Fanthorpe, Patricia, and Lionel Fanthorpe. *The Holy Grail Revealed: The Mysterious Treasure of Rennes-le-Château.* North Hollywood, Calif.: Newcastle Press, 1982.

———. *The Oak Island Mystery: The Secret of the World's Greatest Treasure Hunt.* Toronto: Hounslow Press, 1995.

———. *Rennes-le-Château.* Middlesex, UK: Bellevue Books, 1991.

Farmer, D. H. *The Oxford Dictionary of Saints.* Oxford: Oxford University Press, 1982.

Fath, Edward Arthur. *The Elements of Astronomy.* New York: McGraw-Hill, 1934.

Faust, Patricia L., ed. *Historical Times Illustrated Encyclopedia of the Civil War.* New York: HarperCollins, 1991.

Fell, Barry. *America B.C.: Ancient Settlers in the New World.* New York: Pocket Books, 1989.

———. *Bronze Age America.* Toronto: Little, Brown, 1982.

Feugère, Pierre, Louis Saint Maxent, and Gaston de Koker. *Le Serpent Rouge.* SRES Vérités Anciennes, 1981.

Finnan, Mark. *The First Nova Scotian.* Halifax: Formac, 1997.

Fleming, Thomas J. *The Louisiana Purchase.* Hoboken, N.J.: John Wiley and Sons, 2003.

Foote, Henry Wilder. *Thomas Jefferson: Champion of Religious Freedom, Advocate of Christian Morals.* Boston: Beacon Press, 1947.

Ford, Paul, ed. *The Works of Thomas Jefferson,* vol. 10. New York: G. P. Putnam's Sons, 1905.

Franklyn, Julian, and John Tanner. *An Encyclopaedic Dictionary of Heraldry.* Oxford: Pergamon, 1969.

Fraser, Mary L. *Folklore of Nova Scotia.* Antigonish, Nova Scotia: Formac, 1928.

Frazer, James G. *The Golden Bough.* New York: Macmillan, 1923.

———. *Magic and Religion.* London: Watts, 1944.

Frith, Henry. *The Romance of Navigation: A Brief Record of Maritime Discovery.* London: Ward, Lock, and Bowden, 1893.

Furneaux, Rupert. *The Money Pit Mystery.* New York: Fontana/Collins, 1976.

Ganong, William Francis. *Crucial Maps.* Toronto: University of Toronto Press, 1964.

Gardner, Laurence. *Bloodline of the Holy Grail.* Rockport, Mass.: Fair Winds Press, 2002.

———. *Genesis of the Grail Kings.* London: Bantam, 1999.

———. *Lost Secrets of the Sacred Ark.* London: Thorsens, 2003.

Gaustad, Edwin. *Sworn on the Altar of God: A Religious Biography of Thomas Jefferson.* Grand Rapids, Mich.: William B. Eerdman, 1996.

Geoffrey of Monmouth. *History of the Kings of Britain.* Edited and translated by Lewis Thorpe. Harmondsworth, UK: Penguin, 1966.

Gilbert, Adrian. *The New Jerusalem.* New York: Bantam, 2002.

Gill, Brendan. *Many Masks: A Life of Frank Lloyd Wright.* New York: Putnam, 1987.

Gimbutas, Maria A. *The Language of the Goddess.* San Francisco: HarperSanFrancisco, 1991.

Giraud, V. *Bibliographie de Taine.* Paris: n.p., 1902.

Goode, J. Paul. *Goode's World Atlas.* New York: Rand McNally, 1991.

Goodrich, Norma Lorre. *King Arthur.* Danbury, Conn.: Franklin Watts, 1986.

Gordon, Cyrus L. *Before Columbus.* New York: Crown Publishers, 1971.

Goss, John. *The Mapping of North America.* Secaucus, N.J.: Wellfleet Press, 1990.

Gould, R. F. *Gould's History of Freemasonry.* London: Caxton, 1933.

Grant, Michael. *Myths of the Greeks and Romans.* New York: New American Library, 1962.

Graves, Robert. *The White Goddess.* London: Faber and Faber, 1961.

———. *The White Goddess: A Historical Grammar of Poetic Myth.* New York: Farrar, Straus, and Giroux, 1966.

Graves, Robert, and Raphael Patai. *Hebrew Myths: The Book of Genesis.* Garden City, N.Y.: Doubleday, 1964.

Greenberg, Joseph H. *Indo-European and Its Closest Relatives: The Eurasiatic Family,* vol. 2. Stanford, Calif.: Stanford University Press, 2002.

Grigsby, John. *Warriors of the Wasteland.* London: Watkins, 2002.

Guirdham, A. *Catharism: The Medieval Resurgence of Primitive Christianity.* Paris: St. Helier, 1969.

———. *The Cathars and Reincarnation.* London: Neville Spearman, 1976.

Gurney, Gene. *Kingdoms of Europe.* New York: Crown, 1982.

Haagensen, Erling, and Henry Lincoln. *The Templars' Secret Island: The Knights, the Priest and the Treasure.* Gloucestershire, UK: Windrush Press, 2000.

Haliburton, Thomas Chandler. *History of Nova Scotia.* Belleville, Ontario: Mika, 1973.

Hall, Manly P. *The Lost Keys of Freemasonry.* Richmond, Va.: Macoy Publishing and Masonic Supply, 1976.

Hancock, Graham. *The Sign and the Seal: The Quest for the Lost Ark of the Covenant.* Toronto: Doubleday Canada, 1992.

Hanna, Leslie F. *The Discoverers.* New York: Random House, 1983.

Hannay, James. *The History of Acadia (1605–1763).* St. John, New Brunswick: J. and A. McMillan, 1879.

Hapgood, Charles. *Maps of the Ancient Sea Kings.* Kempton, Ill.: Adventures Unlimited Press, 1997.

Harden, Donald. *The Phoenicians: Ancient People and Places.* London: Thames and Hudson, 1963.

Harris, Reginald V. *The Oak Island Mystery.* Toronto: Ryerson Press, 1967.

Hart, Gerald E. *Fall of New France: 1755–1760.* Montreal: W. Drysdale, 1888.

Hawkins, Gerald S. *Stonehenge Decoded.* New York: Doubleday, 1965.

Heindenreich, C. E. *Cartographica: Explorations and Mapping of Samuel de Champlain, 1603–1632.* Toronto: University of Toronto Press, 1976.

Heinlein, Robert. *Beyond This Horizon.* Baen, 2001.

Hickey, Donald. *The War of 1812: A Forgotten Conflict.* Champaign: University of Illinois Press, 1989.

Higenbottam, Frank. *Codes and Ciphers*. London: English Universities Press, 1973.

Hill, Kay. *Glooscap and His Magic: Legends of the Wabanaki Indians*. Toronto: McClelland and Stewart, 1963.

————. *More Glooscap Stories: Legends of the Wabanaki Indians*. Toronto: McClelland and Stewart, 1988.

Hitchcock, Henry Russell. *In the Nature of Materials: The Buildings of Frank Lloyd Wright, 1887–1941*. New York: Da Capo Press, 1975.

Hitsman, J. Mackay. *The Incredible War of 1812*. Toronto: University of Toronto Press, 1973.

Hodges, Henry. *Technology in the Ancient World*. London: Penguin, 1970.

Holroyd, Stuart, and Neil Powell. *Mysteries of Magic*. London: Bloomsbury Books, 1991.

Holt, Elizabeth Gilmore, ed. *Literary Sources of Art History: An Anthology of Texts from Theophilus to Goethe*. Princeton, N.J.: Princeton University Press, 1947.

Holy Bible Containing the Old and New Testaments, New Revised Standard Version (Catholic edition). Catholic Bible Press: 1993.

Hope, Joan. *A Castle in Nova Scotia*. Kitchener, Ontario: Kitchener Printing, 1997.

Horne, Alex. *King Solomon's Temple in the Masonic Tradition*. London: Aquarian Press, 1971.

Horsman, Reginald. *The Causes of the War of 1812*. New York: Octagon Books, 1972.

Hutchinson, William. *The Spirit of Masonry*. Whitefish, Mont.: Kessinger, 2004.

Hyde, William. *Encyclopedia of the History of St. Louis*. 4 vols. New York: Howard Conard, 1899.

Israel, Gerald, and Jacques Lebar. *When Jerusalem Burned*. New York: William Morrow, 1973.

Izzo, Alberto, and Camillo Gubitosi. *Frank Lloyd Wright: Three Quarters of a Century of Drawings*. New York: Horizon Press, 1981.

Jackson, Donald. ed. *Letters of the Lewis and Clark Expedition with Related Documents*. 2 vols. Champaign: University of Illinois Press, 1979.

Jackson, Kenneth. *Language and History in Early Britain: A Chronological Survey of the Brittonic Languages, 1st to 12th century* A.D. Edinburgh: University Press, 1971.

Josephus Flavius. *The Complete Works*. Translated by William Whiston. New York: Thomas Nelson, 1999.

Jung, C. G. *Collected Works*. London: Routledge, 1953–69.

————. *Memories, Dreams, Reflections*. London: Fontana, 1972.

————. *Synchronicity*. London: Routledge, 1972.

Kerr, D. G. G. *Historical Atlas of Canada,* 3rd rev. ed. Don Mills, Ontario: Thomas Nelson and Sons, 1975.

Knight, Christopher, and Robert Lomas. *The Book of Hiram: Freemasonry, Venus and the Secret Key to the Life of Jesus.* London: Century, 2003.

———. *Uriel's Machine: The Prehistoric Technology That Survived the Flood.* London: Century, 1999.

Knight, G. *The Secret Tradition in Arthurian Legend.* Wellingborough, UK: Aquarian Press, 1983.

Kostof, Spiro, and Greg Castillo. *A History of Architecture.* New York: Oxford University Press, 1995.

Krupp, E. C., ed. *In Search of Ancient Astronomies.* Columbus, Ohio: McGraw-Hill, 1979.

Kukla, Jon. *A Wilderness So Immense: The Louisiana Purchase and the Destiny of America.* New York: Alfred A. Knopf, 2003.

Laidler, Keith. *The Head of God: The Lost Treasure of the Templars.* London: Weidenfeld and Nicolson, 1998.

Laseau, Paul, and James Tice. *Frank Lloyd Wright: Between Principle and Form.* New York: Van Nostrand Reinhold, 1992.

Law, Vivien. *The History of Linguistics in Europe: From Plato to 1600.* Cambridge: Cambridge University Press, 2002.

Lescarbot, Marc. *History of New France,* vol. 2. Translated by W. L. Grant. Toronto: The Champlain Society, 1911.

Lethbridge, Thomas Charles. *Herdsmen and Hermits: Celtic Seafarers in the Northern Seas.* Cambridge: Bowes and Bowes, 1950.

Levi, Eliphas. *History of Magic.* London: Rider, 1968.

———. *The Key of the Mysteries.* London: Rider, 1968.

———. *Transcendental Magic: Its Doctrine and Ritual.* Whitefish, Mont: Kessinger, 1942.

Lincoln, Henry. *The Holy Place: Saunière and the Decoding of the Mystery of Rennes-le-Château.* New York: Arcade, 2004.

Linklater, Eric. *The Royal House of Scotland.* London: Macmillan, 1970.

Lomas, Robert. *The Invisible College.* London: Headline Books, 2002.

Longfellow, Henry Wadsworth. *Evangeline.* New York: Pelican, 1999.

Loomis, Roger Sherman. *Celtic Myth and Arthurian Romance.* New York: Haskell House, 1967.

———. *The Grail: From Celtic Myth to Christian Symbol.* Princeton, N.J.: Princeton University Press, 1991.

———. *Studies in Medieval Literature: A Memorial Collection of Essays.* New York: B. Franklin, 1970.

MacCulloch, John Arnold. *The Religion of the Ancient Celts*. Edinburgh: T. and T. Clark, 1911.

Mackey, Albert G. *An Encyclopedia of Freemasonry*. Whitefish, Mont.: Kessinger, 1991.

———. *The Symbolism of Freemasonry*. Chicago: The Masonic History Company, 1926.

Mackey, James P., ed. *An Introduction to Celtic Christianity*. Edinburgh: T. and T. Clark, 1989.

MacKenzie, Kenneth. *The Royal Masonic Cycolopedia*. Whitefish, Mont.: Kessinger, 2002.

Mallery, Arlington. *Lost America*. Washington, D.C.: Overlook, 1951.

Mallery, Arlington, and Mary Harrison. *The Rediscovery of Lost America*. New York: E. P. Dutton, 1979.

Mann, William F. *The Knights Templar in the New World*. Rochester, Vt.: Destiny Books, 2004.

Markale, Jean. *The Church of Mary Magdalene*. Rochester, Vt.: Inner Traditions, 2004.

———. *The Templar Treasure at Gisors*. Rochester, Vt.: Inner Traditions, 2003.

Mathers, S. Liddell MacGregor. *The Kabbalah Unveiled*. New York: Weiser, 1970.

———. *The Key of Solomon the King*. London: George Redway, 1888.

Matthews, John, ed. *The Household of the Grail*. London: Aquarian Press, 1990.

Matthews, Caitlín. *The Elements of the Celtic Tradition*. Shaftesbury, Dorset, UK: Element Books, 1989.

Maunder, E. W. *The Astronomy of the Bible*. London: Hodder and Stoughton, 1909.

McCluskey, Stephen C. *Astronomies and Cultures in Early Medieval Europe*. Cambridge: Cambridge University Press, 1998.

McFarlane, Peter, and Wayne Haimila. *Ancient Land, Ancient Sky: Flying Canada's Native Canoe Routes*. Toronto: Alfred A. Knopf, 1999.

McGhee, Robert. *Canada Rediscovered*. Ottawa: Canadian Museum of Civilization, 1991.

Meiss, Millard. *French Painting in the Time of Jean de Berry: The Limbourgs and Their Contemporaries*. New York: George Braziller, 1974.

Melanson, Margaret C. *The Melanson Story: Acadian Family, Acadian Times*. Moncton, New Brunswick: Self-published, 2003.

Menzies, Gavin. *1421: The Year China Discovered America*. London: Bantam Press, 2002.

Merot, Alain. *Nicolas Poussin.* New York: Abbeville Press, 1990.

Miller, Crichton E. M. *The Golden Thread of Time.* Warwickshire, UK: Pendulum, 2001.

Milton, John. *Paradise Lost.* Edited by John Leonard. New York: Penguin, 2003.

Moncrieffe, Iain. *The Highland Clans.* New York: Clarkson N. Potter, 1967.

Morison, Samuel Eliot. *The Great Explorers: The European Discovery of America.* New York: Oxford University Press, 1978.

Morrison, N. Brysson. *Mary, Queen of Scots.* New York: Vanguard Press, 1960.

Moscati, Sabatino, ed. *The Phoenicians.* New York: Abbeville Press, 1988.

Moulton, Gary E., ed. *The Journals of the Lewis and Clark Expedition.* Lincoln: University of Nebraska Press, 1988.

Mouni, Sadhu. *The Tarot.* London: Allen and Unwin, 1962.

Mowat, Farley. *West Viking.* Toronto: McClelland and Stewart, 1965.

Munro, R. W. *Highland Clans and Tartans.* London: Peerage Books, 1987.

Murray, Margaret A. *The Divine King in England.* London: Faber, 1954.

Nutt, Alfred Trubner. *Studies on the Legend of the Holy Grail.* New York: Cooper Square Publishers, 1965.

O'Connor, D'Arcy. *The Big Dig.* New York: Ballantine, 1988.

———. *The Money Pit.* New York: Coward, McCann, and Geoghegan, 1976.

Ondaatje, Christopher. *The Prime Ministers of Canada.* Toronto: Pagurian, 1985.

Ovason, David. *The Secret Architecture of Our Nation's Capital: The Masons and the Building of Washington, D.C.* New York: HarperCollins, 2000.

Parkman, Francis. *Pioneers of France in the New World.* New York: Library of America, 1983.

Parton, James. *Life and Times of Benjamin Franklin.* 2 vols. Boston: Houghton Mifflin, 1897.

Penhallow, William S. "Astronomical Alignments in the Newport Tower." *NEARA Journal* (March 21, 2004).

Philip, J. A. *Pythagoras and Early Pythagoreanism.* Toronto: University of Toronto Press, 1966.

Phillips, Graham. *The Templars and the Ark of the Covenant.* Rochester, Vt.: Bear and Company, 2004.

Picknett, Lynn. *Mary Magdalene.* New York: Carroll and Graf, 2003.

Picknett, Lynn, and Clive Prince. *The Templar Revelation.* New York: Touchstone, 1997.

Platt, Colin. *The Atlas of Medieval Man.* New York: St. Martin's, 1994.

Poe, Edgar Allan. *The Complete Tales and Poems of Edgar Allan Poe.* Toronto: Vintage, 1975.

Pohl, Frederick J. *Americus Vespucci, Pilot Major.* New York: Octagon Books, 1996.

———. *The Lost Discovery.* New York: W. W. Norton, 1952.

———. *Prince Henry Sinclair: His Expedition to the New World.* London: Davis-Poynter, 1974.

Pope, Marvin H. *Song of Songs.* Garden City, N.Y.: Doubleday, 1983.

Quarrell, Charles. *Buried Treasure.* London: MacDonald and Evans, 1955.

Ralls, Karen, and Ian Robertson. *The Quest for the Celtic Key.* Edinburgh: Luath Press, 2002.

Ramsay, Raymond H. *No Longer on the Map.* New York: Ballantine, 1973.

Rand, Silas Tertius. *Legends of the Micmacs.* New York: Johnson Reprint Corp., 1971.

Regardie, Israel. *The Golden Dawn,* 3rd ed. St. Paul: Llewellyn, 1970.

———. *Roll Away the Stone.* St. Paul: Llewellyn, 1968.

———. *The Tree of Life,* 2nd ed. New York: Weiser, 1969.

Reuter, Timothy, ed. *New Cambridge Medieval History,* vols. 1–3. Cambridge: Cambridge University Press, 1999.

Rhonda, James P. *Lewis and Clark Among the Indians.* Lincoln: University of Nebraska Press, 1988

Rhys, John. *Celtic Folklore.* New York: Gordon, 1974.

Robertson, John Ross. *History of Freemasonry in Canada.* Whitefish, Mont.: Kessinger, 2003.

Robinson, John J. *Born in Blood: The Lost Secrets of Freemasonry.* New York: M. Evans and Co., 1989.

Roche, O. I. A., ed. *The Jeffersonian Bible.* New York: Clarkson N. Potter, 1964.

Ross, Anne. *The Pagan Celts.* Totowa, N.J. : Barnes and Noble, 1986.

Rutherford, Ward. *Celtic Lore.* London: Aquarian Press, 1993.

Ryan, Peter. *Time Detectives: Explorers and Mapmakers.* London: Belitha Press, 1989.

Sadler, Henry. *Masonic Facts and Fictions.* Wellingborough, UK: Aquarian Press, 1985.

Sanford, Charles B. *The Religious Life of Thomas Jefferson.* Charlottesville: University Press of Virginia, 1984.

Schick, Edwin A. *Revelation, the last Book of the Bible.* Philadelphia: Fortress Press, 1977.

Schwartz, Lilian. "Leonardo's *Mona Lisa.*" *Art and Antiques,* January 1987.

Scott, Martin. *Medieval Europe.* London: Longmans, Green and Co. Ltd., 1967.

Secrest, Meryle. *Frank Lloyd Wright: A Biography*. Chicago: University of Chicago Press, 1998.

Sede, Gérard de. *L'Or de Rennes*. Paris: J'ai Lu, 1967.

Sedgwick, Henry D. *The House of Guise*. Indianapolis: Bobbs-Merrill Co., 1938.

Silberer, Herbert. *Hidden Symbolism of Alchemy and the Occult Arts*. New York: Moffat, Yard, and Co., 1917.

Sinclair, Andrew. *The Discovery of the Grail*. London: Century, 1998.

———. *The Secret Scroll*. London: Birlinn, 2002.

———. *The Sword and the Grail*. New York: Crown, 1992.

Smith, John. *A Map of Virginia. With a Description of the Countrey, the Commodities, People, Government and Religion*. Oxford: Joseph Barnes, 1612.

———. *The Complete Works of Captain John Smith*. Edited by Philip Barbour. Chapel Hill: University of North Carolina Press, 1986.

Smollett, Tobias, ed. *The Works of Voltaire: A Contemporary Version*. Translated by William F. Fleming. New York: E. R. DuMont, 1901.

Smyth, Albert Henry, ed. *The Writings of Benjamin Franklin*. 10 vols. New York: Macmillan, 1905–06.

Sora, Steven. *The Lost Colony of the Templars*. Rochester, Vt.: Destiny Books, 2004.

———. *Secret Societies of America's Elite*. Rochester, Vt.: Destiny Books, 2003.

Spicer, Stanley T. *Glooscap Legends*. Hantsport, Nova Scotia: Lancelot, 1991.

Starbird, Margaret. *The Woman with the Alabaster Jar*. Rochester, Vt.: Bear and Company, 1993.

Starkey, Dinah. *Scholastic Atlas of Exploration*. New York: HarperCollins, 1993.

Stearns, Peter N. ed. *The Encyclopedia of World History: Ancient, Medieval, and Modern, Chronologically Arranged*, 6th edition. Boston: Houghton Mifflin, 2001.

Steiner, Rudolf J. *Mysticism at the Dawn of the Modern Age*. New York: Steinerbooks, 1960.

Stoddard, Whitney S. *Art and Architecture in Medieval France: Medieval Architecture, Sculpture, Stained Glass, Manuscripts, the Art of the Church Treasuries*. Boulder, Colo.: Westview Press, 1966.

Stokstad, Marilyn. *Medieval Art*. Boulder, Colo.: Westview Press, 1986.

Sugden, John. *Tecumseh: A Life*. New York: Henry Holt, 1998.

Sumption, Jonathan. *The Albigensian Crusade.* London: Faber and Faber, 1978.

Tafel, Edgar. *Years with Frank Lloyd Wright.* Peter Smith, 1985.

Taylor, F. S. *The Alchemists.* New York: Schuman, 1949.

Temple, Robert. *The Sirius Mystery.* Rochester, Vt.: Destiny Books, 1998.

Tennyson, Alfred Lord. *The Holy Grail and Other Poems.* London: Stanan and Co., 1870.

———. *Idylls of the King.* London: Penguin, 1961.

The Hours of Jeanne d'Evreux: Queen of France at the Cloisters. New York: The Metropolitan Museum of Art, 1957.

Thiering, Barbara. *Jesus and the Riddle of the Dead Sea Scrolls.* Toronto: Doubleday, 1992.

Thomas, Charles. *Celtic Britain: Ancient Peoples and Places.* London: Thames and Hudson, 1986.

Thomas, Lowell. *The Untold Story of Exploration.* New York: Dodd, Mead and Company, 1935.

Thomas, Marcel. *The Golden Age: Manuscript Painting at the Time of Jean, Duke of Berry.* New York: George Braziller, 1979.

Thwaites, Reuben Gold, ed. *The Jesuit Relations and Allied Documents,* vols. 1–71. Cleveland: Burrows Brothers, n.d.

Tompkins, Peter. *Secrets of the Great Pyramids.* New York: Harper and Row, 1971.

Trefethen, Joseph M. *Geology for Engineers.* Princeton, N.J.: Van Nostrand Co., 1959.

Trento, Salvatore Michael. *The Search for Lost America.* Chicago: Contemporary Books, 1978.

Verendrye, Pierre Gaultier de Varennes de la. Burpee, Lawrence J., ed. *Journal and Letters of Pierre Gaultier de Varennes de la Verendrye and His Sons.* New York: Greenwood Press, 1968.

Vermaseren, M. J. *Mithras, the Secret God.* London: Chatto, 1959.

Vermes, Geza. *The Dead Sea Scrolls in English.* Harmondsworth, UK: Pelican, 1962.

Verne, Jules. *Journey to the Centre of the Earth.* London: Penguin, 1965.

Voragine, Jacobus de. *The Golden Legend: Readings on the Saints,* vols. 1 and 2. Translated by William Granger Ryan. Princeton, N.J.: Princeton University Press, 1993.

Waite, Arthur E. *The Hidden Church of the Holy Grail.* London: Rebman Limited, 1909.

———. *The New Encyclopaedia of Freemasonry.* New York: Weathervane Books, 1970.

Waldman, Carl. *Encyclopedia of Native American Tribes.* New York: Facts on File, 1999.

Wallace-Murphy, Tim, and Marilyn Hopkins. *Rosslyn, Guardian of the Secrets of the Holy Grail.* Shaftesbury, Dorset, UK: Element, 1999.

———. *Templars in America.* York Beach, Maine: Weiser, 2004.

Wallace-Murphy, Tim, Marilyn Hopkins, and Graham Simmons. *Rex Deus.* Shaftesbury, Dorset: Element, 2000

Walsh, Michael, ed. *Butler's Lives of the Saints: Concise Edition,* rev. ed. San Francisco: HarperCollins, 1991.

Ward, A. W., and A. R. Waller, eds. *The Cambridge History of English and American Literature.* 18 volumes. Cambridge, England: Cambridge University Press, 1907–21.

Ward, J. S. M. *Freemasonry and the Ancient Gods.* London: Baskerville, 1926.

Warhaft, Sidney, ed. *Francis Bacon: A Selection of His Works.* Toronto: Macmillan, 1965.

West, John Anthony. *Serpent in the Sky.* Wheaton, Ill.: Theosophical Publishing House, 1983.

Williamson, Hugh Ross. *The Arrow and the Sword.* London: Faber, 1947.

Williamson, John. *The Oak King, the Holly King, and the Unicorn.* New York: Harper and Row, 1986.

Willis, Peter. *Dom Paul Bellot: Architect and Monk.* Newcastle-upon-Tyne, UK: Elysium Press, 1996.

Wilson, Colin. *The Occult.* London: Hodder, 1971.

Wilson, Ian. *The Columbus Myth.* Toronto: Simon and Schuster, 1991.

Wilson, John A. *The Culture of Ancient Egypt.* Chicago: University of Chicago Press, 1951.

Wind, E. *Pagan Mysteries in the Renaissance.* London: Peregrine, 1967.

Wolf, J. B. *Louis XIV.* New York: Norton, 1968.

Wolff, Hans, ed. *America: Early Maps of the World.* Munich: Prestel, 1992.

Wolkstein, Diane. *Inanna: Queen of Heaven and Earth, Her Stories and Hymns from Sumer.* New York: Harper and Row, 1983.

Wood, David. *Genesis.* Kent, UK: Baton Press, 1985.

Wright, Frank Lloyd. *Frank Lloyd Wright: An Autobiography.* Quartet Books, 1943.

Wroth, Lawrence C., ed. *The Voyages of Giovanni da Verrazano, 1524–1528.* New Haven, Conn.: Yale University Press, 1970.

Yates, F. A. *The Art of Memory.* London: Routledge, 1966.

———. *Giordano Bruno and the Hermetic Tradition.* London: Routledge, 1964.

———. *The Rosicrucian Enlightenment.* London: Routledge, 1972.

Young, G. *Ancient Peoples and Modern Ghosts.* Queensland, Nova Scotia: self-published, 1980.

Index

Page numbers in italics refer to maps, photographs, and illustrations.

Books of Related Interest

The Knights Templar in the New World
How Henry Sinclair Brought the Grail to Acadia
by William F. Mann

The Lost Treasure of the Knights Templar
Solving the Oak Island Mystery
by Steven Sora

The Lost Colony of the Templars
Verrazano's Secret Mission to America
by Steven Sora

Secret Societies of America's Elite
From the Knights Templar to Skull and Bones
by Steven Sora

The Knights Templar in the Golden Age of Spain
Their Hidden History on the Iberian Peninsula
by Juan Garcia Atienza

The Secret History of Freemasonry
Its Origins and Connection to the Knights Templar
by Paul Naudon

The Magus of Freemasonry
The Mysterious Life of Elias Ashmole—Scientist,
Alchemist, and Founder of the Royal Society
by Tobias Churton

The Mystery Traditions
Secret Symbols and Sacred Art
by James Wasserman

Inner Traditions • Bear & Company
P.O. Box 388
Rochester, VT 05767
1-800-246-8648
www.InnerTraditions.com

Or contact your local bookseller